THE RISE OF THE
CHICAGO POLICE DEPARTMENT

The Rise of the Chicago Police Department

Class and Conflict, 1850–1894

SAM MITRANI

UNIVERSITY OF ILLINOIS PRESS

URBANA, CHICAGO, AND SPRINGFIELD

Library of Congress Cataloging-in-Publication Data
Mitrani, Sam.
The rise of the Chicago Police Department : class and conflict,
1850–1894 / Sam Mitrani.
pages   cm. — (Working class in American history)
Summary: "In this book, Sam Mitrani cogently examines the
making of the police department in Chicago, which by the late
1800s had grown into the most violent, turbulent city in America.
Chicago was roiling with political and economic conflict, much
of it rooted in class tensions, and the city's lawmakers and
business elite fostered the growth of a professional municipal
police force to protect capitalism, its assets, and their own
positions in society. Together with city policymakers, the
business elite united behind an ideology of order that would
simultaneously justify the police force's existence and dictate
its functions. Tracing the Chicago police department's growth
through events such as the 1855 Lager Beer riot, the Civil War,
the May Day strikes, the 1877 railroad workers strike and riot,
and the Haymarket violence in 1886, Mitrani demonstrates that
this ideology of order both succeeded and failed in its aims.
Recasting late nineteenth-century Chicago in terms of the
struggle over order, this insightful history uncovers the modern
police department's role in reconciling democracy with industrial
capitalism. "— Provided by publisher.
Includes bibliographical references and index.
ISBN 978-0-252-03806-8 (hardback)
ISBN 978-0-252-09533-7 (ebook)
1. Chicago (Ill.). Police Department—History. 2. Police—
Illinois—Chicago—History. 3. Law enforcement—Illinois—
Chicago. I. Title.
HV8148.C4M58   2013
63.209773'1109034—dc23   2013020895

To All My Parents and Grandparents

CONTENTS

Acknowledgments   ix

Introduction   1

Chapter 1. Drunken Immigrants, Businessmen's Order,
and the Founding of the Chicago Police Department   14

Chapter 2. Paternalism and the Birth
of Professional Police Organization   34

Chapter 3. The Police and the First May Day Strike
for the Eight-Hour Day   57

Chapter 4. The Native-Born Protestant Elite's Bid
for Control in the 1870s   72

Chapter 5. 1877 and the Formation of a Law-and-Order Consensus   112

Chapter 6. Carter Harrison Remakes
the Chicago Police Department   134

Chapter 7. Chicago's Anarchists Shape the Police Department   166

Chapter 8. The Eight-Hour Strikes, the Haymarket
Bombing, and the Consolidation
of the Chicago Police Department   185

Epilogue: The Pullman Strike
and the Matrix of State Institutions   208

Notes   219

Index   247

Illustrations follow page 100.

ACKNOWLEDGMENTS

This book owes an enormous intellectual debt to those historians who have already written the history of Chicago and its class relations, especially Richard Schneirov and John Jentz. Their excellent work informed the questions and underlying analysis of this book.

I would also like to especially thank Richard John. He provided firm guidance when necessary, and let me find my own way when that was more useful. Leon Fink, Michael Perman, Perry Duis, and Amy Dru Stanley gave necessary insights and crucial support.

A number of colleagues also provided important help along the way, especially John Flores, Joey Lipari, Anne Parsons, John Rosen, Mohan Sing, and Benn Williams.

I also received excellent and timely advice and criticism from Laurie Matheson, James Barrett, and my anonymous readers through the University of Illinois Press. I would like to thank the rest of the University of Illinois Press staff, and also Deborah Oliver for her careful reading of the manuscript.

Finally, this project would not have been possible without the help and support of my wonderful family, especially Karen Swan and Yeti Mitrani, who read the manuscript at critical stages, and Juanita "Sugar" Del Toro and Peanut Del Toro, who loved, supported, and advised me throughout.

INTRODUCTION

On August 26, 1765, a crowd holding him responsible for the Stamp Act attacked the Boston home of Massachusetts lieutenant governor and chief justice Thomas Hutchinson. The attackers spent the entire night sacking Hutchinson's mansion, carrying off his valuables, and using axes to dismantle the wooden portions of the building. Hutchinson and his family fled and survived without bodily harm, but his home was largely destroyed. As the rioters worked throughout the night dismantling Hutchinson's house and looting his possessions, no forces of order arrived to eject them or to protect the property of this powerful and wealthy man. Hutchinson and his family fled to protect their lives, but not to summon police or militia to save their home.[1]

This incident from the early stage of the American Revolution might seem a strange opening for a history of the Chicago Police Department, which was not formed until almost ninety years later, but it illustrates a basic fact of colonial and early American life: the police simply did not exist. Armies, courts, sheriffs, and armed militias were common enough, but neither the northern colonies nor the early republic built police departments. In the major disturbances of the revolutionary and early republican period, crowds instead confronted other types of armed forces. A Boston mob confronted the British army during the Boston Massacre. Daniel Shays's compatriots took over courthouses and fought the state militia. Whiskey rebels in the 1790s also stopped court proceedings and confronted federal marshals, state militia, and army units, but no police. By the 1830s and 1840s, various forms of disorder had become the norm in U.S. cities.[2] Throughout the 1830s, Whigs and Democrats rioted regularly during election seasons.[3] Working people took over the streets of Philadelphia at Christmas and reveled in the violent inversion of social norms with no force to stop them.[4] Abolitionists and free black workers faced riotous mobs throughout the north, let alone the south, and workingmen's strikes and political demonstrations often became riotous by later standards.[5] Part of the reason that disorder became so prevalent in the 1830s and 1840s was that no U.S. city possessed an institution that modern observers would recognize as a police force. Even as late as 1849, the Astor Place rioters of New York easily overwhelmed the nascent city police and were only put down by the state militia.[6]

In fact, the development of police forces marked something entirely new in human history. Since the first civilizations, the maintenance of order was embedded within the economic and social organizations of society. The modern idea that economics, politics, and family life can be separated did not apply to any society before the development of capitalism. As Moses Finley points out, between Xenophon's *Oikonomikos* in fourth-century BCE Athens and Francis Hutcheson's 1742 work, *Short Introduction to Moral Philosophy*, Western thinkers considered production, trade, the maintenance of order, and family relations as inextricably bound responsibilities of local elites. In ancient Greece and Rome, the head of the household had power and responsibility over all the objects and people in that household, including children and slaves.[7] Big slave rebellions like the Spartacus revolt in the 70s BCE faced Roman legions, not local police. Similarly, a feudal lord was not just a rent collector. He was also the local representative of state power. In England this evolved into the system of justices of the peace. King Richard I commissioned knights to maintain order in restive areas in 1195, and by 1361 King Edward III instructed that "good and lawful men" be appointed in each county to keep order. These men were not organized into a bureaucracy commanded by the king. Rather, they were local elites given the authority to keep order as part of their overall position in society. Until the nineteenth century, the justices of the peace had a variety of responsibilities, including fixing wages, building roads and bridges, and administering poor relief. They were not paid because "for centuries most JPs were well-to-do landowners who would not bother about 'expense accounts.'"[8]

The American colonies inherited this system and continued to adapt it until the 1840s. When necessary, locally elected part-time constables raised posses or called on volunteer militias, but these groups did not regularly patrol the streets. These constables were part of a broader paternalistic system of social control inherited from the colonial era. They did not resemble the police departments of a later era, and cities did not distinguish between the authority of these part-time lawmen and other municipal officials, such as the mayor or the aldermen.

Then, between the 1840s and the end of the 1880s, every major northern city built a substantial police force.[9] These new police departments were disciplined, bureaucratic, organized on military lines, and capable of patrolling entire cities. They were in many ways the standing armies that the founding fathers feared. Twelve hundred Chicago policemen at the end of the 1880s is a small number compared with big-city police departments in the twentieth century. At the end of 2010, the Chicago Police Department had 13,857 employees for a city less than three times as populous as the Chicago of 1890.[10] In other words, Chicago today has more than four times as many police officers per person as in 1890. Still, the 1890 police department dwarfed any force designed to control the northern population before the Civil War, both in terms of manpower and organizational capabilities. If a mob had assaulted the house of a leading Chicago citizen in 1890, such as had occurred at the house of Thomas Hutchinson in Boston in 1765, a massive armed force of policemen would have immediately set upon it.

Why did cities rush to build police departments in such a short period of time, when they had failed to do so earlier? The most basic answer is that the leading businessmen who dominated both urban economies and their politics pushed city governments to build powerful armed institutions that could defend their property and their interests from the new threats that accompanied the development of a wage labor economy. Chicago built its police department to maintain order while it grew from a minor outpost in the west to the nation's second largest city. But the city did not simply create the police because it became too big. While it grew, Chicago's economy also changed dramatically. In 1850, petty proprietors formed the basis of the city's economy and the wealthiest Chicagoans were merchants and land speculators. By 1890, Chicago had an industrial, wage labor economy.[11] This transformation caused a series of crises that forced Chicago's economic and political elite to create the police department. First, it led to a massive immigration of wage workers who settled in the cities instead of moving out into the countryside, as had earlier immigrants. Then workers sought to improve their situation through increasingly threatening strikes and riots. Businessmen responded to these crises in many ways, but the single most important was the creation of powerful armed forces that could protect the constituted order.

This interpretation has deep implications for our understandings of the development of the American state and the limits of democracy. Over time, police departments developed professional leaderships that removed the crucial aspects of police policy from politics and portrayed their activities as a politically neutral municipal service. By the end of the nineteenth century, electoral influence over the police was largely confined to the margins. Questions like police corruption and whether or not to enforce temperance regulations dominated political discussions of the police, while the deeper question of whether or not municipalities should maintain massive organizations of armed men to enforce order on the population was effectively removed from the political debate. This allowed police departments, along with allied institutions such as state militias, to use violence to reconcile democratic politics with the deeply exploitative industrial capitalist order that developed in late-nineteenth-century cities, including Chicago. As Richard Bensel has pointed out, the United States was the only country to remain a democracy with a high degree of popular participation in elections while it industrialized.[12] This was possible in large measure because police departments acted outside the immediate control of those elections and protected the extant political and economic system from the real threat posed by the new working class.

The development of police forces also raised the stakes for debates over government policy. The police are, in the last analysis, an organization aimed at forcing people to do things they would not do voluntarily. Once such a force existed, government acquired the possibility of assuming an entirely new role in reshaping society. This first manifested itself in the fight over regulating drinking, but it also opened the possibility for a whole series of progressive reforms. In this way, it made the struggle between parties potentially much more significant, especially on the local level. It also gave the courts a whole new enforcement mechanism. The antilabor injunctions of the late nineteenth and early twentieth centuries that played such a big role in limiting the labor movement, for instance, were only relevant because bodies of armed men, police, state militias, and the U.S. Army, enforced them.[13] Once police departments had been built, the potential power of those directing them increased exponentially.

At the same time, police departments made possible a large expansion of municipal patronage. In this way, their development went hand in hand with the growth of urban political machines based on patronage politics. These machines also helped keep order by integrating a section of the working-class population directly into the order-keeping apparatus. This aspect of police departments ran counter to the desire of reformers to create bureaucratic, efficient forces that could implement unpopular regulations, like temperance. From the very beginning, bureaucratic-style reformers clashed with more pluralistic patronage bosses. Both models of policing, however, relied on the newly built departments to maintain order among wage workers and the unemployed in the vast new cities of the late nineteenth century. They received support from various, often contending, sections of the elite. But these divisions represented, at base, different policies aimed at achieving the same end.

This book is a case study of the Chicago Police Department, but Chicago was not unique. By the late nineteenth century, police were so ubiquitous that even contemporary observers forgot how recent an invention they were. Chicago does not serve as a representative case since it was certainly a unique city in the nineteenth century. But because Chicago grew so spectacularly in so short a time, it illustrates in the most dramatic fashion the process by which a nation historically lacking permanent, specialized armed bodies of men created large bureaucratic military-style institutions aimed at controlling the population in every major city.

During the late nineteenth century, Chicago was the most violent, turbulent city in the country. It was the city in which the crises accompanying industrialization and the development of a wage labor economy reached their most threatening peak. From the Lager Beer riot of 1855, through the Civil War, the 1867 strikes for the eight-hour workday, the 1871 fire, the 1877 strike and riot, the May Day strikes and the Haymarket bombing, and the Pullman strike, Chicago was roiled with political and economic conflict. Other cities faced similar disturbances, but no other city experienced so many crises with such intensity. In his recent environmental history of industrialization, Harold Platt calls Chicago a "shock city," and this was as true for the social fabric of urban life as for its environment.[14]

Chicago's lawmakers had to overcome many serious obstacles in order to build a force that could protect the constituted economic and political order. The United States had little military precedent for instilling large numbers of men with the necessary discipline, esprit de corps, and physical power. Also, before the late nineteenth century, municipalities had very limited tax resources. Creating a police department was expensive, but creating an adequately paid, professional department cost even more. The less policemen were paid, the greater their incentive for corruption and the less likely they were to feel allegiance to the force. To be effective, the police also needed horses, station houses, telegraph systems, uniforms, and weapons. Wealthy citizens could be convinced to tax themselves and pay for all of these things only if they felt that the police protected their vital interests.

To help solve these difficulties, advocates of the expansion of the police developed a concept of order as a central political ideology. This concept reinforced police legitimacy among the entire population of the city, defined the role of policemen in municipal affairs, and fit with the broader push for order of all types, including moral order, business order, and social order, in the second half of the nineteenth century.[15] To maintain order, the police first of all protected property and suppressed street disturbances. They also arrested thousands of people for drunk and disorderly behavior and attempted to control the behavior of prostitutes. On the margins, groups of immigrants, religious leaders, businessmen, unions, and anarchists hotly contested what counted as "disorderly." Was drinking on Sunday a threat to order? Were peaceful union meetings? Riots were clearly a threat to order, but were anarchist meetings at which peaceful speakers denounced the behavior of the police? What about picketing to enforce a strike? The slipperiness of the concept of order allowed it to serve as a legitimating ideology for people with radically different political goals and positions in society. By the 1880s, this ideology of order shaped both the behavior of the police and a significant portion of municipal politics to such an extent that the entire history of Chicago in the late nineteenth century can be recast as a struggle over order.

The law was essentially irrelevant to police behavior. The police received no legal training, and they mostly charged those they arrested with broadly defined offenses such as "disorderly conduct."[16] The police justices who tried most arrestees also received no legal training, and the police ignored many laws on the books. They did enforce city ordinances, but the police superintendent and the mayor decided which ordinances the police would enforce and which they would ignore. In some cases, such as the repression of the anarchists after Haymarket, the police chose its course of action for political reasons and found a legal justification later. In addition, when lawmakers tried to increase their legal reach by regulating such diverse behaviors as wooden construction, skinny-dipping, and roller-skating, the effects of these regulations were determined by the department's organizational capabilities, rather than the desires of the mayor or city council. For this reason, those who set police policy, including mayors, police commissioners, extralegal organizations of businessmen, and the police leadership itself, had much more power over the department than those who wrote and interpreted the laws, including the city council and judiciary. These policy-making organizations figure much more prominently in the story of police development than the legal system.

Chicago's business class grew in wealth and power and politically consolidated itself at the same time that it spurred the city to build the police department. From its early days, Chicago possessed a clearly defined elite of native-born "Yankee" Protestants who dominated business, politics, and the major professions and played the leading role in pushing the city to build its police force. This elite came west in the 1830s and 1840s mostly from New York and New England. It retained close ties to the East Coast, both culturally and economically, and its members considered themselves part of the national elite. As numerous nineteenth-century observers pointed out,

Chicago's elite included a disproportionate number of "self-made men" and a small proportion of what British journalist William Stead called the "disreputable" idle rich.[17] The elite tended to adopt the viewpoints that anyone could make it in the modern city and that poverty and disorder resulted from the moral failings of the poor or the cultural baggage of European immigrants. They were particularly concerned with limiting charity to only the "deserving poor." This elite was conscious of itself from the city's beginning, but as it grew in size, wealth, and power, it increasingly organized itself into a clearly defined class with its own organizations and political agenda. Historian Frederick Jaher identifies ninety-three capitalists, lawyers, and politicians who dominated the city in the antebellum period. The early elite included families like the Kinzies, who were regional agents for John Jacob Astor's American Fur Company. The Kinzie family produced the first sheriff of Cook County, James, and the first president of the Village of Chicago, John H. These brothers also worked as real-estate speculators, insurance agents, auctioneers, and bankers. Another example is William Ogden, who became the town's first mayor and was also the foremost investor in real estate, a banker, lumber company owner, director of the Chicago Board of Trade, and a financier of agricultural machinery magnate Cyrus McCormick.[18]

Throughout the antebellum period, members of Chicago's elite had diverse business interests and also dominated politics. From 1837 to 1868, seventeen of the nineteen mayors were prominent businessmen. Most had a variety of commercial interests, including Levi Boone, Thomas Dyer, and John Wentworth, all of whom played important roles in the early development of the police department.[19] By 1870, the richest 20 percent of Chicago families controlled about 90 percent of the city's wealth, and almost all of them were native born. The poorest half, meanwhile, possessed less than 1 percent.[20]

Between the Civil War and 1890, Chicago experienced the most rapid population and economic growth of any city in the history of the world to that point, which produced a new, more powerful elite as well as extreme strains on the preexisting political system. The city quickly became the second largest in the United States and the center of the transportation system. It became the second center of commerce in the country with the development of an extensive wholesale commodity trade as well as dry-goods retailing. It also grew to have an enormous and diversified manufacturing economy that produced everything from meat to railcars. This growth was dominated by a larger elite dominated by a few men with enormous fortunes. By 1892, Chicago was home to 278 millionaires, but a small number stood above the rest. Stead identified meatpacking magnate Philip Armour, department store merchant Marshall Field, and railroad car manufacturer George Pullman as "the Chicagoan trinity" of millionaires in 1893.[21] To this group must be added real-estate tycoon Potter Palmer, dry-goods merchant John V. Farwell (at least in the early period), Marshall Field's partner Levi Leiter, agricultural implements manufacturer Cyrus McCormick, and iron pipe and machine manufacturer Richard Teller Crane. These were only the most prominent among a large group of extremely wealthy men who dominated business and politics in Chicago. They knew one another; worked together on the boards of Chicago banks, brokerage houses, and insurance firms; speculated together in real estate and grain; and ran the city's charitable organizations, including the Relief and Aid Society, the Chicago Historical Society, and the YMCA.[22]

The city's middle-class, working-class, and poor populations are much harder to delineate clearly, though the economic, political, and cultural definitions of these groups were key to the development of the police. This is partially because the nature of the working population changed dramatically over the period of this study. On one side, Chicago always possessed a large number of very small businessmen who operated stores, saloons, small workshops, and other establishments. This traditional middle class generally wanted to protect order, but some of its members, especially saloonkeepers in the immigrant neighborhoods, were also closely tied to the wage workers they served. As the city became a business center, it also experienced a consequent growth in white-collar workers who were more likely to identify with their employers. The number of wage workers grew steadily, first in the primary goods processing industries and transport, then increasingly in the various branches of manufacturing. As the city was constantly expanding, many people also worked in construction and in the brickyards. Over time, the proportion of wage workers employed by large firms such as the railroads, factories, and lumberyards increased, while that employed by small firms or individuals declined, though the number continued to grow in absolute terms. On the other side of the working class, Chicago possessed an ever-present layer of people who worked occasionally, worked in the illicit economy, or did not work at all: prostitutes, hustlers, gambling operators, and the chronically unemployed.[23]

Equally important, Chicagoans' perception of class changed dramatically over this period, and this changing perception helped create the fear of disorder among the elite that drove police development. Before the Civil War, Chicagoans generally shared the free-labor ideology of much of the rest of the north, though they did not agree on exactly what "free labor" meant. This ideology drew no hard line between wage workers and small proprietors, and it lauded labor as the means to acquire wealth. The free-labor ideology assumed that young men might work for wages during part of their lives, but would eventually acquire their own farm or shop. U.S. senator Zachariah Chandler described this cycle thus: "A young man goes out to service—to labor if you please to call it so—for compensation until he acquires money enough to buy a farm . . . and soon he becomes himself the employer of labor."[24] In the antebellum period, this ideology reflected one aspect of the social and economic reality of an economy dominated by very small producers and with a large degree of upward mobility, particularly in the west. But from the 1850s on, and at an accelerating pace after the Civil War, this ideology did not capture the social reality of cities, including Chicago. Increasing numbers of young people found themselves stuck as wage laborers, with little possibility of securing the economic independence so central to antebellum free labor ideology. This caused an ideological crisis along with a material one.[25]

Chicagoans seeking to explain these phenomena came up with a variety of answers. Wealthy and many middle-class residents blamed the poor for their inability to follow in the footsteps of their betters: they drank too much, failed to work industriously enough, or lacked the proper morals for success. Wealthy Chicagoans often blamed immigrants for failing to adapt to American ways.[26] This response to the failure of free-labor ideology drove much of the elite's attempt to regulate working-class behavior. On the other side, many trade unionists, Knights of Labor activists, socialists, and anarchists blamed the monopoly of wealth and power exercised by the elite for the fate of the working class.[27] Their increasingly strident critique of industrial capitalism and the wage system also pushed the elite to turn toward the police to protect the established order. A whole range of intermediate positions flourished, with many skilled workers and small businesspeople clinging to some version of the older conception of free labor.[28] The increasing perception of permanent class divisions and the variety of political reactions to those divisions drove the development of the police department as much as the abstract conception of order.

The development of a wage labor economy and widening class divisions were accompanied by a dramatic change in the ethnic makeup of large northern cities, among them Chicago, which possessed a majority immigrant population for most of the nineteenth century. Chicago's class divisions correlated with the city's ethnic makeup, but not precisely. The native born comprised the bulk of the city's elite, but as time went on, some immigrants and their children joined it. Many native-born Chicagoans also worked as skilled laborers, and some fell into poverty. Notable among immigrants were

Germans, who fanned across the socioeconomic classes: by the late 1870s, there were prominent German businessmen active in the main civic organizations of the elite, large numbers of German small-property owners, many German wage workers, and some extremely poor Germans. Many Germans also served on the police force in all ranks from superintendent to patrolman. The German population also became increasingly divided politically as nativism declined and class questions came to the fore.[29] The Irish population was generally poorer than the German and formed a larger share of the city's unskilled wage workers and a smaller share of its businessmen, but it was also divided along class lines. The Irish figured especially prominently in arrest records, especially in the early years of the department, out of all proportion to their share of the city's population. Throughout this period, the Irish never accounted for more than 20 percent of the city's population, but they accounted for as many as two-thirds of all arrests.[30] The Irish share of arrests declined throughout the nineteenth century, as their share in the police department increased. In fact, integration into the ranks of the police department through patronage politics was probably one of the most important ways that Irish immigrants were turned away from radical politics.

Irish and German Chicagoans also brought their own political ideas to the city, though in both cases immigrants arrived with a range of ideas that led to clashes among people sharing the same ethnic backgrounds.[31] A large portion of the city's Germans tended to vote Republican, while the Irish tended to vote Democrat, but those generalities do not hold well throughout the late nineteenth century. Germans became important businessmen and members of the Republican Party, but they also brought anarchist and socialist ideas to the city. Irish immigrants eventually became prominent within the Democratic Party machine, formed their own state militia, and joined the police force in large numbers, but some Irish nationalists in Chicago echoed the violent rhetoric of German anarchists, and planned invasions of Canada and dynamite attacks on London from Chicago.[32]

The police department was also internally divided along class and ethnic lines. In its early years, native-born Protestants dominated the ranks of the department, but this made controlling a working class composed largely of Irish Catholics and Catholic and Protestant Germans even more difficult. In part because the elite of all shades recognized this difficulty, and also because the Irish in particular organized politically and secured employment from all branches of the city government through patronage, the police department became increasingly composed of immigrants. Nonetheless, it was always commanded by men with close ties to the city's leading businessmen and politicians, who often had considerable experience within the department and, after the Civil War, in the army. Patrolmen, on the other hand, were largely drawn from the city's working class. They were poorly paid and expected to work long, dangerous hours, like other workers in the city. They also faced considerable pressures from their commanders to carry out unenviable or in some cases impossible tasks and to accept reduced compensation in times of economic crisis.

The ordinary policemen, however, were not ordinary workers. Their relationship with the rest of the city's working class was contradictory. On the one hand, as historian Erik Monkkonen points out, a large portion of what he calls "class control" carried out by the police force consisted of activities that social service organizations would later assume.[33] The police lodged "tramps" in station houses, returned lost children to their parents, controlled stray dogs, enforced health and building codes, picked up dead horses, and even provided first aid to injured people. The police were never very effective at controlling crime, but they provided other useful services. More importantly, however, they were charged with maintaining order among the rest of the working class, and with deploying force to do so. They did this daily, largely by arresting people for drunkenness, disorderly conduct, or prostitution. Most of those they arrested worked for wages and came from the poorer layers of society. At other times, the police intervened in large numbers to put down riots or break strikes. While these were not daily occurrences, they took place often enough throughout the late nineteenth century to remain in the forefront of the popular perception of the role of the police. Both of these types of activity set policemen off from the rest of the city's population. They engendered resentment among the policed and disdain for ordinary people among the police. Thus, while the police were wage workers themselves in the sense that they were largely drawn from the working class and were paid wages to carry out often difficult work, they were separated from the rest of the working population because they regularly deployed violence against that population. The social separation between the police and the rest of the city encouraged the development of a specific police ideology that included many of the free-labor ideas of the elite, but also included a deeply pessimistic view of human nature.[34]

The police department was also a distinctly male institution. Throughout the nineteenth century, every member of the police department was male, as was every city councilman or mayor who directly influenced police policy. The elite institutions built starting in the 1870s were also exclusively male. Some working-class organizations included women, notably the Knights of

Labor and the International Working People's Association, but they were still generally led by men.[35] Men also constituted the overwhelming majority of those the police arrested. Prostitutes were by far the largest category of women facing arrest, but their numbers were dwarfed by the numbers of men arrested for drunkenness or disorderly conduct.[36] This is not to say that women did not play an important role in police development, both in the highly gendered language of the family used by politicians of all stripes when discussing policing, and in the temperance and moral activism of middle- and upper-class women that helped push police policy, especially from the 1870s. Women's lives were also dramatically affected by the growth of police departments, as the new, male-dominated institution increasingly policed unwanted pregnancy, prostitution, and female political activism. However, it is crucial to recognize that, ultimately, police departments were created by men in order to control the behavior of other men.

This project illustrates the crucial role of state institutions in the development of capitalism. Even as the free-labor ideology of the antebellum period morphed into its caricature, the laissez faire ideology of the Gilded Age, the state apparatus grew at a remarkable pace. In fact, the role eventually played by the police departments of every city could not be played by private organizations, such as the Pinkerton Detective Agency. Private forces lacked the manpower, the legitimacy, and the will to replace the police. They could track down items stolen from an express company, spy on unions or the Molly Maguires, but they could not consistently break strikes. The Pinkertons, unlike the police, actually lost many armed conflicts with strikers throughout this period, most famously at Homestead. More crucially, private organizations such as the Pinkertons could not enforce order over entire cities because they could not turn a profit by doing so. Only municipalities, states, and nations had the resources and will to create legitimate, permanent, professional, armed organizations dedicated to the maintenance of order, broadly defined. Armed public institutions like the police, then, played an integral role in the nation's economic development well before the growth of the welfare state.

This book also illuminates how businessmen shaped these state institutions to meet their needs. Chicago's business elite disagreed on many important political questions and was never able to get exactly what it wanted even when it did agree. Nonetheless, the city's elite reached a sufficient consensus and possessed enough power to create radically new, powerful, armed institutions that could protect their economic interests, even as the city's development was turning them into an increasingly isolated minority within a sprawling multiethnic, working class metropolis. This insight illustrates the limits of American democracy in the second half of the nineteenth century.

At the same time, the elite did not get exactly what it wanted. Elite projects for social control failed more often than they succeeded. Chicago built a police force that could break strikes, destroy anarchist organizations, and protect property, but that police force never succeeded in controlling daily life in the working-class neighborhoods. Sunday drinking, prostitution, gambling, and petty crime continued unabated by the growth of the police department, however much elements of the elite would have liked to check them. Ordinary Chicagoans thus set severe limits on the power of coercive state institutions from the beginning.

This book examines the development of the Chicago Police Department from the 1850s through the 1880s. It does so by exploring how the various political and economic groups in Chicago shaped this institution, as well as how the police shaped the relations between those groups. But in another way the subject is broader, for the police became the central arm of state power aimed at the domestic population. Answering how and why this institution developed in the nineteenth century will help explain the nature of state power and capitalism into the twenty-first.

CHAPTER 1

Drunken Immigrants, Businessmen's Order, and the Founding of the Chicago Police Department

On April 21, 1855, an angry crowd of German immigrants assembled at Chicago's court house on Clark Street between Randolph and Washington. They loudly demanded that the court release nineteen imprisoned saloonkeepers. Ten had been arrested for refusing to pay the new $300 liquor license fee, up from $50, and nine had been arrested for serving alcohol on Sundays.[1] Operating taverns on Sunday violated an old, never-before-enforced municipal ordinance, but it was the only day off for most workmen. This crowd of immigrants confronted Kentucky-born, anti-Catholic Mayor Levi Boone. Boone headed a Law and Order ticket that had swept the city elections the month before with a temperance platform. He had immediately raised the liquor license fee and began enforcing the Sunday laws—earning him the wrath of drinkers throughout the city.[2]

Thus began the first major clash between "disorderly" immigrants and Chicago's proponents of law and order. This clash was part of the wave of nativism that swept the country in the 1850s and led to the brief rise of the Know Nothing or American Party. On the most basic level, this nativist upsurge was made possible by the development of a wage labor economy in northern cities, among them Chicago. The demand for wage workers attracted immigrants particularly from Ireland and Germany, who stood out culturally and religiously from their Anglo predecessors. This difference manifested itself most forcefully in the realm of public drinking. Just as mid-nineteenth-century Protestant moral reformers were gaining in influence, new groups of immigrants arrived in the country with social drinking habits they were loath to surrender. To the German and Irish immigrants, drinking beer on Sundays was an orderly and habitual way to spend their one day off. To many native-born Chicagoans, Sunday drinking was a disorderly and wasteful use of God's holiday. Yet on a deeper level, this clash over drinking marked the opening salvo in a struggle over how the new class of wage workers would spend their time. Employers sought to control the time that workers spent on the job, of course, but they were also increasingly critical of workers' leisure activities. Workers sought to acquire as much free time as possible, along with the right to make use of that time however they saw fit. This struggle lay at the heart of the conflicts that eventually gave rise to the Chicago Police Department.[3]

The proponents of anti-drinking law and order had a problem. In March 1855, when Boone was elected, Chicago lacked a force capable of enforcing his temperance policy or of dispersing crowds like the angry Germans who would soon assemble in front of the courthouse, as the city only employed seventy part-time watchmen for an estimated population of eighty thousand.[4] Realizing this, Boone and his Law and Order Party colleagues proposed to reorganize and enlarge the police department with native-born officers in order to enforce their anti-liquor program. Immediately upon taking office, Boone hired eighty special policemen, all native born, and put them under his control as mayor.[5]

Mayor Boone ordered these new police to break up the crowd that surrounded the courthouse. They accomplished this with no injuries and only arrested a few of the demonstrators. But another contingent of armed demonstrators assembled in the city's North Side German neighborhood and decided to rescue the imprisoned tavern keepers. Boone immediately deputized an additional 150 special policemen to reinforce the 80 he had hired immediately after his inauguration. While these special policemen assembled, the bridge tender raised the Clark Street drawbridge to cut off the crowd. Once the police were ready, Boone ordered the drawbridge lowered, allowing the rioters to confront a solid mass of 270 deputies and police. Boone also declared martial law and called in the volunteer state militia companies: the Chicago Light Guards, the National Guards, and the Chicago Light Artillery.[6] When the North Side Germans came across the drawbridge, the armed forces of the state met them with overwhelming force. In what came to be known as the Lager Beer Riot, at least one rioter was killed according to official accounts, although records of North Side funerals indicated that the number was probably higher. One police officer lost his arm, and 60 rioters were arrested.[7]

The Lager Beer Riot was a founding moment for the Chicago Police Department. On April 23, just two days after the riot, respectable Chicago citizens held a "Law and Order" public meeting at South Market Hall in order to push for a larger, stronger, and more stable police force. Participants in this meeting appointed a committee to work with the city government and to ensure that their demands for a strong police department were met.[8] This committee succeeded: the city council passed a series of modernizing reforms just one week later. In a pattern that would be repeated time and again, a crisis of order prompted a major reform of policing in the city. These reforms amounted to the founding of the Chicago Police Department.

This Lager Beer Riot was one example of the disorder engendered by the growth of a wage labor economy and the beginnings of urban industrial capitalism. As a result of these economic developments, mid-nineteenth-century northern cities became increasingly polyglot and ceased to be bound by traditional social, economic, or political ties. They were beset by divisions and conflicts operating on many different levels: between workers and their employers, between immigrants and the native born, between Catholics and Protestants, between drinkers and temperance advocates, between vice operators and moral reformers, and among Democrats, Know Nothings, Whigs, and Republicans. These conflicts did not line up neatly. For instance, most immigrants were working-class Catholic Democrats who opposed temperance, but the Democratic Party also attracted southern Protestant businessmen such as the agricultural equipment magnate Cyrus McCormick. Many German immigrants, meanwhile, were Protestant artisans who strongly opposed temperance, but who eventually supported the new Republican Party because of its free-labor ideology. But the Republican Party also attracted the staunchest temperance reformers. These multifaceted divisions broke the old personal, paternalistic system of social control and created a smoldering crisis of order that occasionally flared up in events like the Lager Beer Riot. This disorder prompted businessmen in cities across the country to push for the creation of new public institutions that could protect urban order: the police.[9]

Chicago's municipal armed forces had already undergone nearly twenty years of evolution by 1855, but they did not yet constitute anything recognizable as a police department. Before 1853, Chicago possessed a small force of armed municipal officials, but the Cook County sheriff was the main official responsible for policing the city. As in other cities and towns in the first half of the nineteenth century, Chicago had a constable system that was modeled on the colonial and English systems. The town elected constables and night watchmen along with its other municipal officials, but these constables and night watchmen held other jobs to supplement their paltry public salaries, and they lacked uniforms or other markers to separate themselves from the population as a whole. The original city charter of 1837 called for the establishment of a municipal court with constables attached to it. This charter established one constable for each of the six wards, acting under a high constable, but these men were officers of the court, rather than officers of the municipal government.[10] In fact, throughout the 1830s, the city did not even employ all seven constables required under the charter. In 1839, the *Daily American* complained that Chicago employed only two constables. As late as 1850, Chicago employed only nine constables and watchmen for a city of almost thirty thousand people.[11]

Over the first half of the 1850s, elite Chicagoans confronted two interrelated problems of order that prompted them to create a police force: the need to protect their property and the property of visiting businessmen, and the need to enforce order more generally among a largely immigrant class of wage workers who were not bound by earlier forms of social control. As with other cities in the United States and England, the broader issue of riots and strikes played a much larger role than crimes committed by individuals.[12]

It was not so easy, however, to see how elite Chicagoans could create such a system. While the development of the modern police seems inevitable in hindsight, a curious document from December 8, 1851, offers a glimpse of an alternative possibility. On that date, Edward Bonney sent a letter to the city council requesting authorization to establish an "independent"—by which he meant private—police force. He proposed that such a force be "clothed with the same power to do criminal business, that the regular police constables now are," but that "such an independent police . . . should depend solely and at all times upon their employers for compensation for services rendered." Bonney proposed that Chicago hire him to provide these police services. He would make a profit by collecting fines from those arrested and by collecting fees from the victims of crime who engaged his services. This was not a novel idea—private security firms played a large role throughout the nineteenth century, and the profession of "thief takers," who were hired by individuals to track down stolen property, dated to eighteenth-century London.[13] The city council's Committee on Police recommended that the council reject Bonney's proposal not because it was a bad idea, but because Bonney was not a resident of Chicago. But the city council never pursued the idea with a Chicago businessman or security firm, either.[14]

Bonney's letter indicates the inadequacy of public forces in the early 1850s.[15] He claimed that Chicago was "considered about the safest place of refuge for rogues in the Union," largely because the system of constables and watchmen that preceded the establishment of the police proved ineffective.[16] Indeed, the watches of all nineteenth-century cities were undermanned, especially given the part-time nature of police employment.[17] The limited scope of the early police is demonstrated by their budget: for fiscal 1852, the estimated expenses for the police and the city bridewell (jail) were just $8,009.20, excluding the costs of the police court. The wages of fourteen watchmen at $8 per week plus one constable at $10 per week constituted the single largest expense. In 1852, the population of Chicago was about forty thousand. The fourteen-man, part-time watch did not even pretend to patrol the whole city, instead mostly watching for fires.[18] A large part of the problem was that the municipal government had almost no resources for citywide institutions like the police. As Robin Einhorn has explained, local residents paid for street and sidewalk construction through a system of special assessments, rather than through a general municipal fund. The city levied few general taxes, and its citizens were loath to pay any. The city thus had little money to deal with larger municipal problems by creating institutions such as a police department.[19] As a result, the bulk of the city's population, already primarily immigrant workingmen, lived almost entirely outside the direct control or supervision of the government in their day-to-day lives.

Because of this deficiency, private security firms played a large role in nineteenth-century Chicago, as throughout the country. Private warehouses, railroads, and other companies hired night watchmen to guard their property, and these watchmen received official authorization but no pay from the city. Allen Pinkerton moved to Chicago in 1850 and soon thereafter opened his private detective agency. His business expanded rapidly, and by the end of the 1850s he had a large staff who served some of the city's most important businesses. Notable among Pinkerton's clients were the railroads, with whom he contracted in 1855. Pinkerton men guarded railroad property across the nation, mostly away from big cities where there was no public law enforcement whatsoever, but they also guarded railroad property within city limits.[20] While private police like the Pinkertons never took on the primary role of law enforcement as Bonney envisioned, the two types of police worked closely together in the 1850s, and the differentiation between detectives hired by private agencies and those hired by the city was not yet as clearly defined as it would become in subsequent years.[21] Still, private police could not solve the problem of order that worsened during the 1850s and beyond. Private police could protect property, but private individuals would never pay to extend the power of the municipal government over the entire city unless taxation compelled them to do so. As Chicago attracted increasing numbers of immigrant wage workers, the municipal government felt increasingly compelled to do just that.

Chicago could look to eastern and southern precedents for solutions to its burgeoning problem of order. In fact, the first military-style police departments in the United States were founded in the South in order to control large concentrations of slaves. These police departments evolved from a very different colonial heritage, notably the tradition of slave patrols that organized white men in militia-like organizations to track down runaways and prevent any possible slave revolts.[22] New Orleans was probably the first U.S. city to develop a military-style police department in the early nineteenth century in order to control that city's slaves.[23] However, Chicago looked more to eastern examples than southern ones. New York founded its police department in 1845, which was in turn modeled after the London Metropolitan Police Service that dated to 1829.[24] These departments were distinct from the older system of constables and night watchmen because they consolidated their respective cities' municipal forces in one military-style organization. New York and London did not create their police departments to control slaves—rather, they created them to deal with the same kinds of threats to order increasingly facing Chicago in the 1850s.[25]

In reaction to the inadequacy of the constable system, the city government decided to formally found a police department distinct from the municipal court in 1853. This action did not fundamentally change the shape of the constable system or even strengthen the municipal government's ability to control the city, but it did create the original legal framework for the department. The newly created Chicago Police Department formalized the rights and powers of constables and consolidated them under the control of a police marshal. The city council gave policemen an extraordinary amount of discretionary authority. It ordered them to "devote their attention to the preservation of the peace, quiet and good order of the city and the enforcing of the ordinances thereof, more especially in their respective wards and districts." The council did not yet make the position of constable a full-time job, but it did instruct these men to carry out only police business while on duty, and assured them that they would be paid accordingly.[26]

From the beginning, the city government ordered police officers to enforce "order" and "quiet" as well as city ordinances. It also granted them the right to "arrest all persons in the city found under suspicious circumstances and who cannot give a good account of themselves." In addition, officers had "the power and authority in a peaceable manner or if refused admittance after demand made, with force, to enter into any house, store, shop, grocery, or other building whatever, in the city, in which any person or persons may reasonably be suspected to be for unlawful purposes." They had the right to arrest anyone suspected of committing a crime, or the "violation of any ordinance for the preservation of the peace and good order of the city." Thus, the city government gave the police very broad powers to enforce a vaguely defined peace and order. They could enter any home, question any citizen, and arrest anyone who could not provide a convincing account of his or her activity.[27]

The city council also established the police as a direct extension of municipal authority and made no distinction between police officers and other members of the city government. The aldermen and the mayor granted themselves police powers, and the mayor was given control over the police marshal and, consequently, over the entire force. The mayor had the power to establish "Police Rules" at his own discretion, with the aim of making the various officers "efficient, vigilant, prompt and useful to the city." The city council gave itself the final authority to appoint and remove police officers, and it directed the mayor to regulate the department in his "Police Rules."[28]

Although the city government gave police officers considerable legal authority in 1853, it did not yet create a police department in any recognizable sense. Constables remained part-time employees and were expected to have other remunerative occupations. The newly consolidated force remained minuscule, given the scale of the city. Perhaps most importantly, the 1853 ordinance kept intact the division of the force into night watches and daytime constables. The position of constable as defined in the ordinance of 1853 was much the same as previously: constables had broad powers, but few specific directions and little professional cohesion. The 1853 founding was so unremarkable that neither the *Tribune* nor journalist John Flinn's otherwise exhaustive *History of the Chicago Police* written in 1888 make any mention of the police department's founding ordinance. It was not even clear precisely what constituted the tasks of the police force. While the city council instructed constables to answer to the mayor, it did not establish any standardized set of police procedures. The city council's Committee on Police, for instance, was still the body that Lake Street merchants approached to request that the city construct draymen's stands—an issue that had nothing to do with enforcing the laws.[29] In other words, it was not yet clear exactly what the police were supposed to do, and the difference between their responsibilities and those of other city officials remained ill-defined. In 1854, for instance, Isaac Milliken served simultaneously as both mayor and police justice.

The new police force soon confronted its first strike and revealed its limitations to Chicago employers. On Saturday, August 6, 1853, several hundred workers, mostly construction laborers, accompanied by a "band of music" quit work and paraded through the streets from workplace to workplace, demanding to work only eight hours on Saturdays. The strikers marched to the corner of Randolph and LaSalle, where Mayor Charles Gray urged them to disperse. The following Monday, August 8, the strike continued and shut down the building sites of the city. That day, construction employers submitted a petition to the city council with dozens of signatures requesting that the police stop the strike. The petition claimed that "a number of persons have this day been traversing our streets for the avowed purpose of preventing those who did not fall in with their peculiar views from prosecuting their ordinary daily labor, in many instances using force and threatening in some cases the lives of those who refused to leave their work." The petition argued that the strikers' activities tended "to disturb, and endanger the peace and good order of the city" and that they were damaging to the "pecuniary [interests of] many of our citizens." For the first time, employers invoked the rhetoric of disorder in order to prompt the police to protect their financial interests. But the police were incapable of putting down the strike. The mayor refused to give in to the strikers' demands that he ring the city bell marking the end of the workday at four o'clock on Saturday afternoons, but he was also unable to call in the police to help the employers because there simply were not enough men to intervene effectively.[30]

On Tuesday, August 9, the "employers of the city" assembled to discuss what action they should take. The *Chicago Journal* reported that these employers represented fifty establishments that employed about two thousand workers. The employers adopted a resolution that expressed their "determination never to yield to so unjust and unreasonable a demand" as the strikers' desire to work only eight hours on Saturdays. They also appointed a committee of twenty to coordinate employer resistance to the strike. This new "Business Committee" represented the city's "principle Mechanical Departments of Industry," indicating that the strike had spread beyond the building trades. The formation of an employers' committee was an early precursor to a development that became increasingly common in the coming decades. Throughout the rest of the century, when labor disturbances threatened Chicago's employers, they almost instinctively united in committees that pushed the city government to strengthen the police force and encouraged the department to act in their interests.

Despite the lack of a strong police force, the employers were able to wait out the strikers. By Friday, the newspapers reported that a majority of strikers were back at work, and by the following Wednesday they declared that the strike had been completely defeated.[31]

For the first time, the threat of organized wage workers prompted a section of Chicago employers to unite, if temporarily. These employers turned to the city government and used the language of order to plead for an armed force that could control these wage workers. While the city government lacked the forces to respond at that moment, this threat of disorder prompted Chicago to increase the number of men at its disposal to fifty-five men six months later in the spring of 1854. It also helped create a sentiment among employers that a stronger police force would be useful.

Yet in 1853 and 1854, the relatively new police authority was not universally respected, by either the citizenry or the press. The *Tribune* reported that "in arresting a man yesterday . . . two policemen went altogether too far in the use of their authority." The man was "refractory and partially intoxicated" and infuriated the policemen by refusing to cooperate. One of them struck the man repeated blows to the head and cut a deep gash in his face. This incident was not remarkable. The *Tribune*'s coverage of it, however, shows that this mouthpiece of the city's business interests had not yet developed the habit of deferring to the police interpretation of this type of event. Such incidents would become increasingly common as the police department grew, but in 1854 neither the press nor the population was yet used to dealing with an institution granted almost unlimited discretionary authority.[32]

Despite their general support for the police department, businessmen were not immune from injury at its hands. For instance, in December 1854, innkeeper Peter Connerton petitioned the city council for release from a fine imposed on him by overzealous policemen. Connerton kept a lodging house on New North Water Street. He claimed that sometime in June 1854, the night police entered his house and arrested some people for offenses they had committed elsewhere. In the process of making the arrest, "the Windows of Petitioner's house were damaged to a considerable extent." When he complained about the damage, the police took Connerton into custody and fined him $25. He claimed that he did not interfere with the "duties of the officers, although his said remarks touching the damage to his windows were so construed." Ultimately, the city council rejected Connerton's request that the fine be canceled, because his version of the story did not accord with the version related by the policemen involved. Not surprisingly, the city council chose the account given by its own forces over that of an unknown and apparently uninfluential citizen. Whichever story is accurate, this encounter illustrates a basic tension that would only increase over time as the police force grew. In order to effectively carry out their tasks, the police needed considerable latitude. That latitude gave them the possibility of acting in heavy-handed and often corrupt ways. This type of behavior could alienate Chicagoans of various class backgrounds and ethnicities and undermined the legitimacy of the police among all sections of Chicago's population.

Other petitions reveal that the police force established in 1853 still did not meet the needs of Chicago's businessmen for a municipal service that could protect their property. On February 5, 1855, at the Sherman House hotel, thieves robbed Albert Deshow of his watch and some belongings. Deshow offered a reward of $100 for the return of his property and the police subsequently arrested the culprit and returned Deshow's watch and all of his property except for $20.[33] Deshow paid the police a reward of $50 and an additional $13.25 "for Policemen's Expenses in looking for the thief." A short time later, he submitted a petition to the city council asking to be reimbursed the sum of $63.25 for all the expenses he incurred as a result of the ordeal. The Committee on Police advised the council that "the amount of $13.25 should be remitted, but they are not satisfied that the city should pay rewards offered by individuals for the recovery of their own property."[34] This petition reveals, first, that the city still had a "cash-and-carry" police force. Given that constables were poorly paid and only worked part-time, this was neither a bribe nor police corruption. That this practice was still routine is shown by the fact that, rather than hiding his reward, Deshow tried to get the city council to pay him back. By 1855, the thief-taking system was in decline, and Deshow's case illustrates the transition. While the city council did not reimburse Deshow for the money he offered as a reward, they did pay him the $13.25 that he spent on police expenses. The city council accepted that Deshow had the right both to hire the city's police to carry out the task he desired and to be reimbursed, since the city had assumed the responsibility for preventing theft.

As a wealthy visitor from out of town, Deshow belonged to the group that city officials most wanted to impress. Throughout the late 1850s and 1860s, city council members reiterated again and again the importance of making a positive impression on eastern businessmen. Chicago rose to become the dominant midwestern metropolis in large part through the booster system. In the 1850s, many of Chicago's wealthy citizens had acquired their wealth through land speculation, and their success depended on the city's continued growth. That growth, in turn, depended on Chicago's relationship with eastern business interests.[35] The police were charged with protecting these businessmen. In that context, it is not surprising that the Committee on Police would recommend that Deshow be reimbursed for at least part of his expenses. The fact that Deshow needed to offer a reward and to pay expenses in the first place was a sign that, in early 1855, the police force did not automatically protect even the interests of potential eastern investors in the city without additional financial incentives.

Thus, by 1855 Chicago's political and economic elite felt the need for a police force like those already established in London, New York, Philadelphia, and Boston. They needed a force that could break strikes, like the one that shut down construction sites in August 1853. They also needed a force that could protect eastern investors like Albert Deshow and their investments. Finally, and most importantly, they needed a force that could extend the power of the municipal government into the apparently lawless and disorderly immigrant neighborhoods, where in the eyes of the native-born elite, traditional ties of deference and paternalism had not developed. It was in this context that Levi Boone's Law and Order party won control of the city government and embarked on an anti-immigrant temperance policy.

Boone and his Law and Order compatriots failed to enforce this temperance policy. The Lager Beer Riot led to a compromise in which the city council agreed to lower the liquor license fee to $100. This was still double the old $50 license fee, but was much less than the $300 demanded by Levi Boone. By a close vote, the council decided not to release those imprisoned for failing to pay the $300, although most of those arrested in the riot were released without charges. Neither the nativists nor the rioters could impose their will.

This prompted Law and Order politicians to shift their focus from temperance to policing and to create the Chicago Police Department. On April 30, 1855, just nine days after the confrontations at the courthouse and the Clark Street Bridge, the council passed a series of modernizing police reforms that amounted to the department's real founding. Part of the motivation for the reform was that even Levi Boone's enlarged force of deputies could not put down the riot without the help of the militia. The militia was inordinately expensive: the bill for the deployment of the Chicago Light Guards, the National Guards, the Chicago Light Artillery and the various special deputies during the Lager Beer Riot amounted to at least $4,223.50, plus doctors' fees. Chicago needed a force of its own. The new police reforms met considerable opposition from the same forces that opposed temperance. The ordinance creating the new department passed by a vote of 8–7, against the opposition of every North Side aldermen, whose constituents were predominantly German immigrants. Thus, the modern Chicago police force was born in the aftermath of a riot that the existing force had been unable to put down without substantial assistance, and it was born over the opposition of the city's immigrant political leaders.[36]

The new department was not simply the creation of a flash in the pan, nativist political coalition—it had the backing of some of the most important businesses in the city. In fact, the document the city council's Committee on Police submitted to justify the reorganization was printed on Illinois Central Railroad stationery. The Illinois Central Railroad letterhead is crossed out on each page, but it is clearly legible.[37] The precise significance and source of this letterhead is impossible to determine today, but it suggests that the railroad's motives and opportunities for promoting the police department warrant further investigation. This railroad was a lynchpin in the Chicago economy. It connected Chicago to its hinterland and helped make the city the premier midwestern metropolis. The railroad was also a heavy investor within Chicago. The corporation's directors estimated that they had spent a million dollars on construction in Chicago alone in the year prior to March 19, 1856.[38]

From its inception in 1851, this corporation was connected to the government at all levels. Governor William Bissell, elected in 1856, had been a solicitor for the railroad. He had also been the main proponent in the U.S. House of Representatives of the bill granting the railroad its right of way. In 1852, the railroad secured its entrance to Chicago along the lakefront after heated debate in the city council. Even after this legislative coup, the Illinois Central maintained close relations with the council. On August 4, 1853, for instance, the superintendent of the railroad invited the entire council on a free day trip to Kankakee.[39] The Illinois Central was also tied to U.S. Senator Stephen Douglas, who had helped the railroad acquire its approach to Chicago through Indiana. In 1855, Douglas bought a valuable piece of real estate from the Illinois Central at a low price. Abraham Lincoln helped the railroad secure its charter in 1861, and his law practice included at least fifty cases with the Illinois Central, for which he received a retainer and free rail passes.[40] While investors from the East Coast and Europe owned most of the stock of the Illinois Central, historian Bessie Pierce estimates that about $150,000 of its capital stock was held by residents of Chicago. The Illinois Central Railroad was one of the biggest players in the city's economy and government, and all of the city's business leaders recognized it as such.[41]

The Illinois Central needed police protection.[42] To meet this need, the Illinois Central, Rock Island, Burlington, and other railroads hired Allan Pinkerton to establish a police agency in Chicago devoted to protecting their property. For obvious economic reasons, the Illinois Central would have preferred to rely on a police force funded by the public.[43]

Crime was not the only reason the Illinois Central needed police protection. Like other large enterprises that employed many unskilled wage workers, the Illinois Central also had a problem enforcing labor discipline. Historian Carlton Corliss estimates that the railroad itself was responsible for bringing a hundred thousand men to Illinois to work on construction, and these workers had a history of rebellion.[44] In 1853, workers laying track for the Illinois Central between Bloomington and La Salle rioted and killed Albert Story, one of the railroad's contractors. The state militia put down the riot, and 150 workers walked away from the construction project.[45]

Colonel Roswell B. Mason, the chief engineer, argued that "these scenes of violence are the result, in most cases, of the free use of Whiskey by the men, which has been the cause of more delay, more violence and bloodshed, than any other one thing."[46] This interpretation fits with Mayor Levi Boone's equation of drinking, immigrants, and disorder, and with a long and inaccurate tradition of blaming ethnic rivalries and drink for worker discontent. In 1834, for instance, Irish workers building the C&O Canal in Maryland fought each other in a pitched battle. Contemporaries blamed the clash on age-old conflicts between Irish clans, but historian Peter Way illustrates that the fight was really about who would have access to jobs in a period of layoffs. As canal construction accelerated, these types of fights, along with strikes and other forms of disorder, increased to the point that, between 1829 and 1834, soldiers put down strikes or riots among canal workers thirty-two times.[47] Railroad construction was no different.

That Mason and Boone blamed workers' use of drink for disorder is emblematic of the emerging elite critique of working-class leisure activities that would only accelerate in subsequent years. In the colonial and early national period, patrons of various classes, races, and ethnicities mixed in the same taverns. As a result, late-eighteenth-century Philadelphians, for instance, "drank in ways that confirmed their sense of hierarchy," rather than in ways that reinforced class consciousness.[48] In the early nineteenth century, apprentices, journeymen, and master artisans all drank together in the course of the workday, discussing politics, religion, and social questions while they did so.[49] As some masters became capitalists and others were ruined, as cities grew and immigration increased, and as the elite increasingly separated itself from the working class and the poor, the social ties that bound urban residents across class lines were severed.[50] As a result, by the middle of the nineteenth century, across the urban north, mixed-class taverns were giving way to saloons segregated by class and ethnicity. These saloons gave workers the chance to socialize free from elite eyes. For this reason, they were symbols of the growing class divisions within northern, urban society and were potential threats to the order that elites were so anxious to secure.[51] This helps explain why Levi Boone, Roswell Mason, and others were so anxious about the drinking habits of immigrant workers.

It would be a mistake to make too much of this use of the Illinois Central's letterhead: clearly, the Chicago Police Department was not created at the behest of just this one corporation, however important. Nonetheless, the interests and influence of the Illinois Central illustrate how nativism, temperance, and worker disorder dovetailed to overcome businessmen's reluctance to tax themselves and create a more powerful police department.

The city council's Committee on Police made it clear from the outset that it was creating a military-style police department to keep order in the face of the threats posed by a mobile class of wage workers, not to fight crime. The city council also made clear its intention to protect out-of-town visitors in order to attract eastern capital. Chicago needed to host meetings of "the Scientific, the Mercantile, the Political and religious Communities of the Union." The council lamented that the police consisted of "a force scarcely sufficient to diligently watch at and guard our Public wharves, Steam Boat landings, and our several Rail Road Depots, not to mention the Constant attention of the Police that ought to be given day and night to our most public thoroughfares."[52] In creating the new force, the committee wrote that Chicago is "the receptacle in transit of a class of persons against whom a Vigilant Police can alone protect us, and from among whom nineteen twentieths of the Criminals Convicted in the Recording Court are Taken." This "class of persons" in transit differentiated stable, property-owning Chicagoans from the wage-working renters, usually immigrants, that so incensed the nativists. The committee explained that, to keep this population under control, the police had to have broad powers, since "matters not criminal in particulars, but which if permitted to go unchecked in a dense population like ours, would result very injuriously to the city." Because of what the police force did once it was created, these "matters not criminal" probably refer to the drinking and disorderly behavior for which the police subsequently arrested so many Chicagoans. The Committee on Police, then, wanted to be able to enforce order as they understood it on the laboring population, even when no obvious criminal activity was involved.[53]

To accomplish these goals, the city council undertook a dramatic reorganization of the police department from a system of constables to one made up of full-time officers expected to act in a disciplined manner. The council divided the police into the ranks of marshal, captain of police, lieutenant, second lieutenant, sergeant, police constable, and policemen of the city and defined the roles of each. It also strengthened the mayor's power over the police and abolished the differentiation between the constabulary and night watch. The council made provision for riots, divided the city into three police districts, and provided the police with uniforms. This last is perhaps the most important single change since it visually set the police force off from the rest of the population. A policeman in uniform was a representative of municipal authority rather than a private individual who happened to have the power to act as a constable. In sum, the police were transformed from an unorganized, undisciplined, and poorly defined group of citizens into a well-ordered hierarchy organized along military lines and clearly differentiated from the rest of the population by their uniforms.

The city council's resolution of April 30, 1855, marked the crucial founding moment, when Chicago created a force similar to the London Metropolitan Police Service, the New York Municipal Police, the Philadelphia Police, and the Boston Police Department. Each of these cities founded their departments in almost precisely the same way. They each abolished the division between night watchmen and constables, organized the police on a military basis, divided their cities into precincts, and provided their policemen with uniforms. While the Chicago city council made no mention of any other city's police department in the ordinances reorganizing the department, they were no doubt aware of their eastern and perhaps foreign predecessors and created a force that closely resembled them.[54]

New York, Boston, and Philadelphia similarly founded their police departments in response to increasing disorder caused by immigration and the development of a wage labor economy that broke down earlier forms of social control. Philadelphia in particular founded its police department as a result of a series of disturbances similar to the Lager Beer Riot. Like other northern cities, it experienced regular riots throughout the 1830s and 1840s. In 1838, for instance, a crowd burned to the ground the newly constructed Pennsylvania Hall, a meeting place for reformers. This was possible because no police force existed in that city that could effectively cow the crowd. The commission charged with investigating the violence urged the city to establish a more powerful police force, arguing that "because conditions such as these had been rare, a strong police had 'never yet been required. . . . A moral force . . . has heretofore always sufficed to preserve the public peace.'"[55] Then, in 1844, widespread violence broke out between anti-Catholic nativists and Irish immigrants. In the confusion, the state militia fired on an already pacified nativist crowd, killing a number of bystanders. After these riots, many prominent Philadelphians, as well as the grand jury that investigated the violence, called for the organization of a strong municipal police force that could respond to riots, and the existing force of constables began to be reorganized along more military lines.[56] Over the next five years, as public violence between native-born and immigrant fire companies and gangs increased, calls grew stronger for a consolidated police force that could stop riots. This culminated in an 1850 reorganization of the Philadelphia police along lines similar to the New York and London police departments. The result was a marshal's police organized to arrest "idle, suspicious, or disorderly persons" and "to put down riots anywhere in the county."[57]

Like London, New York, and later Chicago, Philadelphia experienced an increase in disorder as a wage labor economy grew. This new economy created a mass of native-born workers with few prospects for becoming independent free laborers at the same time that it attracted increasing numbers of immigrants, especially from Ireland. At first, the degradation of journeymen led to the birth of America's first Workingmen's Parties and the labor movement in the 1820s and 1830s, but as Irish immigration especially increased, the labor movement declined because of increasing ethnic divisions among workers. Nonetheless, both the immigrants and the native born were cut from the traditional ties of deference and authority that sufficed to keep order, at least usually, in colonial cities and in the early cities of the republic.[58] Disorderly crowds were certainly part of the urban landscape before this period, as the American Revolution or the violence surrounding the election of 1800 demonstrated.[59] But those earlier crowds were often cross-class alliances, organized within the context of elite politics even though they sometimes exceeded the desires of the elite. As the wage labor economy grew, the scale of disorders and the difficulty of reining them in grew apace. New York, Philadelphia, Boston, and Chicago all created police departments in this context. Thus, the need for a bureaucratic, military-style police department charged with maintaining order among the anonymous crowds arose directly from the increasing class divisions brought about by the transformation of the northern economy in the middle of the nineteenth century.

Professional police officials emerged to take charge of the new departments. In Chicago, Mayor Levi Boone appointed Cyrus Bradley captain and acting chief over the new force of seventy-three men after the Lager Beer Riot.[60] Bradley was the individual most closely connected with the early history of the Chicago police. In addition to serving as the city's first chief of police, he would also be appointed superintendent of police by the police board created in 1861. He was born in Concord, New Hampshire, in 1819 and came to Chicago when he was eighteen years old while the city was first developing. He first entered public life in 1849, when he was appointed tax collector for the town of South Chicago. He then served as sheriff of Cook County in 1854 and 1855, before he was appointed the first chief of police. In 1856, when he was removed from his post by the newly elected Mayor Thomas Dyer, Bradley started a private detective and collection agency. This kept him in close contact with the force, even though he was no longer chief. He was also a member of the Chicago Light Artillery, a militia unit that helped to put down the Lager Beer Riot and later served in the Civil War. Bradley was intimately connected with the leaders of Chicago's Republican Party, and he worked closely with them until his death in 1865. Although he was not a politician, he instead became one of the city's first experts in police affairs.[61] He was a professional police officer, the first of his kind in Chicago.

Although Bradley shaped the new police department into an institution that protected order on the city streets, the fledgling police force had little effect on crime. Because patrolmen faced attack from those they sought to arrest and had no easy means to call for reinforcements, they traveled in pairs. This meant that the whole city of about eighty thousand people was covered by only twelve beats. Bradley personally solved a number of important murder cases, but neither he nor his police force could adequately protect Chicago's property owners. Mayor Boone received frequent letters from store owners and clerks complaining of the lack of adequate police protection. Because of this, businesses in the city continued to rely on an extensive system of private security guards to keep watch over their property.[62]

The police primarily arrested working-class immigrants for nonviolent charges. The Irish accounted for two-thirds of the 3,716 arrests during the first six months of the new department's operations. The Irish were the city's poorest large ethnic group and most likely to work for wages in Chicago's growing lumberyards, meat-processing facilities, and brickyards. Yet the Irish accounted for only about one-fifth of Chicago's total population.[63] Germans were the next largest ethnicity represented in the arrest figures, accounting for 17 percent of the total. This is entirely consistent with the rhetoric that accompanied the founding of the new force. It also illustrates the divergence between the clash over German drinking habits symbolized by the Lager Beer Riot and the reality that Irish immigrants, not Germans, made up the bulk of the poor population more likely to live outside the traditional bounds of social control and more likely to behave in "disorderly" ways. Black people accounted for less than 1 percent of the total, which can be accounted for by the tiny size of the city's black population. The police only recorded 11 percent of those arrested as "Americans." While immigrants formed the majority of the city's population by this time, the native-born certainly accounted for more than 11 percent.[64] The bulk of those arrested also had working-class occupations. The police identified a little more than half of all arrestees as laborers or mechanics. Prostitutes, hackmen, draymen, and peddlers accounted for most of the remainder. Members of the last three professions were implicated in the traffic disorder that marked every city in the country in the middle of the nineteenth century. The only arrestees who were not part of or tied to the city's growing working class were four ministers, eight doctors, and four lawyers. In a city where a large number of people still owned their own shops, where manufacturing was still generally carried out in small concerns with owners who worked alongside their employees, it is significant that the vast majority of those arrested were wage workers rather than small-business owners.[65]

The new police force kept order on the streets, but the prison system remained small. Eighty-six percent of cases serious enough to go to the police court ended in a fine. The average fine was $5.38, an onerous sum for Chicago's poorest residents, but mild by later standards. The police courts sentenced only 113 people, or 3 percent of those arrested, to the bridewell (city jail), for an average of 35 days each. Given that the police recorded 24 arrests for murder or attempted murder, 7 arrests for rape, 35 for burglary, and 337 for larceny, the chances were small that an arrestee would go to prison even for a relatively major crime. The majority of those arrested even for larceny were released after they paid a fine, and a large number of those convicted of more serious crimes were probably released after relatively short stints in prison. The criminal justice system released 14 percent on examination without fining them or sentencing them to the bridewell. The Chicago justice system, then, meted out remarkably lax punishments by later standards. Police presence on the streets, rather than fear of punishment, kept order.[66]

The police mostly arrested people for offenses related to the maintenance of order. Drunk and disorderly conduct accounted for 64 percent of all arrests. This is not surprising since this police force was created in the aftermath of a major clash over drinking. It was also an indication of things to come; throughout the nineteenth century, the majority of the Chicago Police Department's arrests would be for this offense. It is impossible to say exactly what constituted disorderly behavior, but it is safe to assume that many arrests for drunk and disorderly conduct occurred when there was no other evident criminal activity, in view of the wide latitude granted to individual officers.[67] Most of the other arrests were also for nonviolent and even noncriminal offenses. The violation of city ordinances accounted for about 11 percent of total arrests. These city ordinances covered a wide range of behaviors, but most involved traffic. This was followed by larceny, which was the charge against 9 percent of those arrested, and was the most frequent property crime recorded. Arrests of "Keepers and Inmates of Houses of Ill Fame" accounted for 5 percent of the total, and for the majority of the arrests of women. Of the 3,716 people arrested, only 282 were women, and most of these were prostitutes. Another 130 people were arrested for "Resisting and Interfering" with the police, indicating that working class immigrants continued to contest the operations of the new police force, even after the suppression of the Lager Beer Riot. The frequency of "Resisting and Interfering" arrests would decline in coming years as the police force became more established and legitimate.

Altogether, these statistics paint a relatively clear picture of what the new police force did on a daily basis during its first six months. Policemen on patrol arrested a large number of working-class Irish and German immigrants for drinking. They forced these immigrants to pay a fine, and then released them. They also enforced order on the city streets among the multitude of carts and wagons driving and parking in a disorderly manner. And they occasionally harassed prostitutes, without putting a serious dent in the trade overall. While the police investigated a small number of serious crimes, the bulk of their activity consisted of patrolling the everyday activity of the immigrant working class.

While temperance reform failed, challenging drunkenness and disorderly behavior nonetheless served a vital interest for Chicago's elite. The city's native-born businessmen and politicians felt genuinely threatened by the drinking and perceived disorder of the immigrant neighborhoods, and they created the police in large measure to deal with these threats and enforce order as they understood it. This order took different forms, from protecting out-of-town visitors especially in the city's downtown area to cracking down on saloons that stayed open on Sunday, to breaking strikes. In every case, the city's elite deployed the concept of order to justify deploying ever-increasing force against Chicago's growing population of immigrant wage workers who lived outside the earlier framework of deferential social control. The intermittent police presence in the working-class neighborhoods and their regular harassment of the residents by imposing fines did set limits on working-class behavior. By establishing some authority on the streets with the police, Chicago's city government reinforced its power over the city as a whole. Also, as both businessmen and workers, native-born and immigrants, all knew, the police constituted a force that could be deployed to repress strikes and riots. In other words, the police acted to preserve the businessmen's understanding of order. From the beginning, policemen suppressed disorderly behavior and upheld the broader social, political, and economic order of the day.

Paradoxically, the temperance of the native-born supporters of Levi Boone was one of the biggest threats to police legitimacy in its early days. The equation of drinking, immigration, and disorderly behavior missed the class divisions especially within the German population. In fact, the German saloonkeepers were agents of order in the traditional American sense. They were small businessmen, tied in myriad ways to the artisans and wage workers who frequented their saloons. The saloonkeepers also had a large interest in order, or at least in protecting their property from rowdy drunks or crime. The Lager Beer Riot illustrates not that German immigrants were a threat to the established order, but rather that a significant segment of the German population was willing to take big risks to protect those they saw as leaders of their community. In this way, the Lager Beer Riot can be interpreted much as Alfred Young interpreted the Boston Tea Party, in which working-class Bostonians united with social elites to protect that city's political economy from an intruding state.[68] Just as British attempts to control the colonial economy more tightly drove Bostonians to unite politically across class lines, the nativism of the 1850s pushed immigrants in Chicago to unite in a similar way. Boone's policies created long-term problems for the police by driving immigrant property owners to view the new force as a threat.

The reorganization of the Chicago police was Mayor Levi Boone's most important legacy. He has often been characterized as a flash-in-the-pan, nativist mayor whose attempts at liquor control ultimately failed.[69] Even as insightful a historian as Robin Einhorn characterized Boone's election as the last time that "a small group of extremists could win [an election] surreptitiously."[70] While Boone was certainly a nativist, his brief tenure as chief executive of the city can be better understood by taking the name of his party seriously. He was the Law and Order candidate and, for better or worse, he helped create the main institution that would enforce law and order in the emerging city. His nativism was part of a broader fear of immigrants and the increasing anonymity in big cities. It was also intimately linked to the emergence of "law-and-order" ideology as a driving force in municipal politics.

By the end of 1855, Chicago possessed a new police force with a professional leadership, clad in standardized uniforms, and able to patrol the streets with discipline. Yet the new department's undermanned patrols were unable to enforce order, let alone the law, in wide swaths of the city. The city's elite and politicians continued to disagree over the shape the new force should take. And it confronted a growing population of wage laborers who posed an increasing threat to the old order and who had yet to recognize the department's legitimacy.

CHAPTER 2

Paternalism and the Birth
of Professional Police Organization

On March 12, 1856, the *Chicago Tribune* declared: "[Mayor Dyer's] promises to the rapscallions who electioneered for him, who secured him the fraudulent votes to which he owes his election, who stood for him at the polls to overawe opposition and bully the timid, must be kept." Dyer was the Democratic candidate for mayor, supported by many of the city's workingmen and immigrants and stridently opposed by Republicans like the editors of the *Tribune*. To the *Tribune*, the election turned on the question of order. "We shall probably have as the fruits of the 'great victory,' [of Mayor Dyer] such a police as the mob which rallied in our streets after the battle would elect. What vindicators of law and order they will be let their shouts, blasphemies and orgies on the day of the 'big drunk' bear witness. Before the end of the year, *revolvers* will be a legal tender in Chicago."[1] Despite the *Tribune*'s dire predictions, Thomas Dyer's election as mayor did not make revolvers legal tender. Still, until 1861, the Chicago police were directly answerable to the individual mayor who appointed them, which meant that Dyer's 1856 overturn of Levi Boone's nativist regime did potentially mark a major transformation in the city's young police department. The mayor had the authority to change the entire personnel of the police, to set them entirely new tasks, and to decide which laws they would enforce. Chicago's original police force was so tied to the person of the mayor that a change in party could prompt the *Tribune* to worry about the most basic maintenance of law and order when the Democratic candidate was elected.

Dyer's election in 1856 inaugurated a five-year period of contestation over the basic shape of the new police force. On the surface, this fight pitted law-and-order Republicans against Democratic supporters of immigrants and looser law enforcement. But party politics tells only a fraction of the story, especially since the Republican Party was just coming into being as an antislavery coalition of former Democrats and Whigs and since the sectional crisis increasingly dominated national and local political alignments. As a result, the Republican Party included people who agreed on their opposition to the extension of slavery, but who had very different opinions about how to maintain order in the cities. The Democratic Party, meanwhile, increasingly attracted constituents who favored restraint and accommodation on sectional issues, regardless of their opinions about local politics.

The underlying dispute was between two conflicting visions of the police, each of which had supporters particularly within the Republican Party. Some members of both parties, most notably Democratic Mayor Dyer and Republican Mayor John Wentworth, sought to fit the police into the older paternalistic method of keeping order. The politicians who advocated this police methodology wanted to give elite individuals within the city considerable leeway over law enforcement. According to this view, respectable men could use the police to help them keep order, and they should be able to secure clemency for those connected to them. The police should be part of the traditional, paternalistic system of social control, not a replacement for it. The advocates of this policing ideology also generally advocated giving elected officials considerable control over the department, and argued that this was a way that voters could express their desires about police policy.

Professional police officers, including the first Superintendent of Police Cyrus Bradley and their allies, began to elaborate a countervailing ideology. They argued that order could be better protected if men dedicated to law and order, rather than professional politicians, controlled the police force. These men did not actually argue that the law should dictate police behavior—throughout the nineteenth century, the law was barely relevant to police policy.[2] Rather, they argued that a consistent police leadership should command a well-trained body of policemen who were secure in their jobs. This form of police organization would make the police less open to corruption and less beholden to venal politicians. On the other hand, it would put the police increasingly outside the control of the electorate. As the Civil War approached, members of the Republican Party in Illinois and nationally became increasingly worried about the problems of order that the conflict might engender. As a result, the majority of the Republican Party eventually rallied around this professional, bureaucratic vision of policing and eventually made it the standard model of a big-city police department, rhetorically accepted by Democrats and Republicans alike even while reality on the ground always differed widely from this ideal.

This clash thus foreshadowed the struggle between political machines and professional reformers that would characterize so much of the urban history of the late nineteenth and early twentieth centuries. It is no accident that this early struggle revolved around the police. Police were both a source of patronage and the key arm of the municipal government, necessary to enforce order as well as any proposed reform. The police eventually stood at the heart of machine politics because drawing policemen from immigrant neighborhoods became one of the key ways of integrating immigrant groups—especially the Irish but also the Germans—into a political machine. Political machines in many ways grew out of older forms of cross-class alliance building, and in this way, the promoters of a paternalistic police force, such as Mayors Dyer and Wentworth, served as bridges between the older form of personal party politics and the newer form of machine politics.[3] For the same reason, the police continuously aroused the ire of reformers who saw patronage as an antidemocratic arm of the political bosses.

On a deeper level, however, the stakes were high because the police were the key institution that made the evolving mid-nineteenth-century conception of reform possible. If the municipal government possessed an institution that could remain above the fray to dispassionately enforce rules that were in the best interests of the population, as understood by enlightened reformers, then municipal government might be the key to reforming society. That the police never conformed to this image, and indeed rarely approached it, helps explain the continued attempts by municipal reformers to reshape the department. The men who built the Republican Party in the 1850s, and eventually tried to enforce a bureaucratic, professional vision of the police force, thus represent a bridge between antebellum reformers and those of the late nineteenth century, who increasingly turned to the state to implement their vision of a progressive society.[4]

Chicagoans elected Democrat Thomas Dyer mayor along with a Democratic majority in the city council in 1856 mainly in response to their hatred of Levi Boone's police force. As the *Tribune*'s outrage at his election implies, Dyer was a staunch opponent of temperance. Once elected, Dyer removed most of the personnel of the police force, fired Cyrus Bradley, and appointed his own political allies. But despite the shrill alarm of the *Tribune* and the newly formed Republican Party, the force under Dyer carried out essentially the same activity as under Mayor Boone. Out of 5,008 arrests between January 1, 1856, and January 1, 1857, 1,971 were for drunk or disorderly conduct, and another 1,151 were for the newly recorded but equally vague offense of vagrancy. More than half of those arrests, 2,753, were of Irish immigrants, and another 842 were of Germans, though since some people were surely arrested more than once, the total number of arrestees was lower than these figures indicate. Despite the change in personnel, rhetoric, and support of the mayor, Dyer did not change the basic activity of the force.[5]

While the police force pursued the same crimes and prosecuted the same individuals as under the old regime, the new force was characterized by a paternalism that had not existed in Mayor Boone's anti-immigrant, law-and-order department. Dyer set up a system that sought to gain the approval of his electoral base, both immigrant and native born, with three interconnected aspects. First, the mayor set the rules for the police and appointed to the police force men with whom he had personal ties. While some of these officers eventually served long careers with the Chicago Police Department, they were appointed by Mayor Dyer because of the service they had rendered to him and his campaign, rather than for any particular skills they had as police officers. Thus, policemen under Dyer had personal and political, rather than professional, obligations. Second, people arrested by the new force frequently appealed for release to the city council, while there is no evidence that they did so under Mayor Boone. They appealed to the council's mercy and invoked their allegiance to the Democratic Party, rather than asserting their own innocence. And as long as they exhibited appropriate deference, they were largely successful in obtaining release from fines or imprisonment under the regime of Mayor Dyer. Finally, petitioners to the city council used a highly gendered language that referred to the roles within the family that arrestees were supposed to play. Men appealed for their wives' release on the grounds that those wives were needed for child care, while women appealed for their husbands' release because they needed those husbands to support the family by earning wages. Thus, petitioners placed themselves within a world of hierarchical mutual obligations, rather than in an objective, anonymous, and legal world.[6]

The petitions that arrestees and their families submitted to the city council reveal that the relationship between the Democratic city government and the city's wage working population was based on shared notions of morality, sympathy rooted in hierarchy, and a mutual understanding of the family. In this way, the police under Mayor Dyer most closely approached the ideal of paternalistic policing. Petitioners sought to establish that they were on the same political side as those they petitioned. They repeatedly referred to the crimes for which they were arrested as "sins," and they expressed hope that the council would alleviate their poor circumstances. Nearly every petitioner referred to the impoverishment that an arrest had imposed on a family, but not one petition denied the truth of the charges against the arrested person. In addition, because petitioners appealed to the mercy of the city council, rather than to the police or the justices who sentenced them, they sought to take advantage of the city government's hierarchy by going over the heads of the arresting officers and the sentencing police justices. At least under Mayor Dyer, the city council was disposed to overturn the decisions of the police and the justices. Thus, elected officials rather than the police hierarchy controlled the Chicago criminal justice system. They ran this system in a manner that encouraged deference from their constituents but that offered those constituents potential relief from fines and jail time. In this way, Dyer and his city council sought to deploy the police within the framework of the paternalistic system of order extant before Levi Boone's police reforms.

The petition that Mrs. John Caffrey submitted to the council on March 6, 1856, illustrates how the Democratic Party's victory in the 1856 municipal elections created an opening for arrestees claiming political connections to gain release if they used the right language. "Your petitioners husband," she wrote, "pending the City Election was induced by others to take some liquor, this last Sunday." Later in the same petition, she declared her "confiden[ce] that the *present* counsel will not turn a deaf ear to the prayer of a poor wife and innocent little ones, but that they will at once unbar the gate, and lead the husband forth to life and light, and that he will sin no more." Mrs. Caffrey emphasized that her husband was arrested while working for the Democrats' election, and she underlined the word *present* as if to indicate her faith that the newly elected council would fulfill its side of the paternalist relationship. Mrs. Caffrey also appealed to the council to release her husband because his arrest was harming her and her little ones, since it was his job to earn money for the household. She acknowledged that he had sinned, but maintained that his arrest was punishing her and the children, who had not sinned. This deferential appeal that established the Caffreys' relationship with the municipal leadership and their assumption of appropriate gender roles was successful, and the council released John Caffrey.[7]

Men made similar appeals to the council for the release of their wives, and also called on the council to let their wives resume their assigned roles within the family. On January 26, 1857, the council received a petition from Peter Owens requesting the release of his wife. He reported that she was "presently confined in the workhouse on a charge of Drunkenness" and that he had "an child about fifteen months who it appears cannot live without her mother." He then argued that he could not afford the ten-dollar fine, and prayed that "your hon. body will restore her [his wife] to the child, and by so doing it will enable him [Peter Owens] the sooner to provide for the wants of his family." Like Mrs. Caffrey, Peter Owens did not dispute that his wife was drunk, but instead argued that her arrest had disrupted the family economy. He implied that he had to take care of their daughter instead of working to provide for the needs of his family. If they would only restore his wife, the traditional gender roles of his family could be restored. Unlike other petitioners, Peter Owens did not claim that his wife was normally sober. Still, his use of the same basic gendered reasoning as the other petitioners was enough for the city council to pass his request unanimously. While the police acted to enforce their conception of morality and sobriety under Mayor Dyer as under Mayor Boone, the families of arrested people could successfully sue for their loved ones' release by affirming the authority of the council and their allegiance to the basic social hierarchy.[8]

Mayor Dyer and the Democrats' control over the city government did not survive the swelling support for the newly formed Republican Party. Voters elected Chicago's first Republican mayor, "Long John" Wentworth, on March 4, 1857. Wentworth was a former, six-term Democratic U.S. representative who then joined the Republican Party in response to the Kansas-Nebraska Act. His status as a former Democrat turned Republican allowed Wentworth to build a broad electoral coalition focused on his person, rather than on his new party. Wentworth used this support to continue the personal, paternalistic shape of municipal power under Mayor Dyer even as his party began to advocate an impersonal, professional state apparatus. At the same time, perhaps because he was less dependent on the city's poorer residents for his election, Wentworth quickly made the criminal justice system less responsive to pleas from wage workers and impoverished Chicagoans imprisoned or fined by the police.

It would be a mistake to view Wentworth's election as a reprisal of the 1855 election of Mayor Boone that pitted the city's immigrants against a native-born, elite, nativist Republican Party. The Republican Party was formed to contest over national political issues, and these national positions won it considerable support not only from the native-born elite but also from many German immigrants. The Democrats had garnered considerable support from a section of the city's poorest population through Mayor Dyer's police policies as well as through their opposition to nativism. The Irish in particular formed the Democrats' consistent base, but the party also received support from considerable numbers of native-born wage workers and members of the elite who opposed the Republicans' sectional policies and feared a civil war. Wentworth had made much of his fortune in the newspaper business, and his newspaper was still called *The Democrat* even after he was elected mayor as a Republican. Wentworth's election was thus as much a victory for him as an individual as it was for his newly formed party. And Wentworth was formidable: he stood six feet, six inches tall and weighed over three hundred pounds. His consumption of food and whiskey were legendary. By the time he ran for mayor, in addition to serving in the U.S. House of Representatives and owning and publishing a newspaper, Wentworth had also started a law practice. All of this gave him considerable latitude to set police policy as he saw fit.[9]

The municipal election of 1857, like those before it, was accompanied by a great deal of violence. At least one person was killed at the polls and many were wounded. The *Tribune* and the Republicans generally blamed this violence on the Irish, claiming that Mayor Dyer's police were at best indifferent. In reaction, as Dyer had done before him, Wentworth promptly replaced many of the personnel of the police force. He then added a new requirement for those applying to be policemen: they had to submit with their applications the names of two reputable businessmen who would vouch for their characters. As a member of the city's business class, Wentworth wanted to ensure that his policemen met with their approval. He would deploy the older, paternalistic version of policing to meet the needs of the city's businessmen and ensure order.[10]

Mayor Wentworth initially proposed to solve the problem of disorder by rebuilding the personal, hierarchical policing system of small northern towns in the early nineteenth century. He planned to do this by ensuring that the police were permanent residents of Chicago and that policemen lived in each neighborhood in the city. "Every family will know that there is, within a convenient distance," Wentworth promised, "a house of respectable occupants, where ladies and children, in the absence of husbands and fathers, can leave complaints [about disorderly activity] with confidence that they will meet with prompt attention." Wentworth understood the weakness of the force he inherited. His proposed solution would create a police system embedded within the family and neighborhood structure of the city, manned by "respectable" property owners, rather than an efficient bureaucratic machine. But the time for such a solution had passed, and Wentworth did not pursue it.[11]

Wentworth also bemoaned the system of pardons prevalent under Mayor Dyer because these pardons weakened the authority of the city government. He claimed that "abandoned" women with connections to criminal gangs went from house to house pretending to be the wives of convicts to drum up sympathy and obtain pardons, or offered large sums to get apparently respectable people to advocate for the release of their "husbands," though there is no other evidence that this actually happened. Wentworth claimed that the practice of issuing pardons undercut the operation of the police courts that had to pass harsh sentences to end "the frequent disturbances of violations of our ordinances in the night and on the Sabbath." He also decried the weakness of the police force, which "cannot be relied upon for the preservation of order, as was evinced on the day of our recent election." He pointed to the profusion of private police as further evidence of the failings of the current force.[12]

Wentworth's administration immediately made it more difficult for petitioners to secure the release of their imprisoned family members. On March 23, 1857, Peter Owens submitted another petition requesting the release of his wife from the workhouse after she had again been arrested for drunkenness. He worded his second petition almost exactly the same as the petition two months earlier. He again argued that his wife's confinement disrupted the family economy, and that if she were released "the inconvenience and mental pain under which he labours will be removed and enable him to attend to his calling better and providing for his family." This time, however, the new chair of the city council's Committee on Police, Hiram Joy, responded that "the petitioners furnish no evidence showing the error of the Police Justice . . . but merely appeal to the sympathies of the Council." Joy then pointed out that "as every inmate of the bridewell can do this and as nearly every one has relations or friends outsiders to assist in doing this, as granting request of this kind would be an invitation to all the inmates of the bridewell to make them, he [Hiram Joy] deems it best not to interfere with the judgment of the court and therefore asks to be discharged from the petition." There is no evidence that the council rejected Peter Owens's second petition because his wife was a repeat offender; in fact, it is likely that they did not realize this fact, since Joy referred to Peter Owens as Patrick Owens. Instead, Wentworth and Joy recognized that the system under Mayor Dyer undercut the authority of the police by allowing arrestees and their families to go over the heads of the police and the courts. Wentworth maintained many aspects of the paternalistic order that he inherited, but he sought to reinforce rather than undercut the authority of policemen and police justices personally tied to him and the council.[13]

The Owens case was not unusual. Hiram Joy consistently rejected petitioners' requests for the release of their loved ones if those petitions were based solely on sympathetic pleas. Joy gave increasingly concise reasons for his refusal to release prisoners. When a number of petitioners sought the release of James MacKellroy on May 4, 1857, because "his wife and 3 Children are in Destitute Circumstances, and suffering for the want of his labor," Joy responded curtly using the same reasoning he had deployed against Peter Owens's second appeal. "They furnish no evidence," he wrote, "showing the error of the Police Justice, he [Joy] deems it best not to interfere with the Judgement of the Court and therefore asks to be discharged from the petition." Wentworth's election, then, severely restricted that part of the paternalistic relationship between the city government and Chicago's poorest residents that had allowed those residents some redress from the actions of the police.[14]

A simple appeal to the city council's sympathy was no longer sufficient to secure a prisoner's release, but a petition signed by an employer or other "respectable" citizen usually won its case. On May 26, 1860, during Wentworth's second term, for instance, the city council received a petition from A. Lowenthal testifying that Alexander Henry was "a young man of good character. . . . He worked for Mr. Someweicks at the Boot and Shoe." This was sufficient to secure Mr. Henry's release from the bridewell for having been in a "House of Ill Fame," though he had to pay $10 plus costs. Wentworth himself even intervened occasionally, as in the case of D. L. Hibman. Mr. Hibman was sent to the bridewell for vagrancy but was released when Wentworth reported that "his wife informs me that if he can be released from bridewell, it is her intention to have him sent to an insane asylum." Imprisoned Chicagoans, then, could still secure release if they could get a powerful person in the community to intervene.[15]

The underlying paternalistic relationship between the arrested worker, his employer, and the city had not changed since the regime of Mayor Dyer, despite the tougher policies of Republican mayors Wentworth and his successor, John C. Haines. This basic set of relationships is clearly demonstrated in the single most eloquent appeal of the 1850s or 1860s, made by Edward Kane, arrested for drunkenness. Mr. Kane began by asserting his remorse. "When reason was dethroned," he wrote, "[I] have been guilty of such acts that in my sober moments make me, not only ashamed, but have so confounded me that I am unable to look my friends, or rather acquaintances, in the face." He also claimed poverty and the inability to pay his $25 fine. "We have been compelled to sell our wearing apparel to procure food and shelter," he wrote, "but now we have no recourse under heaven but to apply to the County Agent for a home in the alms house." Mr. Kane begged forgiveness and abased himself before the council. "I have nothing to say in extenuation of my conduct," he wrote, "on the contrary, I acknowledge the justice of my sentence and also feel that I deserve greater punishment for allowing myself to become prey to my base passions while a raving menace through my appetite for the accursed cup." He claimed that his only intention in seeking release was to save his family the indignity of applying for further charity, and that he intended to return to work or leave the city immediately. The determining factor in securing the council's mercy, however, appears to be the inclusion of a letter from his employer, Gates, Warner, Chalmers and Fraser, manufacturers of railroad cars and steam engines. They reported that he was a foreman in the boiler shop and recommended his release, which was duly approved by Wentworth and the council.[16]

Wentworth saw the problem of crime entirely within this paternalistic context. For him, crime was the result of a larger breakdown in the social order that needed to be checked by the reformation of poor criminals at the hands of the authorities. Wentworth's proposed solution to the problem of poverty in the aftermath of the 1857 panic illustrates this outlook. "I am satisfied that paupers are being sent to our city from other cities," he reported to the city council, "and that they constitute a large portion of the persons sent to our city bridewell." Wentworth suggested that these out-of-town paupers, "and especially females," should be sent to the poor farm, where they would labor in return for subsistence. On the farm, there was "plenty of good, healthy work, both for males and females." He further suggested that local farmers might take these individuals under their wing to save them from the evil influences of liquor. As the head of the urban family, he had the right and responsibility to intervene in the lives of these individuals. This stands in marked contrast with the emerging view of the Republican Party leadership, which sought to create strong bureaucratic institutions such as the Illinois National Guard and the U.S. Army, that could enforce order regardless of the plight of the individual involved in a given disturbance.[17]

Wentworth's organizational police policies fit in his broader paternalistic vision of the institution and were consistent with Dyer's method of organizing the force, despite the fact that he was a Republican and Dyer a Democrat. Wentworth took responsibility for the personnel and equipment of the force. He made all appointments, and no officer could be removed without his consent. He rejected the use of police uniforms and claimed to have personally designed the leather badge that the police wore over their ordinary clothes. When Wentworth was reelected in 1860, he mothballed the limited uniforms reinstated by Mayor John Haines, who served between Wentworth's terms, also restoring the leather badges from his 1857 term. He also created a special Mayor's Police that fell under his immediate control.[18]

Soon after his 1857 election, Wentworth launched a campaign against vice in the city that illustrates the results of this personal control. He carried out the anti-vice campaign by deploying the police against specific targets that he chose, often charging into gambling parlors and brothels at the head of his force. On April 20, 1857, soon after he assumed office, Wentworth led the police into Chicago's famous vice district known as the Sands, just north of the Chicago River. He and his subordinates attached hooks and chains to many of the buildings in the district, demolishing nine. In the ensuing melee, six more buildings were burned down, though it is unclear whether these fires were set by residents or by the police. This raid was arranged by William Ogden, who had bought some of the property in the Sands and who had already dispensed an agent to tell the residents to leave. This effort met with general acclaim among the city's business leaders. But the destruction of the Sands did little to stem gambling, drinking, and prostitution in Chicago, as it just dispersed these activities throughout the city. The police also did little to protect those kicked out of their homes. "We are told that last evening, about dusk," the *Tribune* reported, "a shameful outrage was committed upon three of the miserable females who were among those ejected from the dens on the Sands. They had taken shelter for the night in a small shanty near by and the rabble finding them there, treated them in the most shameful and outrageous manner. No arrests were made." Wentworth would use the police to promote the interests of William Ogden and other "respectable" business-men, but not to stop or punish the rape of his raid's victims.[19]

The raid on the Sands also illustrates the limitations of Wentworth's version of policing. Chicago was already too large a city with too many desperate people for one man to keep order by personally directing an armed force. By 1857, Chicago had already become a major commercial hub. Its lumberyards, brickyards, stockyards, rail yards, construction sites, factories, mills, and small workshops attracted thousands of wage workers each year, both from the surrounding countryside and from Europe.[20] Chicago also had a growing reputation as a center for vice, including drinking, gambling, and prostitu-tion, and many out-of-town visitors welcomed the opportunity to partake of the city's illicit offerings. The growing economy, both licit and illicit, also produced large numbers of desperate people. All of these factors combined to make Chicago both increasingly disorderly and increasingly anonymous. Wentworth's vision of stopping vice by destroying the vice district could not work in the new context of the city. The vice operators could easily find new places to reconstitute their businesses, and they quickly did so.

At the same time, while the newspapers and the city's businessmen lauded Wentworth's raid on the Sands, his high-handed actions increasingly caused problems for "respectable" Chicagoans. On July 17, 1857, while continuing his campaign against vice, Wentworth arrested a group of eighteen gamblers who had been operating out of a large house on Randolph between Clark and Dearborn. While attorney Charles S. Cameron was conversing with the arrested gamblers, a policeman ordered him to leave. Cameron refused, asserting that as their attorney, he had the right to converse with the arrested men. Soon after the policeman left, Wentworth arrived with more police, assaulted Cameron, and ordered him locked up. Wentworth himself was consequently arrested for assault and battery, and Cameron sued him for false arrest and imprisonment. When ordered to appear in court, Wentworth refused and denied the court's jurisdiction. Eventually, the case was settled amicably, and Wentworth and Cameron subsequently became friends and political allies, but this case was characteristic of Wentworth's governance style. As head of the city government, he considered himself to be above the law.[21]

Wentworth's high-handed style set him directly against downtown businessmen when, on the night of June 19, 1857, he ordered the police to gather the signs, hogsheads, boxes, pails, grindstones, and other objects cluttering the sidewalks on State Street and throw them into the mud in the middle of the road. The city had passed an ordinance restricting the amount of space that business owners could legally occupy with overhanging signs and merchandise, and business owners had not complied. While the business community generally applauded Wentworth's assault on vice, they were less enthusiastic when he deployed the same force against them. They complained in the newspapers and to him personally, before retrieving their property.[22]

Wentworth's imperious methods also drove important parts of the electorate away from the Republican Party. On October 10, 1857, for example, Wentworth received reports of a rabid dog in a German neighborhood. He sent to the area five police officers and a lieutenant, who shot and killed four leashed dogs, which understandably angered the dogs' owners.[23] The same night, a fire that would be the worst in Chicago history (before the Great Fire of 1871) swept through the same neighborhood and destroyed seventeen buildings. The police were accused of accidentally setting the fire when an ember from a missed shot landed in a pile of hay. The *Tribune*, a Republican paper that had supported Wentworth's mayoral campaign in March of 1857, accused Wentworth of sending the police to kill the dogs out of spite toward the German population. It further accused him of purposefully trying to alienate the Germans from the Republican Party for his own political ends.[24] The Republican Party was making a concerted and largely successful effort to win German immigrants, especially Protestants from northern Germany. Wentworth's police policies, then, caused considerable problems for the Republican Party as it tried to assemble an electoral coalition that could gain control of the nation in the late 1850s.

Wentworth's police also proved unable to deal with the problems caused by the 1857 economic panic, which had drastically reduced the funds available to the city. Wentworth was a committed fiscal conservative, opposed to issuing bonds. He was able to keep the city solvent by vigorously collecting licensing fees, but he was loath to spend more than he felt he had to on the police department. At the same time, the unemployed flooded into Chicago, and the newspapers reported a rash of burglaries. The police force as organized and controlled by Wentworth could do little to halt the spread of crime and disorder. The use of this force as a personal political gang under the mayor's control meant that, although officers did walk beats, they were not trained or organized to stop disorder more generally or protect property. They were much more concerned with arresting drunken immigrants and gamblers, which helped them stay in the good graces of their boss. When, for example, Wentworth ordered the police to arrest people found on the streets after midnight who could not account for themselves, they mistakenly arrested three night watchmen hired by a group of merchants to guard their block.[25]

Partially as a result of Wentworth's questionable stewardship of the police force, John C. Haines replaced him as mayor beginning in 1858 for two one-year terms. During his tenure, Haines allowed the police hierarchy to run the force with little interference. Haines reintroduced uniforms and removed Wentworth's leather badges. He also increased the salaries of officers and hired more police, bringing the total to 117 men. While there is no definitive breakdown of the ethnicity of these men, the overwhelming majority still had Anglo-sounding surnames.[26] During this two-year break between Wentworth administrations, the police department was better funded, better manned, and run more professionally. Under Haines, the police continued to make a majority of arrests for drunkenness and disorderly behavior, and the city council continued to reject most petitions for the release of prisoners based on the poverty of their families.[27] But Haines's direction of the police remained in the long shadow of "Long John" Wentworth, and his reforms were to be short-lived.

In March 1860, Wentworth was reelected mayor in the context of the surging Republican campaign for the presidency. While out of office, Wentworth had spent his time involved in intrigues within the Republican Party, particularly with Norman Judd over the selection of a Republican gubernatorial candidate. These internal faction fights became so fierce that many observers suspected Wentworth would bolt back to the Democratic Party, but he did not. As a result of the internal bickering, Wentworth had to fight to win the Republican mayoral nomination in March 1860, but once the party decided to hold its presidential nominating convention in Chicago that May, the Republicans united behind him. As a former Democrat strongly opposed to the extension of slavery, Wentworth represented a crucial piece of the Republican coalition, but he was completely out of step with the modernizing, former Whig forces within the party. As he had demonstrated in his first term, Wentworth was a fiscal conservative. In order to pay for the expenses of the Republican presidential nominating convention, he cut the police force in half and again decommissioned the uniforms. Part of this move was intended to give the police back the leather badges that Wentworth had supposedly designed himself, but it left the police force in tatters and also turned many officers against him.[28]

Wentworth's second term was overshadowed by the increasingly urgent sectional crisis. While many Republicans, including Wentworth, thought that the South's opposition to Lincoln was all bluster, many others took the threat of secession and war seriously. By the beginning of 1861 when the newly elected Republican legislature of Illinois gaveled into session, Lincoln had already won the presidential election and the Deep South had already seceded. In response, the Republican Party leadership tried to strengthen the state apparatus on every level. Both the incoming governor Richard Yates and the outgoing governor John Wood greeted the new legislature with a call to improve the state militia, both for potential use in war against the South and to enforce order within the state, since laws were virtually unenforced. "The law is inoperative in many parts of our state," Governor Wood said, "and has no perfect application anywhere." A well-regulated militia could ensure that the law was operative everywhere. Governor Yates echoed his predecessor when he claimed that a regular system of uniformed, trained militia would "be of benefit to the state, aside from any purposes of war, because it would encourage a system of physical training and the cultivation of a manly, independent spirit among our youth, and raise up in our midst a generation of men taught to reverence the law, accustomed to obedience, and disciplined and qualified for service in all emergencies." While Yates framed his call for a strengthened militia within the familiar language of manhood, the institution he proposed to create would train its members to defend the law, not any particular political leader. This basic outlook emerged again in Yates's support for the police reform bill passed a few months later.[29]

It is important to remember that Wood, Yates, and other Republicans were starting from a point at which law enforcement barely existed in Illinois. Even the prison system could not yet hold its convicts. The warden of the Joliet prison reported that twenty-one convicts escaped and were not recaptured for the year ending December 1, 1861, out of a total prison population of 672. "The number may appear large," the warden admitted, "but when it is recollected, that they have been worked without the protection of a wall, and were necessarily scattered over considerable territory, in the prosecution of work upon the penitentiary, it is believed the number is not larger than might have been expected." In other words, the prisoners were still in the process of building their prison. Given the enormous strains that all observers knew the war would place on the militia, the police, and the prison system, it is no surprise that the Republican leaders so dedicated to preparing the North for its war effort would be equally concerned with strengthening the organs of coercion within the state. This concern put them at loggerheads with Wentworth over his paternalistic and ill-run police force.[30]

As a result, the leaders of the Illinois Republican Party created a police board to remove control of the Chicago police department from the hands of the unreliable mayor. The state government established this police board because of the weakness of Wentworth's force and his capricious and arbitrary use of it, but it was also part of the general centralization and reinforcement of the Illinois state apparatus in the context of the looming civil war. This police board marked the first important stage in the development of a bureaucratic conception of the role of the police that was opposed to the previous paternalistic order. The establishment of the police board thus represented the victory of the proponents of a professional, bureaucratic police force in the first skirmish with Wentworth, Dyer, and others who sought to maintain a paternalistic, personal system of policing.

The state-appointed police board set out to establish a bureaucracy that would run the Chicago police force according to internally defined rules and a strong hierarchy. The most critical aspect of this transformation was that each policeman from this point forward was accountable to a supervisor within the department, rather than to a set of politicians. The police department was accountable to politicians only at the very highest level. This made it difficult for ordinary citizens to go over the heads of the policemen who arrested them and the police justices who sentenced them, because those policemen and justices answered to other members of the police hierarchy, rather than to elected politicians. Theoretically, the development of this bureaucracy removed policing from politics and put it on the level of any other city service that could be evaluated on the basis of its efficiency, such as the Board of Public Works, also founded in 1861, rather than any political criteria.[31] Of course, in practice this was never the case, and political interests and the ethnic and class context in which the police operated always affected policy at every level. Still, the development of a bureaucratic model of police organization was a crucial step in creating a force that claimed to stand above class and ethnic interests and to protect a neutral "order."

This strengthening of the state apparatus fit with the old program of the former Whigs who now made up a significant part of the Republican Party, including Governor Yates. Illinois Republicans could also look to New York, where the state government had appointed a similar police board to take control of New York City's police force. The appointment of that police board was a partisan move by Republicans in Albany against the Democrats of Tammany Hall who ran city politics.[32] This was not the case in Illinois, where Mayor Wentworth, Governor Yates, and the majority of the state legislature were Republicans. It does suggest persistent differences on local policy between Republicans who came out of the Whig Party versus those who had affiliated with the Democrats before the Kansas-Nebraska Act. That Republicans in New York and Illinois tried to assert control over the police departments in their biggest cities prior to the Civil War illustrates how crucial the issue of policing was in the politics of the day. In both cases, the clash between municipal and state governments foreshadowed the long-running struggle between the nascent big city machines of Tammany Hall and the Chicago Democrats versus reformers in Albany and Springfield who supported professional experts and a bureaucratic police system. However, in Chicago, unlike New York, partisan politics had not yet crystallized.

The example of San Francisco illustrates that similar trends pushed businessmen throughout the country to advocate a bureaucratically organized police force, though they could take different paths to the same end. In that city, as in the rest of the nation, clashes had broken out between the native born and Irish immigrants throughout the 1850s. The Irish largely controlled the Democratic Party and the city government in 1856, just as Mayor Dyer and his allies did in Chicago. Rather than responding by putting up a man like John Wentworth, however, San Francisco's native-born elite organized a Vigilance Committee composed of the city's leading businessmen. In May of 1856, this Vigilance Committee organized an armed force of six thousand men to carry out a coup and eject the duly elected Democratic Party officials from San Francisco. These Vigilantes maintained control for three months, during which time they organized new elections that their party won. While in control, the Vigilance Committee fired the entire old police force and completely reorganized San Francisco's police department along rational, professional lines that removed control of the department from the electorate and established a powerful independent police hierarchy. Policemen in San Francisco received considerable job security and the chance for promotion, but they were also subject to close supervision, were required to submit regular reports, and were required to submit to physicals. The San Francisco police also played a crucial role in maintaining order and loyalty to the Union during the Civil War. While the Vigilance Committee and its successor political party declared themselves to be nonpartisan, they supported the Union war effort and thus acted like Republicans.[33]

Taken together, these conflicts suggest that, before the Civil War, the leaders of the Republican Party began to elaborate a new model for government institutions to help solve some of the problems facing advancing capitalism in the North. The struggle for control of the West and the federal government that culminated in the secession of the Confederacy was by far the biggest of these problems, and the Republican Party was willing to use state power in an entirely new way to solve it. The military that the Republicans created in response to secession was unprecedented in U.S. history in terms of scale, organization, and attempts at professionalism.[34] But the struggle with the slave masters was not the only problem prompting the creation of the Republican Party. The problem of immigration, the rise of nativism, and the growth of a wage labor economy in the burgeoning northern cities destroyed the old party system of Whigs and Democrats as much as sectionalism did.[35] Just as the Republicans were struggling to construct a new way to use state power against the slave masters, they also sought to use state institutions to solve the problem of disorder in the cities. And the most farsighted Republicans recognized that, to do this, they would have to build a new type of police force, governed by professional policy makers rather than the personal politics of local political leaders like Wentworth in Chicago, the Democrats of San Francisco, or those running Tammany Hall in New York. Chicago's path was unique because it remained a relatively small city in a state with a powerful modernizing Republican Party. Wentworth and his allies had much less chance against the Illinois Republican leadership than the Democrats of Tammany Hall had against Albany, and Chicago was not an isolated center like San Francisco, where a municipal coup could be carried out far from other centers of power. Yet despite these unique paths, the similarity of the destination reached by political leaders in these three cities illustrates that this was a national, rather than local, trend.

The key aspect of this professionalizing push was that it made it increasingly difficult for the electorate to influence police policy. The bill establishing the Chicago Police Board removed control of the force from elected municipal officials and put it in the hands of the governor and an appointed group of experts. Certainly, the governor was also elected, and this transfer of power could be interpreted as a simple clash between state and municipal authority. But the governor was much less accountable to the population of Chicago since he was elected by the voters of the entire state. Chicago was full of immigrant workingmen, while the state electorate was still overwhelmingly composed of native-born farmers. Also, the members of the police board were appointed to staggered six-year terms, initially of two, four, and six years, so that even when the state returned the power to select board members to the Chicago electorate in 1863, Chicagoans would only be able to change one out of three board members every two years. In this sense, the police board limited popular control in a similar manner to the U.S. Senate. The commissioners of the police board did have to be residents of the city for five years, and of the division (North, South, and West Sides) from which they were elected for at least one year. Still, this bill made it extremely difficult for Chicago voters to change the leadership of the police force in reaction to any specific incident or policy, as had taken place when Mayor Dyer was elected to replace Mayor Boone after the Lager Beer Riot.[36]

The 1861 Chicago Police Board law also gave policemen substantial job security compared to the previous system of mayoral appointments, which also served to reduce the stakes of elections for the department. Under the new rules, no person could be removed from the position of police officer "except upon written charges proffered against him to the board of police, and after an opportunity shall be afforded him of being heard in his defense." It established three ranks of police officers: captain, sergeant, and patrolman, in addition to one general superintendent and one deputy superintendent for the whole force. The rank of captain was only open to sergeants, and the rank of sergeant was only open to patrolmen, so that no outsider could be appointed into a supervisory position over experienced officers. The combination of these two measures served to ensure continuity in personnel, policy, and basic outlook from one mayoral regime to the next. With such a system in place, even if all of the police board members were replaced when Chicagoans got to elect them, it would be almost impossible to radically change the personnel of the police force.[37]

Mayor Wentworth attempted to resist the power of the newly appointed police board and the governor. On the night of March 21, 1861, he summoned the entire police force to city hall while the new board was holding its first meeting. Once the board adjourned, and Wentworth was confident that its members intended to remove the entire control of the police from him, he had all the police officers assemble in front of him. He told these men that they were the best force ever formed and that the new police board intended to discharge them all. Rather than submit to this indignity, Wentworth fired all of the policemen himself, at 2:00 A.M., which left the city without police protection for the rest of the night. This move illustrates both Wentworth's perception that the creation of the new police board was aimed directly against him and his police force, and the arbitrary behavior that the board was supposed to stop. On a broader level, it was a protest by the Chicagoan who most represented the older, personal, paternalistic brand of politics against the changes in governmental power and institutions wrought by the Republican Party in the 1860s.[38]

The new superintendent, Cyrus Bradley, who had been the first chief under Mayor Boone, along with his deputy superintendent, Jacob Rehm, took a number of immediate steps to ensure the effectiveness of the force they created. First, they introduced physical requirements for all men hired onto the force. They had to be over five feet, eight inches tall, under forty years old, and of stout build. Because "the majority of Germans are men of low stature," Wentworth complained that this rule was adopted to prevent Germans from joining the force, but this objection did not prevent the rule from going into effect.[39] They also put the police in uniforms copied directly from the New York City Metropolitan Police force: dark blue frock coats with big buttons printed with the words "Chicago Police," dark gray pants with blue stripes, and blue caps reinforced with ribbing for protection against bricks. Policemen were allowed to wear whiskers "*a la militaire*," but not full moustaches. Finally, Bradley and Rehm quickly established reputations for severely disciplining their men, both for infractions of the rules and in drills to ensure the new force's effectiveness.[40] All of these reforms were aimed at creating a professional force that presented a standard image to the residents of the city. The reintroduction of uniforms instilled a sense of professionalism in the policemen themselves and enabled them to present a more martial image to the population. At the beginning of the Civil War, when military men in uniform represented the authority of the Union, the connection between the army and the police could only strengthen the authority of the police. The combination of job security, discipline, height requirements, and uniforms created a force whose members were tied to the institution rather than to any political party or politician, and which might develop an esprit de corps that had been impossible to maintain when the personnel were changed at every mayoral election.

In his annual report to the city council in April 1862, Superintendent Bradley made clear what the new force had accomplished and what it was intended to do in the future. He praised the efficiency of the force by noting the "general good order of the city," as evidenced by "*no* riots, or any extensive burglaries or robberies, that have not been detected, and the perpetrators punished" (original emphasis). That Bradley emphasized the lack of riots illustrates that the force was intended to keep order in a time of extreme stress as much or more than it was intended to prevent crime. This was no doubt particularly important given the stresses of the Civil War. Chicago raised sufficient numbers of volunteers by offering high bounties that it never resorted to the draft, and New York had yet to experience its draft riots, but Bradley was already aware of the disorder that might arise from the hardships of war.

The most striking part of Bradley's praise for the force in this report is his repeated use of the word "efficiency." Every time Bradley mentioned how well the new organization functioned, he spoke of how efficient it was in terms of cost and men with respect to the services it provided. This term put the functioning of the police force on objective, businesslike terms, outside of any political considerations. Wentworth had used the analogy of the family to describe the city government and the police force. Bradley shifted to use the analogy of business. Businessmen, not patriarchs, were to run Chicago. The police were supposed to work efficiently to provide a service that could be measured by the number of arrests and the lack of recordable problems. Bradley's police reports themselves were early versions of spreadsheets, neatly organizing records of arrests, of crimes reported, and of the biographical information of arrestees in tables. Bradley modeled the police after a business that issued annual reports to stockholders giving a balance sheet of costs and accomplishments.[41]

Bradley also argued that the police force needed more resources in order to extend this service to every Chicagoan. He pointed out that the police were able to provide adequate protection to only the most densely populated "business" areas of the city. While Bradley contended that most city residents were happy with the new organization of the police, those in outlying areas were understandably dissatisfied by their lack of protection. Bradley cited no evidence for this dissatisfaction among the largely working-class Chicagoans who lived on the city's outskirts. Still, he used the lack of citywide coverage to justify his request for horses in case the police had to concentrate men to quell riots or other large-scale disturbances. To communicate with one another, policemen carried creakers, noisemaking boxes that they could swing to attract attention if they needed help, but with patrolmen on foot and separated by large distances, it would take a great deal of time for a sufficient force to assemble if they were confronted by a crowd. Bradley asserted that since all Chicagoans were taxed to pay for the police, they should all receive its services. This argument defined police protection as a service to be rendered by the city government like any other service, even as it admitted the possibility that a significant portion of the city's population might act against the police in a riot.[42]

Deputy Superintendent Jacob Rehm affirmed this outlook decades later when he looked back on the days of the police board as the best period in his long association with the force.[43] "Back in 1861" when the police board was in control, he recollected, "we had what I believe was the best police force Chicago ever had." He decried the control of politicians and elections over the police. "It is an injustice to policemen to keep up a disturbed condition of affairs in the department by constant changing of rank and file, while the agitation of proposed bills for the department's reorganization does not encourage efficiency." He then made an explicit analogy with skilled labor: "The same principle applies to police work as to any other human activity. If you want carpenter work done, you don't engage a tailor. The men in the department should feel assured of their positions as long as they do their duty." Rehm suggested that the key to successful organization of the police was to keep politicians out of the department's affairs. "If Chief Kipley [police chief appointed in 1897] is allowed to direct police affairs untrammeled by politicians," Rehm argued, "he will give the people a force equal to any in the world." For both Bradley and Rehm, the police would work best when experts like themselves could make objective decisions, and when politicians and by extension the electorate had no control over the force.[44] As would be the case for the rest of the century, these professional police officials stood firmly in the camp of the reformers.[45]

Other than dealing with the problems arising from the Civil War, the daily activity of patrolmen appears to have changed little between 1855 and 1862. Of 8,782 arrests made during the first year of the police board, 3,632 were Irish, though "Americans" now outnumbered Germans. A majority of arrests, 5,108, were still for drunk and disorderly behavior. The next largest category of arrests was for inmates of disorderly houses or houses of ill fame, which accounted for 1,275 arrests. The largest share of those arrested earned their living as laborers (1,339), followed by prostitutes, (771), sailors (576), and soldiers (485).[46] The *Tribune* described those arrested in the course of an average night as "male and female 'drunk and disorderly,' coal thieves . . . women of the town in paint and others and occasionally a gentlemanly persecutor of the other sex, 'pulled' from a house of ill repute; boys who have no parents and no occupation save to steal; girls who are fast approaching nigh the vortex which will eventually sweep them away, and who have been detected in filching clothes from a line . . . professional till-tappers, pick-pockets, and rogues of every description."[47] This description illuminates the *Tribune's* attitude toward the city's poor residents at least as much as it informs us about those residents themselves, but it also illustrates who the department arrested.

The police also continued to enforce the basic social hierarchy in the city, as attested to by the case of Peter Weiner. According to the *Tribune*, he was "a hard looking vagabond" brought up on charges of "grossly insulting a respectable lady." He escaped before her husband could apprehend him, but the crime was severe enough that a police captain personally arrested him.[48]

Against the backdrop of this basic continuity, the new leaders of the force immediately confronted the problems raised by the Civil War. Bradley was prevented from serving with the Chicago Light Artillery only because of his duties as superintendent of police. While he could not serve in the artillery, he worked hand in hand with the military to help meet its needs. Between April 1861 and April 1862, his force spent $999.34 for special policemen to guard the Confederate prisoners of war housed at Camp Douglas, just outside the city. Once the draft began, Bradley placed policemen at the depots of the railroads and at the harbor, and these police officers required every man of draft age leaving the city to prove that he was not doing so to avoid service. Where no officers were posted, railroad and ship agents were forbidden from selling tickets to men of draft age unless they had written authorization from Bradley himself. The police also pursued deserters and bounty jumpers. More than ever before, the Chicago police acted as an arm of a state apparatus that included the U.S. military. The Chicago police were obviously distinct from the military, and the police board commissioners were not under military orders, but at least for the first year when they were all Republicans, these men used the police to ensure Chicago contributed as much as possible to the Northern war effort.[49]

A plank passed at the constitutional convention of the state in 1861 posed a more serious threat to the board of police. This plank provided that at the municipal election of April 15, 1862, Chicago voters would be allowed to print either "For the City of Chicago electing its own officers" or "Against the City of Chicago electing its own officers" on their ballots. If this ballot initiative passed, it would repeal the state law appointing the police board, and make all of the professionalizing reforms of that board moot. This law would not actually enact a situation where Chicago residents elected each officer individually, but would return control over police appointments to the mayor and city council. In other words, Chicago residents were to vote on whether to return to the old system or proceed with the consolidation of the new. In April, the majority of Chicago voters elected to return to the old system, which belies Bradley's argument in his first annual report that "the system under which the force was organized a year ago . . . has met the approval of the people." Whatever efficiency the new force might provide, Chicagoans apparently resented the imposition of state control over a body they alone were taxed to pay for and that policed only residents of the city. But Illinois voters defeated the proposed state constitution as a whole on June 17, 1862, even though the majority of Chicagoans voted for it. This made the city electorate's vote to return to the old police system moot, and left the police board in control. The board of police continued its existence against the electoral will of the majority of Chicago's voters.[50]

The rise of the Republican Party and the Civil War ushered in a new role for the state in American life and helped bring forth a new set of institutions to play that role. During this period, the Republican Party established federal authority to make and enforce policy for the entire nation, set the stage for subsequent national social policy, and established a vital precedent for intervening with armed force both in the South and in New York during the draft riots.[51] Establishing a new, professional vision of policing against its paternalistic antecedents was one aspect of the broader modernizing push of the era. As with other Republican initiatives, however, this one was not entirely successful. Rather, the establishment of state-appointed police boards began the long struggle between big-city politicians and state-capital-based reformers for control of the nation's police departments. These groups advocated different methods of social control: paternalism and cross-class coalitions organized around patronage versus bureaucratic efficiency. And the stakes were high, for if the police were to enforce reforms like temperance, they had to be an efficient tool for enacting policy, rather than an extension of a political party apparatus or the client army of a political chief.

CHAPTER 3

The Police and the First May Day Strike for the Eight-Hour Day

In the period after the Civil War, a new working class emerged in the United States. On the one hand, the nation's economy increasingly relied on wage workers in factories and mills, on the railroads and construction projects, and in lumberyards and mines. Owners and managers sought to strip control over the production process from skilled artisans and direct it themselves to maximize profits, though many skilled workers and artisans retained their strategic economic position in the late 1860s. This created a situation in which a large number of people with little chance of establishing their own shops were forced to sell their labor power to the highest bidder. All of these trends had begun much earlier, but the war and its aftermath gave them a huge boost. At the same time, U.S. workers began to organize themselves in a more class-conscious way than their predecessors. Workers did not share a common set of ideas, and remained divided along lines of skill, ethnicity, race, and gender. Yet by forming unions and working together to promote their interests politically, many workers implicitly rejected the individualism of the dominant culture and saw that collective action on a class basis provided them with a chance of improving their situation.[1] By the 1860s, then, a U.S. working class was coalescing both because an increasing number of people worked for wages and because those wage workers were increasingly coming together in a variety of collective ways to address their common problems.

Chicago was a key center of both aspects of working-class formation. Before the Civil War, Chicago's leading businessmen were boosters who, like William Ogden, made their fortunes through real-estate speculation, and whose success depended on the continued growth of the community. Small enterprises were the primary employer of wage workers. Skilled workers sought to become independent artisans, and often succeeded. Then, during and after the war, Chicago transformed into a manufacturing and distribution center, relying on the labor of thousands of wage workers. Iron manufacturing expanded to employ 9,623 men by 1873, and to service a host of industries that produced finished goods out of iron, such as Cyrus McCormick's giant agricultural implements business. The Civil War created a huge demand for salt pork and cut off Cincinnati's river access to the southern market, allowing Chicago to emerge as the country's leading meatpacking center, and by war's end the city's nine largest railroads and the Pork Packer's Association had formed the Union Stockyards and Transit Company. Leather, gelatin, boot, and shoe manufacturers, and other industries that depended on meatpacking byproducts, expanded accordingly. The size of these industries also grew tremendously, so that by 1870 about 38 percent of Chicago's population worked for wages, 75 percent of them in firms employing more than twenty-five workers. Three giant meatpacking companies, two huge railcar works, two large furniture manufacturers, four agricultural implements companies, and six iron firms each employed hundreds of workers. Because Chicago stood at the center of a vast railroad network and its population was rapidly expanding, these companies drew on a national labor market, and consequently both workers and their employers faced competitive pressures on a national level for wages, working hours, and productivity. By the end of the war, Chicago possessed a large and growing pool of wage workers, many now managed by supervisors and subject to a minute division of labor, pushed to work extremely long hours for low pay, and facing competition for jobs from workers throughout the country.[2]

On a national level, workers' organizations reached a new peak during and immediately after the war. Workers rebuilt the unions that had been set back by the panic of 1857, and they also formed eight-hour leagues in almost every state to push for legislation that would limit the legal workday to eight hours. Immediately after the war these unions and eight-hour leagues embarked on a program of unification under the leadership of William Sylvis, head of the International Molders Union, which eventually led to the formation of the National Labor Union. The newly formed unions also engaged in a number of hard-fought strikes, most notably three Iron Molders strikes in Cincinnati in 1866.[3] These fights were often over control of the production process and the right to hire apprentices.[4] Sylvis and others also famously objected to the wage labor system, and advocated a system of workers' cooperatives as its replacement. There was no single strategy, but in a variety of ways, workers in the 1860s increasingly resisted the development of a wage labor economy with terms set by the market.[5]

In Chicago, workers both formed unions and pushed for legislative reform. Skilled workers had built craft unions for many occupations by the end of the Civil War. The city's typographers built the first craft union in the early 1850s, followed by the mechanics in 1852, the iron molders in 1857, the machinists and blacksmiths in 1859, the shipwrights and caulkers in 1860, the seaman and foundry workers in 1861, the painters and locomotive engineers in 1863, and the plasterers, bricklayers, and stonemasons in 1864.[6] These unions set up apprenticeship programs to recruit new members and to control the supply of workers with their skills. They met with only intermittent success in winning higher wages, but generally built lasting organizations with stable memberships. They also began to ally with each other from the beginning: in 1864, these skilled unions established a trades assembly to support each other in boycotts and in pushing for legislative reform. This federation claimed to represent 8,500 workers, or about 28 percent of Chicago's workforce.[7] And in that same year, the Typographical Union started a newspaper called the *Workingman's Advocate* and edited by Andrew Cameron that became the voice of the city's labor movement.

The division between the skilled and unskilled was the central dividing line in the Chicago labor movement throughout this period, and it largely correlated with ethnicity. By 1870, the wages of skilled workers such as blacksmiths, boilermakers, bricklayers, machinists, and printers, were nearly double those of laborers or hod carriers.[8] The native born and immigrants from England, Scotland and Wales made up the bulk of skilled workers, though some trades had significant numbers of German workers. The largely unskilled Irish were mostly excluded from the organized labor movement, but they had the most pressing grievances. Still, the unions had a multiethnic leadership. In 1864, of 100 union leaders from various organizations, 41 were Anglo-American, 31 were German, and 27 were Irish.[9] Ethnic divisions among the native born, Germans, Irish, and increasingly Bohemians and Scandinavians would remain within the working class, but these divisions did not keep many workers from uniting across ethnic lines. The divisions between the skilled and unskilled would prove a more pressing problem.

By the end of the war, then, Chicago possessed a vast number of wage workers who had begun to organize themselves across ethnic lines and who posed increasing problems for the city government and for its businessmen. These workers remained divided in myriad ways, but they had built class-based organizations. This was a change from the antebellum period, when most workers remained tied to artisanal crafts and ethnic neighborhoods or organizations. The emergence of working-class politics undermined the cross-class politics of the antebellum era both nationally and locally, as workers increasingly raised the question of what the "equality" promoted by the Radical Republicans meant for them. As historian David Montgomery points out, "Class conflict . . . was the submerged shoal on which Radical dreams foundered."[10] Within the city, this class conflict manifested itself as the first open battle between businessmen and workers over the eight-hour day, and raised the question of class order in a more direct way than the conflicts of the 1850s had. And just as the leaders of the Republican Party sought to use the army to remake the south, the business elite that controlled Chicago politics sought to use the police to contain the labor movement, with dramatic consequences for both.

For the police department itself, the war years had been an interregnum. They set the stage for later developments and conflicts, but the operations of the police during the war did not establish basic precedents for police activity or organization because it was such an exceptional period. Many people who would become leading officers served in the war and gained military experience. The police took on many wartime tasks, including arresting deserters from the military and guarding the prisoners of war held at Camp Douglas.[11] Chicago had no draft riot and in fact its residents never faced the draft because the local government offered large enlistment bounties to ensure that its quotas for the military were filled by volunteers.[12] The department was in a state of limbo as the city turned its attention and personnel toward the South.

The end of the war brought new problems of order to Chicago. By 1867, the city's population was about 250,000, but until May, Chicago employed fewer than two hundred policemen. The city was flooded by discharged soldiers looking for work, but with the cessation of hostilities came the cessation of orders from the government for the products of Chicago's food-processing industries, machine shops, and many other small manufacturers that provided a large share of the city's employment. In 1867, then, Chicago had a large population who lacked their own means of subsistence and wanted to work for wages, at the same time that the number of jobs was declining.[13]

This situation created increasing class tension in the city along with problems for and resentment toward the police department. At first tension manifested itself in simple complaints about the department's class bias. In 1866 and 1867, the city's fledgling workers' movement regularly critiqued the police department for its partiality toward the wealthy. Andrew Cameron's *Workingman's Advocate*, for instance, complained that the police issued workers heavy fines and failed to protect them. On September 1, 1866, the *Workingman's Advocate* reported "on last Wednesday night, a milkman was garotted and robbed on Washington Street." Instead of protecting the milkman, "the officer came very near shooting the unfortunate victim. As usual, no arrest has been made." Cameron was not hostile to the institution of the police. He was a major leader in the growing typographical union and in the National Labor Union. He saw skilled workers such as typographers, building trades workers, and iron molders as legitimate members of the civic community, free laborers in the antebellum sense.[14] In this context, he saw workers as having the right to demand the public services provided by the city, including the right to be protected by the police department. Like many other skilled workers and their leaders, he complained of class bias in policing but did not see the police as a potential agent of business against the workers' movement.[15]

This complaint about the department's class bias was not restricted to the labor movement. For instance, on March 10, 1867, James Cleland wrote to the mayor and Common Council of the City of Chicago complaining that "there was one law for the rich and another for the poor." Cleland set forth a number of clear examples: a saloonkeeper was fined $17.75 for selling beer on Sunday when his wealthy patrons who were not only drinking but playing cards were left alone; the mother of a Union Army veteran was arrested for holding a raffle to benefit her son; rich men were allowed to run races on Wabash Avenue in the winter with their "fine horses and splendid critters," whereas, for a parade of draymen, "the bridewell [city jail] would hardly contain them for number." Cleland said that if questioned, he could "point to perhaps hundreds of cases where favour is shown to one which is denied to another."[16]

The city council formally denied the class bias of the police. In response to Cleland's letter, the city council passed a resolution that read: "Ordered—That all city officers and all their employees, and all private citizens, be and they are hereby directed to act honestly, fairly and impartially, in every public as well as every private capacity and to do unto others as they would that others should do unto them." But this passing reference to the Golden Rule could hardly solve the basic problem of policing in a city sharply divided by class, as was Chicago in the early 1860s.[17]

The *Workingman's Advocate* and James Cleland appear to have been correct in their assessment of police bias. While sensational murders and rapes took up most of the newspapers' coverage of the police, most of the department's daily activity continued to consist of arresting Irish immigrants for drinking and disorderly conduct. In the twelve months prior to March 1866, the police arrested 4 people for rape and 14 for murder, while they arrested 4,149 for disorderly conduct, 1,081 for vagrancy, and 960 for being inmates of a disorderly house. Of the 15,035 people they arrested in that year, 3,277 were reported as "American," while 7,404 were "Irish." The next largest group was German, with 1,988 Germans arrested that year. More strikingly, the police aimed the bulk of their activity against that layer of unskilled laborers that was growing quickly with the transformations in the economy wrought by the war. "Laborers" made up 3,264 of those arrested, while another 3,256 were reported to have no occupation. Thus, about half of the total arrestees were unskilled workers or the unemployed. The next largest category of occupation was "prostitute," numbering 1,506, followed by 1,056 housekeepers. Most of the rest had various working-class occupations such as sailors, carpenters, hackmen, and machinists. Despite the image projected in the newspapers of a force of detectives tracking down hardened criminals, most of the real daily activity of the police continued to consist of policing the behavior of the largely Irish immigrant population of unskilled workers and unemployed people.[18] Even before the city's class tension exploded into open class conflict, the police daily conflicted with the city's wage workers.

While they may have resented the police, workers' organizations still looked to the government to solve the problem of overwork. In 1866 and 1867, the labor movement floated laws throughout the nation that defined a legal workday as eight hours, and backed candidates who supported these laws. In Connecticut, for instance, the fight over an eight-hour law led to the collapse of the Republican coalition and the victory of a Democratic candidate for governor in an otherwise Radical Republican state.[19] Connecticut then joined Wisconsin, Missouri, California, New York, Pennsylvania, and Illinois in passing laws defining a legal day's work as eight hours.[20] In Chicago, eight-hour men elected committed supporters to the city council in five of the city's sixteen wards and pushed the Republican Party to endorse the eight-hour day. The Illinois law was supposed to go into effect on May 1, 1867, but like laws in other states, it had a gaping loophole: it stated that a longer workday was legal if it was agreed to in a work contract.[21]

This whole organizing drive was part of labor's reaction to the growth of a wage labor economy that stripped even skilled men of their independence. Skilled workers strove to remain the "free laborers" central to the ideology of the antebellum Republican Party.[22] Many northern workers supported the Civil War to protect the system of "free soil, free labor, free men" that Salmon Chase articulated. This free-labor ideology promoted "self-employment as the end to which all purposeful effort should be directed."[23] But the war had brought the opposite result—the concentration of capital, the growth of factory production, and the rise of a wage labor system that made even skilled men increasingly dependent on their employers. Nonetheless, in Chicago as throughout the country, many workers, especially the skilled, considered themselves to be rightful members of the community that could expect the government to be responsive to their needs and demands.[24] The Chicago workers' movement sought to use government institutions and the Republican Party to check the decline in their status. The eight-hour day would help ensure that workers did not become wage slaves but remained independent free men even if they worked for wages. Yet the eight-hour leagues also generally supported the right to make free contracts (with some exceptions) and did not push for the government to create the type of agency that would have been required to enforce these laws.[25] Ultimately, then, while workers looked to the government to define a legal day's work as eight hours, the enforcement of that resolution would be up to the workers themselves.

As the date approached for the Illinois eight-hour law to go into effect, the city's Republicans divided on the issue, and this was reflected in the newspapers. Andrew Cameron's *Workingman's Advocate* favored the eight-hour day, along with the *Chicago Republican*, the official paper of the Republican Party, which was then in control of the city and state governments. The leadership of the party saw the issue similarly to the way Andrew Cameron and the skilled trade unionists did. It was part of the Republican program of encouraging wage workers to prepare for economic independence. The skilled workers could use their free time to better themselves, perhaps to eventually become independent proprietors. But other important Republicans as well as Democrats opposed the eight-hour day. The *Tribune*, also a Republican paper, and the Democratic *Times* both came out stridently against the eight-hour day. They argued that it was bad for the city because it would increase the cost of doing business. They also insisted that restricting the hours of labor violated the laws of the market by imposing outside limitations on what should be determined by supply and demand.[26] This division marked the beginning of the schism of the Radical Republican bloc, reflected through the lens of Chicago labor.[27]

This schism was driven by the self-confidence, power, and stridency of the city's employers as much as by the labor movement's attempts to cut work hours. The economic growth of the war years had created not just a new working class but also a new class of businessmen in Chicago. These men increasingly relied on wage labor rather than real-estate speculation for their wealth. They emerged from the war more politically confident than ever.[28] Like the city's workers, employers were divided by ethnicity, industry, and political ideology, but the bulk of them opposed the eight-hour workday and did not intend to implement it. While skilled workers were organizing in unions and eight-hour leagues, the city's employers were also meeting to decide how to deal with them. On April 30, employers in the painting industry met with the object of reaching "some mutual understanding in relation to the demands of the workingmen on the eight-hour question." At this meeting, the employers decided to employ men for eight hours, but to pay them at the same hourly rate as before, which would have resulted in a 20 percent pay cut. The Illinois Central Railroad, which employed a thousand men in Chicago, decided to enforce the ten-hour day and was prepared to close its shops for three months rather than shorten the workday.[29] Most employers, small and large, were against giving in to the workers' movement.

Meanwhile, workers were also meeting to discuss their demands and non-electoral means of enforcing them. Machinists and blacksmiths resolved in mass meetings to work only eight hours, even if it meant a pay cut, and many other trades followed suit. The trades assembly eventually adopted this position for the entire city.[30] Some workers were willing to compromise. Journeymen painters, for instance, resolved that they were "willing to meet [their] employers half-way: eight-hours work for nine hours pay."[31] Overall, however, the workers' movement was prepared to attempt to force employers to accede to their demands.

The unions organized a mass demonstration for the first of May, a Wednesday, backed by the threat of a strike if the employers did not give in. This demonstration was not intended to produce a violent confrontation with either employers or the city government, since after all the leadership of the Republican Party had supported the eight-hour demands. A detachment of police and a number of the aldermen who had supported the state's eight-hour-day law marched at the front. Workers marched with signs of their trades. The marble cutters had a truck with samples of monumental sculptures, the mill stonecutters with large millstones on a truck. Even the laborers were represented by a truck with workmen holding "various implements." While this parade was designed to promote the eight-hour day, it was also a demonstration of artisan pride and contained no threat of riot. In addition to the signs of their trades, workers carried banners with slogans like "Labor No Longer the Slave of Capital," and "Eight Hours we want, and Eight Hours we'll have." The march was enormously successful in attracting participants and halting production. The newspapers reported that no work took place that day.[32] The movement remained peaceful, orderly, and within the bounds of traditional republican politics.

On the same day, workers staged demonstrations in other cities throughout Illinois and in St. Louis. In Springfield, Peoria, Quincy, and Aurora, workers staged mass meetings. Skilled railroad shop workers took the lead in all four of these cities. Fifty workers of the Chicago and Alton Railroad Company in Springfield refused to work after the company remained unmoved on the ten-hour workday. In Aurora, workers at the carshops of the Chicago, Burlington, and Quincy paraded and resolved to work only eight hours from that point forward. In St. Louis, six thousand demonstrators from all the different trades came out for the eight-hour day and threatened to strike if employers would not accede to their demands. In every city that these demonstrations took place, the marchers and strikers were organized and peaceful on May 1, but they expressed their determination to push for the eight-hour day, even if employers would not give in.[33]

These demonstrations failed to convince employers to adopt the eight-hour day. As the *Tribune* reported, "It may as well be understood at once that there is no intention on the part of the employers to yield to the demand of the eight hour rule." As they had planned, workers throughout Illinois and in St. Louis struck on May 2. In Chicago, this strike spread to a large portion of the workforce. The *Tribune* estimated that Chicago's workers were divided into three segments: those who were willing to fight for eight hours "at all hazards, utterly reckless of the consequences to themselves, to employers and to the general public"; those who were for the eight-hour workday but unwilling to strike or take less pay; and those who were willing to work for eight hours at reduced pay. A large number of workers took a wait-and-see attitude to the strike, rooting for it, hoping that they might gain by the success of strikers, but unwilling to risk their livelihoods by striking themselves.[34]

The intransigence of the majority of employers and the determination of the organized workers broke the Republican Party coalition that had stood through the Civil War and that had maintained order in Chicago. Now skilled workers and their unions faced employers in a growing battle over the meaning of free labor. The contestants also squared off over government policy. The unions and eight-hour leagues had succeeded in getting government to back their demands so far, at least symbolically. But it remained to be seen how the government would react to the battle.

Soon, the skilled workers and their unions lost control of the strike because it attracted a large number of young men who were not organized in the skilled trades. These included unskilled factory workers, construction workers, laborers in brickyards, and probably some of the unemployed, the same groups that figured most prominently in the arrest figures quoted above. The *Tribune* described them as boys, and many were probably quite young. Many were also Irish immigrants or their descendants, with longstanding grievances against both the police department and their employers. While they had been neglected by the unions' organizing attempts, the broad class appeal of the march and the eight-hour leagues brought them into the movement.[35]

Unlike the skilled workers who could withdraw their labor without fear that they would be easily replaced, these unskilled workers had to bar others from taking their places in order for the strike to be effective. The unskilled workers also had fewer ties to the Republican Party and fewer illusions that the state would intervene on their behalf. Thus, from the moment they entered the field, the unskilled workers made the strike both more militant and, from the perspective of the employers and the city government, more disorderly. As soon as they struck and tried to picket, the police intervened to stop them. On May 2, at the Michigan Central freight depot, a crowd set upon a few men engaged to work for ten hours and drove them from the depot. Twenty policemen eventually arrived and dispersed the crowd. At the freight yards of the Galena Division of the Northwestern railroad in Chicago, crowds of fifty and then a hundred men tried to enforce the strike, but in both cases they were met by the police, who intimidated the crowds into leaving. Nearly two hundred strikers tried to prevent strikebreakers from working at the freight depot of the Fort Wayne railroad, but again, the police drove them off.[36]

But there were too many strikers for the police to check them all. At the King Brothers lumber yard, the strikers convinced those who initially continued to work on the ten-hour basis to join their strike. This crowd marched south through the lumber yard district and forced almost all the yards to shut down. In Bridgeport, a large crowd of young men marched down Archer Avenue and shut down the meatpacking factories. At other workplaces, workers took different actions on their own. At the McCormick Reaper factory, all the workers quit at four o'clock, after they had put in eight hours. Virtually all of the machine shops, factories, and foundries in the city were closed.[37]

The employers and city authorities were alarmed by the breadth of the strike, and it even surprised the organizers of the movement. The leaders of the unions who had called for the original march and strike disassociated themselves from the unskilled workers who attacked strikebreakers.[38] The newspapers, including the *Republican* and others that supported the eight-hour workday, condemned the strikers for engaging in violence and using compulsion against other workers. They reported that rumors of violence and lawlessness were overblown, but the newspapers' need to refute these rumors indicated the scale of the fear among the propertied residents of Chicago as much as the relative orderliness of the strike. The *Republican* insisted that, while it still defended the eight-hour day, the strikers had gone too far and should be suppressed.[39] The Democratic *Times* and the Republican *Tribune* called for more vigorous repression of the strike. The *Tribune* understood that "it is the purpose of the Mayor and police authorities to employ the force at their disposal as far as it will go, and make a thorough trial of strength with the rioters before calling the military into requisition or appealing to the State Government. . . . If it appears necessary, however," the *Tribune* continued ominously, "more effective measure will be taken today than were employed yesterday, and arrangements will be made to put the city on a war footing at the shortest notice."[40] The *Times* insisted that "the mobs of yesterday should not be allowed to make the slightest headway today. If they must be dispersed by violent measures—if artillery must be unlimbered in their front—it is humane that these measures be taken at once."[41] Although these two papers were divided over Reconstruction, the main political issue of the day, they were united in their opposition to and fear of the strikers. This unity seemed to sum up the general mood among the employers.

The positions of the *Republican* and the *Tribune* on the eight-hour day, the strike, and Reconstruction reveal a great deal about the evolution of the free-labor ideology of the Republican Party during Reconstruction. Both of these papers were committed to free labor, and both were in favor of taking radical measures to ensure the enforcement of a system of free labor in the South. They were also united on the limits of that free-labor system: workers were free to contract with their employers and should work to improve themselves, but they should not be free to unite, to strike, or to threaten the property rights of their employers. The old ideology of free labor, in which people might work for wages for part of their lives, but would eventually establish an independent farm or business, was already running up against the growth of a wage system that rendered "independence" on the part of most workers an unrealistic goal.[42] In this strike, three competing conceptions of how this free-labor system might evolve were deployed. The *Tribune* and the employers wanted to maintain the form of the old ideology of independent men contracting with one another, even though individual workers were not able to negotiate with large employers on equal terms and the chances that workers would be able to establish an independent livelihood were greatly reduced. Andrew Cameron and the skilled workers in the trades assemblies maintained that they were free men and free laborers despite their status as wage earners, and that they needed to unite to counter the combinations of capital in increasingly large businesses, such as the railroads. They argued that the contest between themselves and their employers should be arbitrated by a neutral state in which they had an equal stake with the capitalists. This motivated their successful drive to get the eight-hour state law passed. The unskilled workers elaborated the third definition of free labor when they united on the streets against their employers, and posed the question in stark class terms that were only resolved in a physical confrontation between police and strikers.

On the afternoon of May 2, many of the city's employers met to decide what action to take. This meeting was attended largely by the small employers, such as lumber mill owners, rather than big corporations like the railroads. Each reported on the conditions in his mill or factory, and repeated that the greater part of the skilled workmen were willing to keep working for ten hours, but that a rabble of youth and unskilled workers made up a mob that forced the strike forward. Many employers also insisted that a properly organized police force could have dispersed the crowd. In fact, where the police had been present, the strikers had failed to force out workers willing to labor for ten hours. But the police were badly outnumbered. As Alderman Russel pointed out, "the police force would scarcely number one to each factory in the city." The employers made a number of proposals to solve their problem. First, they planned to assemble men to be sworn in as special policemen. Superintendent of Police Jacob Rehm sent word that any officer could call on bystanders to act as special policemen. At the end of the meeting, the employers resolved "that we call upon the authorities to furnish an adequate force to protect our property and our employees in the prosecution of their work from the lawless depredations of the mob."[43]

At the same time, the police board was meeting to decide how to deal with the strike. First, they organized a *"corps de reserve"* at the central police station, consisting of as many men as could be spared by each station. The board prepared this reserve to be sent to any area where a crowd assembled. Despite the pleas of some business leaders, Superintendent Rehm declined to appoint a large number of special deputies, and added only twenty-three men. Rehm insisted that the forces at his disposal were sufficient to deal with the threat. The mayor backed up the police by declaring that, despite his previous support for the principle of the eight-hour-day, the city would use whatever force was needed to suppress the strikers. "Eight hours or ten hours," the mayor proclaimed, "increased or reduced wages, employment or unemployment—these things are all subordinate to public order, and to the protection of property and honest labor." In the face of the strike, the newspapers, the employers, and the city government united to call for repression by whatever means were necessary. This is not to say that all the politicians and employers were united on the issue of reform. They had divided over the eight-hour-workday law, and a segment of employers did eventually give in to that demand. They were united, however, on the need to maintain order as they understood it, and at all costs.[44]

By May 3, the police managed to regain control of the situation. Many workers remained out on strike, but there was much less violence because the police force effectively prevented it. Once again, large crowds of mostly Irish young men gathered around the lumber and planing mills, the railroad depots, and in Bridgeport. The strikers managed to force many workers in the packing houses and planing mills to join the strike, but police assembled to guard the mills and depots, attacking the group of strikers and arresting nine leaders of the group, effectively dispersing the crowd. Later that day at an outdoor mass meeting of strikers around the mill district, the police listened for those issuing "incendiary" statements, and arrested them. The *Tribune* summed up the overall effects of this activity: "The efficient service performed by the police who were constantly moving from one point to another throughout these localities had a good effect in overawing the idlers and inspired the laborers [who had not joined the strike] with fresh courage." At the same time, the unions led by Andrew Cameron held a mass meeting at which they reaffirmed their commitment to the eight-hour day but condemned the lawless unskilled workers.[45]

For the next few days, the police patrolled the city vigorously, breaking up any crowds that began to assemble and arresting incendiary speakers. The strike continued on the railroads and among the skilled workers, but the police kept crowds off the streets. This made it impossible for the unskilled workers to force compliance with the strike. Most employers succeeded in maintaining the ten-hour day, though a few gave in. The painters, for instance, won nine hours' pay for eight hours' work.[46] But despite their general victory, many employers were not satisfied with the police response. The Illinois Stone Company went so far as to notify the mayor that "this company will hold the city responsible in damages accruing from such violent proceedings, we claiming the protection of the law, and further, we believe it in the power of the city authorities to prevent such acts of violence." Most employers did not sue the city for its failure to provide protection, but they did clamor for a stronger police force. And the city responded. On May 3, the city council passed an ordinance authorizing the police board to hire fifty additional patrolmen at municipal expense.[47] On May 4, the police commissioners issued a notice informing employers that they could specify any men they trusted to be sworn in as special police officers to defend their property. In the aftermath of the strike, the city dramatically increased the total size of the police force by over 44 percent, from 173 to 250 men.[48]

The defeat of the strike in Chicago had wide-ranging political implications. It sounded the death knell for labor's 1860s attempt to enforce the eight-hour day throughout the Midwest, and was thus a major victory for employers.[49] It also signaled the demise of the labor-employer coalition in the Chicago Republican Party. From this point forward, Chicago's labor movement increasingly rejected the Republicans, backing Democrats or labor candidates. The labor movement would still attempt to wrest reforms from the state in the future, but many workers' expectations on this front in Chicago were reduced. This defeat also led to a short-term decline in the labor movement and exacerbated divisions between the skilled and unskilled.[50]

This strike was also the first time that the Chicago Police Department confronted large crowds of angry workers organized as such, and the department proved unequivocally which side it was on. Unlike during the Lager Beer Riot, the strikers were not mobilized directly against the city government or the police force itself. Rather, the police acted to defend the interests of the city's business class. Certainly, the unskilled strikers behaved in a disorderly manner, blocking strikebreaking workers from entering their places of employment and shouting threats. But because of the large number of unemployed people in the city and the nature of unskilled work, the unskilled strikers had little choice if they wished to be successful. Also, the strikers could point to the eight-hour law on the state books as justification for their position in the dispute. But there was no question about which side the police would intervene on. There was no possibility that the police would go from workplace to workplace and order work to stop after eight hours to enforce the state law. This strike therefore stands as a milestone in police-labor relations. Police policy toward strikes had been established, and employers and the city's workers alike knew it.

The strike also drove employers to unite as a class as never before. These employers were divided among themselves on a range of issues, including the original question of the eight-hour day and the broad political questions of Reconstruction. Some of them were small proprietors of painting companies that employed a few journeymen, while others, among them the meatpacker Philip Armor and the railroad corporations, already employed thousands of men. Many supported the Republicans, while others, including reaper magnate Cyrus McCormick, were Democrats. But they were united in their opposition to the threat of striking workers, and they had relied on the police to protect their position. The city's businessmen still distrusted the police department and looked to the army and the state militia as more trustworthy guarantors of their interests. Still, from this point forward, the city's business leaders would respond to every threat from below by clinging together, organizing themselves more closely into a coherent class, and strengthening the institutions committed to defending their power. The period after the Civil War was in this way as much a period of class formation for businessmen as it was for workers.

CHAPTER 4

The Native-Born Protestant Elite's Bid for Control in the 1870s

During the 1870s, it became increasingly clear that the promise of "free labor" would not be met. Rather than an expanding economy of small proprietors, the North was becoming more and more divided along class and ethnic lines. New York, Philadelphia, Boston, Chicago, and other cities were full of immigrant working men who were not about to become the free laborers of antebellum mythology. Many of these wage workers did not adhere to the developing norms of middle-class respectability, nor did many of them even speak English. In addition, the unemployed of all ethnicities swarmed into the cities especially once the economic crisis began in 1873.[1] Native-born Protestant urban elites across the country felt as if the cities were slipping into the grasp of these immigrant workingmen and unemployed vagrants. In response, the Protestant elite attempted to tighten its control over the nation's cities. In Chicago, the traditional native-born, Protestant elite attempted to enforce stricter temperance laws, regulate economic life, especially construction, and gain tighter control over the municipal government itself. However, this elite faced two enormous problems in carrying out this program. First, it was an increasingly small electoral minority. Chicago, New York, and Philadelphia were among the cities with majority immigrant populations and increasing numbers of wage workers who were unwilling to ally politically with their bosses. Second, the state apparatus was not strong enough to implement elite plans for regulating either economic or leisure activity.

The police stood at the center of this struggle. Police departments were expected to enforce temperance regulations, house vagrants or evict them from the cities, and control unruly workers, at the same time that businessmen were loath to tax themselves to pay for municipal services of any sort. Police departments also came under increasing criticism for corruption and inefficiency, which were often valid charges.

These problems raised a series of questions about the nature of policing. Did maintaining law and order mean enforcing Sunday closing laws, or did it just mean protecting lives and property? Were the police primarily responsible for creating an orderly society, free of rabid dogs, as well as free of larceny and murder, or were they primarily responsible for maintaining the specific political and economic order that kept the business elite in control? The traditional Protestant urban elite in Chicago began the decade with an aggressive program for controlling as many aspects of urban life as possible. This would only be possible if the traditional elite could seize control over municipal governments and craft powerful police forces that would enforce their program.

This process began in New York. That city's elite particularly felt the threat of immigrant working men in the aftermath of the draft riot of 1863 and the growth of an immigrant-based Democratic machine run by Boss William Tweed out of Tammany Hall. The New York elite attempted to overcome these problems by banding together politically. First, important businessmen formed a so-called Committee of Seventy to carry out a municipal coup against Boss Tweed's Democratic machine in 1871. This coup installed a probusiness municipal government that, among other things, ensured the New York City police would intervene against any strikes. The New York elite even contemplated disfranchising the city's workers. According to historian Sven Beckert, throughout the rest of the 1870s, New York businessmen increasingly united to retain control of city government and to form themselves into a cohesive class that could ensure the state at all levels acted on their behalf.[2]

Chicago's elite faced even deeper problems. It was considerably weaker and less cohesive than New York's. Chicago did not yet possess the millionaires who would emerge in the 1880s. Many of its wealthiest citizens were still real estate speculators who banked on the city's continued growth, yet to ensure that growth they needed to ensure that the city would be safe for investment. Chicago also possessed a sizeable population of middle-class and wealthy Germans, who were culturally distinct from the native-born members of the elite but who had similar class interests. In addition, Chicago was growing at a tremendous clip during this period, from about three hundred thousand people in 1870 to half a million by 1880. While the city's growth presented many new business opportunities, it also attracted hundreds of thousands of new immigrant wage workers who would have to be fed, housed, and controlled. Finally, Chicago's police force was even weaker and less developed than New York's.

The struggles of the early 1870s revealed important fault lines within the elite about how to address these problems, between those who favored a strong, centralized municipal authority that could enforce reforms, and those who favored a more inclusive style of politics. In this way, the clashes of the 1870s reprised the fights that culminated in the establishment of the police board in 1860. Once again, the native born clashed with immigrants, temperance reformers fought those in favor of drinking rights, and promoters of professionalism decried corruption and sought to militarize the police department further. Chicago's business community did not resolve these divisions or solve any of its problems in the 1870s. In fact, the elite's attempted solutions exacerbated ethnic and class tensions, weakened its control over the municipal government, and left the police department in disarray for a period. Through their failures, though, native-born businessmen and the city's political leaders gained a clearer understanding of the limits and dangers of their position. This decade of crises also shifted the terrain of Chicago's political conflicts from what were, at least on the surface, ethnic divisions to much more sharply posed class conflict.

These problems were greatly exacerbated on October 8, 1871, the most disorderly night in Chicago history. That night, a fire started on the city's West Side and fed by strong, steady winds and the mass of wooden buildings, it grew so hot that it melted brick and stone. By the time it burned itself out the following day, the Great Chicago Fire had consumed a huge portion of the city. It killed three hundred people and left a third of the city's three hundred thousand residents homeless. The Chicago fire destroyed eighteen thousand buildings, including all those in the city's downtown, along with many homes and small businesses in outlying areas.[3]

Karen Sawislak, the premier historian of the fire, points out that while contemporaries expected the destruction of so much wealth to "burn the barriers" between the classes, in fact the fire had the opposite effect. While it destroyed the homes of rich and poor alike, the policies enacted after the catastrophe ensured that relief and reconstruction efforts would be organized to protect the interests of the mostly native-born, Protestant large property owners, rather than to assuage the suffering of the thousands rendered homeless by the blaze, including many German homeowners. Countless accounts produced soon after the fire described the plight of wealthy and middle-class Chicagoans fleeing from the flames and watching their possessions go up in smoke, yet the city's poor were the main victims of the fire: most of those killed in the fire lived in the Irish neighborhoods on the South Side near where the fire started, so they had little chance to flee. But it was wealthy Chicagoans who controlled the city government, the resources that could be used for relief, and the media outlets that told the initial story of the fire. The policies that the elite enacted in the fire's aftermath engendered considerable resentment among poorer Chicagoans and helped prompt renewed political activism by people denied relief and by small-property holders.[4]

In addition, in the fire's immediate aftermath, fear of the city's working class gripped wealthy and middle-class Chicagoans. The *Times* falsely accused an exiled Communard from Paris of intentionally setting the blaze because of his jealousy of the rich.[5] Even the infamous story that Mrs. O'Leary's cow started the blaze when it knocked over a lantern carelessly left burning laid the blame squarely on the immigrant Irish working class that so frightened Chicago's wealthy citizens. After the fire, the wealthy feared that poor people and workers would take advantage of the crisis to loot the burned buildings. In response to this fear, the city's business elite united around a concerted effort to strengthen their control over the city.[6]

With this in mind, the Chicago city government sought to maintain order in the city above all else. While the fire was still burning itself out on October 9, the mayor, comptroller, and the presidents of the police board and the common council declared that "with the help of God, peace and private property shall be preserved."[7] The next day, Mayor Roswell B. Mason issued a proclamation that included the assertion that "Public order will be preserved. The police and special police now being appointed will be responsible for the maintenance of the peace and the protection of property."[8] In order to accomplish this, the city appointed everyone who worked for the fire or health departments as special police. The mayor also requested that citizens organize "a police" for each block and send reports of those organizations to police headquarters. Later that day, the mayor proclaimed that he would appoint five hundred additional special policemen from each district, and hundreds of volunteers went to the city headquarters to be sworn in.[9] Each special policeman was to be placed under the command of the sergeant for his district, who would get orders, supplies, and rations from the superintendent of police. The city government made preparations as if it expected the fire to be the opening act of an impending insurrection.[10]

The newspapers fanned the fear of the poor by printing sensational accounts of looting and rioting, though later investigations reveal that these reports were almost entirely fabricated. Certainly, the fire broke down the normal functioning of the legal system, but a deeper problem was that the city's leaders did not consider the police department up to the task of maintaining order. As historians Carl Smith and Karen Sawislak argue, this fear shows how divided Chicago was along ethnic and class lines, with little understanding across them. Fear of the poor was not entirely without cause— Chicago was home to hundreds of thousands of harshly exploited people living in squalor next to elaborate mansions and imposing hotels and office buildings. The city's workers had already organized a large strike in 1867, and Chicago's elite was all too aware of the precedents for disorder set by the Paris Commune and the New York draft riots of 1863.[11]

During those draft riots just eight years earlier, crowds of mostly Irish young men had overwhelmed the New York Metropolitan Police Department. The police superintendent himself had been beaten badly. Even when police did charge the crowd with revolvers drawn, they were overpowered. The New York rioters burned the mayor's house along with two police stations. They killed at least 120 civilians and estimates of property damage ranged widely from one million to five million dollars. The New York draft riots only ended when federal troops and New York state militia entered the city in sufficient numbers to control the streets and subdue a massed and angry crowd.[12]

Chicago's political and business leaders feared a repeat of New York's experience. They decided to invite a stronger force into the city before things could get out of hand, and three days after the fire, the infantry arrived. On October 11, Mayor Mason entrusted "the preservation of the good order and peace of the city" to Lieutenant-General Philip Sheridan and the U.S. Army. Sheridan had a considerable force at his disposal: ten regular infantry companies of a hundred men each, plus a volunteer regiment of eighteen additional companies composed largely of Civil War veterans.[13] This boosted the total occupying force to about 2,800—or about seven times the number in the police department. The army also brought in supplies to help those rendered homeless in the catastrophe. At the same time, the police commissioners revoked the powers they had granted to special policemen the day before and ordered the regular police to cooperate with and obey General Sheridan.[14]

In fact there was little cause for alarm. General Sheridan sent a number of letters to the mayor remarking on the peacefulness and calm of the city's residents. He wrote that, contrary to newspaper reports, he had heard no news of attempted arson, hanging, shooting, or even of disorder in general. On October 17, more than a week after the fire, he insisted that "there has been no case of violence since the disaster of Sunday night and Monday morning. The reports in the public press of violence and disorder here are without the slightest foundation."[15] By October 22, Mayor Roswell Mason asked General Sheridan if he thought the troops needed to stay in the city to preserve "the lives and property of the citizens," and the General replied that they did not. The board of police commissioners was already annoyed at the military's usurpation of their powers, and after Mason consulted with them, he and the police reclaimed control of the city the following day.[16]

The military and special police proved more hazardous to Chicagoans than the feared mobs of arsonists and looters. "That a number of persons met death at the hands of excited citizen-policemen is most probably true," wrote John Flinn, the 1888 historian of the police, "but that the number exceeded, or even reached, half a dozen, all told, is very improbable."[17] Given that there were no reported deaths at the hands of looters and no evidence of arson, half a dozen deaths at the hands of the military and special policemen loom large in comparison to the threat these forces were supposed to protect Chicagoans from. Indeed, the end of military government was hastened when a volunteer militiaman shot and killed Thomas Grosvener, the prosecuting attorney for the city in the police courts. According to Elias Colbert and Albert Chamberlain, Grosvener was returning home after midnight when a sentinel named Treat accosted him near Douglas University. When Treat said that he would fire if Grosvener did not stop, Grosvener reportedly retorted "fire and be damned," upon which Treat shot him in the chest.[18]

The elite reaction to the fire thus reveals that the city's elite was both extremely class conscious and aware that it had little power over or even knowledge of the city's poor and working-class residents. In the short term, the elite organized in the Chicago Relief and Aid Society and the city government was mostly concerned with preventing a working-class uprising. In the longer term, though, this crisis pushed the city's elite to attempt to extend its power and control over the entire city, to discipline the working class and ensure a permanent order. However, in 1871, these elite fears were almost entirely unfounded. Poor Chicagoans caught up in the fire's aftermath were struggling to survive and to put back together the pieces of their lives, not organize against the rich. Yet the anxiety of the wealthy and their reaction to the crisis would increasingly push Chicago's poorer residents into a class consciousness of their own.

Chicago's business elite and politicians responded to their fears by forming an electoral coalition that could extend elite control over the city more fully. In December 1871, a combination of reformers from the Democratic and Republican Parties elected Joseph Medill mayor on the Union Fire-Proof ticket. Medill was a Republican and part owner of the *Tribune*. His election continued the period of party reorganization in the city that had begun with the 1869 election of a "citizen's" ticket against corruption and which lasted through the 1870s. In fact, during this entire decade, the two national parties failed to hold together broad coalitions, and elections were fought between shifting groups assembled on the basis of immediate issues like the fire or the enforcement of Sunday drinking laws. Medill was elected by a diverse group of Chicagoans who were against corruption and who were determined to prevent another disastrous fire, and who were on a deeper level anxious to extend order over the city. Medill's party was almost entirely dominated by the native-born elite, at the expense especially of German immigrants who had been key in the Republican coalition of the 1860s. This elite sought to use the municipal government to enact the policies they thought crucial, and extend their control over the city by force, rather than bring together elements from various ethnic groups and neighborhoods. In this way, Medill's mayoralty represented a new iteration of the reform policies first elucidated by the wing of the Republican Party that had established the police board against Mayor Wentworth in 1860. Medill was the antithesis of a machine politician, but his policies would do more to reveal the need for inclusive, machine or patronage-style politics than any other mayor in Chicago history.

The first problem facing a mayor who sought to extend the city government's control was that the police were themselves untrustworthy wage workers. Immediately after he took office, Medill and the police commissioners tried to address this by rooting out corruption and instilling greater military discipline in the force. They first tried a number of police officers accused of bad behavior. One had stolen money from a drunken tourist, another assaulted a horse-car driver, and a third had been off-duty without permission for five days. Then, the police commissioners ordered that patrolmen salute their officers and that the superintendent and deputy superintendent of police wear their uniforms when on the street.[19] These were largely symbolic gestures because Medill and his allies knew that the discipline of the policemen was a serious problem, but they did not yet have a clear solution.

Another immediate problem for the police was that, because tax receipts were sure to plummet with the loss of so much property in the fire and the city had to raise money to rebuild the burned public buildings, the city was desperately trying to reduce its expenses. All municipal workers engaged in jobs that were not absolutely critical were laid off.[20] One of the police commissioners, Jacob Rehm, proposed to cut the pay of the three state-appointed, but municipally funded, police commissioners from $3,000 a year to $500, at a time when patrolmen were paid $1,000 a year.[21] The other commissioners agreed with Rehm, especially since, as one commissioner pointed out, "he saw nothing to do sitting around the office."[22] This was again largely symbolic, however, since the pay of the commissioners was only a small share of total police expenses. This again raised the problem of police discipline. How could the city ensure that patrolmen would be satisfied workers while at the same time cut payroll? The lack of solution to this question contributed to the elite's continued dissatisfaction with the police department.

Medill's party provoked its first serious political crisis by attempting to enforce an antifire measure that divided the upper layers of the elite from everyone else in the city: an ordinance that only brick buildings be allowed within the city limits. This law threatened small-property owners who could not afford to build buildings of brick, as well as real estate investors, such as M. D. Ogden, who hoped to profit by subdividing their extensive property on the edges of the city and selling small lots to people who could afford only wooden construction. Irish and German politicians on the North Side, led by Anton Hesing, the owner and editor of the Republican *Illinois Staats Zeitung*, organized opposition to this ordinance in defense of the actual and potential owners of wooden buildings. If the city allowed only brick buildings, they argued, only the wealthy could afford homes. Hesing and his compatriots sent a petition to the city council, and then, on January 15, 1872, they organized a massive march on city hall.[23]

The marchers arrived during a regular city council meeting that had yet to take up the issue of fire limits. Up to that point in the meeting, the council had fixed the salary of the bridewell inspector, appointed a new oil inspector, and granted a petition from a businessmen to allow his storefront to extend three feet into the sidewalk.[24] While the council was discussing a motion to remove two "pest houses" or quarantines, the large crowd arrived and broke up the meeting. The eight to ten police officers present tried their best to prevent the crowd from entering the chamber, but they were overwhelmed. First, the anti-fire limit demonstrators thrust a Union flag and a German flag into the council chambers. Then, they forced entry into the meeting and caused the council to adjourn and vacate the premises. Anton Hesing made a speech calling for stringent fire limits, but not so stringent as those proposed by Medill. When a few brickbats flew through the windows and into the crowd, injuring some demonstrators and policemen, everyone left the chambers.[25]

The demonstration succeeded in pushing the council to allow wooden buildings in many parts of the city.[26] More importantly, it began the process of forcing the native-born elite to pull back from their most severe program. Anton Hesing was not opposed to the constituted government or to ensuring that Chicago was safe from a fire. The small-property holders who so angrily opposed the new fire limits were exactly the group that the businessmen needed electoral support from if they hoped to maintain control over the city government. In fact, Hesing articulated a vision of a property-holding working class that offered a potential bulwark against the radical left. This demonstration began the long process of demonstrating to the most uncompromising members of the native-born elite, like Medill, that they would have to bend and work with moderate immigrant leaders like Hesing if they wished to rule.[27]

The success of the crowd in overawing the city council also illustrates once again the weakness of the police force, both physically and morally. One of the

crowds' participants was an alderman, and Anton Hesing was a newspaper-
man heavily involved in local politics. That these politicians were willing to
lead a crowd against the police showed that they neither feared nor respected
its authority. The native-born business interests that controlled both the city
government and the police force (which was still directly run by a board of
police commissioners, two out of three of whom had been appointed by the
state legislature) framed the conflict in terms of democratic legitimacy and
the protection of order, rather than simply the question of the fire limits.[28]
While Medill and his allies yielded on the question at hand and agreed to
more modest fire limits, they moved to ensure that similar disturbances of
the normal functioning of government could not recur. The police force was
the main tool at Medill's disposal to protect the city government from such
intrusions in the future.

The police were thus immediately involved in the conflict. Seventy-eight
police officers bearing six-shooters guarded the next city council meeting.[29]
Mayor Medill submitted a formal letter to the meeting insisting that the
council take action against the alderman who had participated in the "mob."
He also promised that, in the future, the council would be protected. "The
Police Commissioners will take such measures as will secure your adequate
protection hereafter when in discharge of your duties," he wrote, "and will
deal with such riotous bodies in the future in a summary manner. The peace
good order and dignity of the City and the supremacy of the laws shall be
maintained at all hazards and if the organized police force of the City should
at any time prove inadequate, the military power of the state will be promptly
invoked."[30] Here again, even while the mayor insisted that he would use the
police to defend the city council, he recognized their weakness. In essence,
Medill and his allies wanted a police force they could count on to enforce
any regulations they chose to pass, however unpopular. This was impossible,
of course, but it would take a few more defeats for the elite to learn that fact.

Rebuilding Chicago after the fire presented new threats as thousands of
newcomers flooded into the city in the spring of 1872. During this period,
there was no way the police force could accomplish what was requested of
them. Even many of the mundane tasks the city government required were
beyond the reasonable scope of the police force. For instance, on June 15,
Alderman Daggy from the Fifth Ward asked the committee on police to
"inquire what if any legislation may be necessary to prohibit boys of all ages
and sizes from jumping on the rear end of horse railway streetcars while in
motion."[31] Similarly, on April 17, 1872, the city council ordered the board of
police commissioners to make the police stop railroad cars from blocking
city streets.[32] Given the size of the force and the city, it is inconceivable that

such ordinances, if passed, could be enforced. The department employed 425 patrolmen, twenty sergeants, three captains, one clerk, one custodian, one secretary, and one superintendent to guard a city of over three hundred thousand people, with additional thousands pouring in every month.[33]

As Chicago was rebuilt, the municipal government also assumed full responsibility for policing the city, which was a mixed blessing for Medill. On July 1, 1872, the mayor regained control of the board of police commissioners under the terms of a March state law granting mayors the power to appoint all the members of municipal boards in the state, subject to the approval of the city council. On the one hand, this gave the mayor increased authority over the police. He could now appoint the members of the police board, a power he promptly used to appoint Ernst Klokke to replace the venerable Jacob Rehm, who had retired from the board in May.[34] He could also appoint any policeman. But it also meant that the mayor was now responsible for the efficiency of the police and that police policy could once again become an object of contention in local politics. The state had retained official control over the police board since the days of Long John Wentworth in 1860, even though it had generally appointed board members who met with the approval of Chicago's city government. Under the board of police commissioners, the police force had been much more consistent in personnel and policy than before. No longer was the entire force replaced at each mayoral election. But now that possibility was reopened.

As the press began to report an increase in crime in the summer and fall of 1872, some newspapers began calling on the mayor to reconstitute the force wholesale. The *Tribune* began reporting in June that crime was plaguing the West Side and declared the "utter demoralization of the second precinct police force."[35] On July 8, the *Tribune* editorialized that the police force was full of stupid and incompetent men. It cited a recent robbery of a jeweler, during which the thieves held the stolen goods for ransom at some safe place in the city that the police never discovered. The *Tribune* also reported the rumor that any robber or thief could go about his business, so long as he reserved 20 percent of the proceeds for the police. The *Tribune* dismissed this accusation, arguing not that the police were honest, but rather that they were so incompetent that no criminal would agree to share his profits with them. It called on Mayor Medill to follow the example of Philadelphia, where a few years previously the mayor had fired at once all eight hundred men working for the Philadelphia Police Department and hired their replacements wholesale.[36] A few weeks later, when reporting on a case of attempted burglary on the West Side, where "it is doubtful that ever a policeman has been seen," the *Tribune* asserted that "If some of the sturdy scoundrels in want of prey would only break into and rob the homes of all the Police Commissioners, Superintendent, Captains, sergeants, detectives and patrolmen, and in addition garrotte old Talcott, Sheridan and Klokke [the police commissioners], it would be a stroke of poetic justice that would tickle the public."[37] Distrust of the force had reached such a pitch that the *Tribune*, a paper partially owned by the mayor, essentially called for criminals to assault and even kill the leaders of the police department.

Neither the police commissioners nor the mayor had a clear solution to the perceived inadequacy of the police. In retrospect, it is easy to see that what was asked of the force was well beyond their means. The city was full of half-burned buildings that served as easy hiding places. It was populated by newcomers who were generally unknown to the police on their beats, and who often did not speak English. With just 425 patrolmen, the force was woefully undermanned and spread thinly across a great area. But the actions taken by the police leaders did not help. On July 22, the commissioners resolved to fire any patrolmen found to be drunk, which only provoked more ire from the press since it confirmed their impression that officers were frequently intoxicated on the job.[38]

In fact, the fear of crime that gripped Chicago in the summer of 1872 had at least three distinct sources. First, as both Karen Sawislak and Carl Smith have pointed out, the massive influx of foreign-born construction workers heightened the native-born's already considerable fear of the city's immigrants. Much of this fear was exaggerated, as we have seen in the response to the fire itself. But middle- and upper-class Chicagoans probably did feel uncomfortable and unsafe in a city that no longer felt like their own. Second, there was real crime, both of the spectacular type like the murders and robberies constantly reported in the *Tribune*, as well as the everyday brawls and rowdy behavior in nineteenth-century Chicago. It is difficult to tell whether the increase in crime was actually out of proportion to the increase in the city's population. The crime wave of the summer of 1872 seems very unspectacular to modern eyes—the *Tribune* reported three murders during this period, one of a policeman. The Northwestern University homicide project lists only one murder for the entire year of 1872.[39] As Jeffrey Adler points out in *First in Violence, Deepest in Dirt*, murders were still quite rare in this period, so reports of three murders in a summer might seem like a crime wave to people at the time, even if they fade in comparison to the hundreds of murders that would become common each summer in the twentieth century.[40] The third cause of alarm, and most important for this study, was that few in the city had faith in the ability of the police force to protect the population.

In response to the perceived crime wave, the ineffectiveness of the police, and their desire to assert greater control over the city more generally, concerned members of the elite reinvigorated the "citizens' committees" formed immediately after the fire in late July 1872. They consolidated these committees to form a Committee of Seventy, likely named after the Committee of Seventy that had taken over New York's municipal government earlier that year, since it did not denote the actual number of participants.[41] The Chicago Committee of Seventy was not a permanent political association, but it could mobilize a formidable section of the city's business and political elite. These included many of Chicago's most prominent businessmen and politicians. It was chaired by Judge S. B. Gookins, a lawyer from Indiana, and often presided over by John V. Farwell, a merchant and investor.[42] The committee brought together representatives from the board of trade and other important business and political figures, including former mayors like John Wentworth, senators, and aldermen.[43] The committee alternately called its electoral candidates the Temperance Party and the Law and Order Party. The Committee of Seventy intended to form an organization that could pressure city government to do what it desired, and for more than a year it succeeded. Because Mayor Medill had been elected with the support of the leaders of the Committee, he was particularly vulnerable to their influence.

The Committee of Seventy immediately attempted to put one of their own in charge of the police in order to reshape the department. On July 29, 1872, they pushed Mayor Medill to fire Superintendent Kennedy and appoint Elmer Washburn to replace him.[44] Washburn was warden of the Illinois penitentiary in Joliet at the time of his appointment and had served as the head of the federal secret service during the Civil War.[45] Before that, he had been a division superintendent for the Illinois Central Railroad.[46] He had no experience as a policeman or with the city of Chicago, but he was well-liked by the leading members of the Committee of Seventy. In discussing whether or not to recommend that Washburn be confirmed, the city council's Committee on Judiciary and Police was reluctant, but they also came under pressure from the Committee of Seventy. One alderman related that he had at first been opposed to the confirmation because Washburn lacked experience, but some of the city's "best men" had visited him and convinced him to change his mind. On August 12, 1872, the council confirmed Washburn.[47] That Washburn owed his appointment to the Committee of Seventy rather than to the established city government gave him wide latitude to try and reform the force, but it also raised the ire of the career officers, who were now commanded by an outsider.

The Committee of Seventy dictated policy to Washburn, and sought from the start to discipline the police force, so that it could in turn discipline the city. Just a month after his confirmation, on September 17, Washburn met with leading members of the Committee of Seventy to decide how to "remedy the existing social conditions." The committee members thought that the jury system put the law in the hands of the ignorant. They also accused the police of corruption and of lacking discipline. They complained that officers took bribes to return stolen property. They thought that individual policemen were too hard to fire. They also complained that policemen could never be found to enforce the laws. For instance, the mayor had issued a proclamation against young people racing omnibuses on Wabash Avenue, but no police could be found to enforce it. The Committee of Seventy, then, viewed the problem as wealthy men were accustomed to: their employees, the police, were lazy and undisciplined, and they needed a strong leader who could whip them into shape. They hoped that Washburn could be that man.[48]

Washburn evidently recognized the difficulty of the position he had been thrust into. He denied the charges of corruption and insisted that the problem was leadership, perhaps realizing that a campaign against corruption would not be the best way to win the allegiance of the force. He also asked for more resources. Washburn pointed out that the police force did not have a single mounted patrolman, and that it was severely undermanned.[49] In other words, he immediately adopted the viewpoint of the institution and reiterated the frequent requests of superintendents since Cyrus Bradley in 1855. This time, however, he directed his request not to the city council, but to the self-appointed Committee of Seventy.

Washburn and the Committee of Seventy's power over the force was also limited given the political nature of police hiring. When the city did agree to hire an additional hundred policemen in 1873, the hiring process was extremely political and remained in the hands of the police board. Francis O'Neill, later famous for collecting and publishing traditional Irish music, was hired only when he secured the backing of his alderman, after failing to secure a position earlier despite support from a member of Congress, the superintendent of the Chicago and Alton Railroad, and Superintendent Washburn himself.[50]

O'Neill's story also illustrates how Germans and especially Irishmen came to be so heavily represented on the police force. O'Neill worked for John V. Farwell's dry-goods business before he joined the force. Farwell was a leading member of the Committee of Seventy, and in his business, O'Neill had found himself blocked from promotion by his lack of connections and probably his Irish roots, despite a classical education in Ireland.[51] Yet because of the political nature of police hiring, once Irish and German immigrants established their own neighborhoods and became a force in city politics, they could get their own hired on the department. This field was not open to everyone: O'Neill, for instance, had considerable references and connections with politicians and businessmen, an impressive educational background, and a lot of tenacity, yet he was only able to secure a position with great difficulty. Still, this was one of the few avenues of advancement open to ambitious Irish immigrants who lacked even the small amounts of capital needed to open a saloon or boardinghouse and who faced considerable difficulties securing promotion within established firms. And while the pay of one thousand dollars a year for a patrolman in 1873 was no fortune, it was considerably more than Irish immigrants could earn in most other jobs.

While the influx of immigrants for reconstruction, the increasing importance of wage labor, and the weakness of the police were the most important factors contributing to upper-class perceptions of disorder, in 1872, temperance ideas were again growing in popularity, especially among Protestants. The Women's Temperance Crusade would not break out in Upstate New York until the following year, but the ideas that informed it were well rooted and already in widespread circulation throughout the country. Between 1873 and 1874, women in more than nine hundred towns throughout the north gathered, demonstrated, prayed, and pleaded with saloonkeepers to shut down in a mass movement that would eventually give birth to the Women's Christian Temperance Union.[52] This movement was gathering strength below ground, and helped provide an answer to why the promise of a society of free, independent laborers had not been realized after the Civil War. Temperance dramas had spread around the country in the 1850s—by 1851 the American Tract Society alone had distributed nearly five million temperance tracts. These dramas followed the same narrative path—a husband takes to drink and impoverishes himself and his family both morally and materially, before finally abandoning alcohol and redeeming himself. These narratives linked drink and disorder in clear ways—the drunkard behaves in a disorderly way both within his own family and in the wider social world, leading to personal degradation and social disorder.[53] They helped explain the poverty of a great many Chicagoans. It was not the fault of low wages or lack of jobs; rather, families were impoverished because their fathers were drunks, lacking the self-discipline necessary to become independent free laborers. In this way, temperance was an ideology that was equally attractive to middle-class and elite Protestants, in ways that limiting wooden construction, for instance, was not.

Temperance also became increasingly attractive in the 1870s because working-class saloons had become a permanent fixture of the urban landscape, key sites of working-class socializing outside the realm of the elite. Historian Roy Rozenweig points out that, in its initial form, temperance was as much an ideology of self-control as social control, aimed at instilling the self-discipline needed to become a free laborer. But over time, temperance ideology was shifting toward "a more exclusive concern with the external threat posed by working-class drinking and particularly by the working class saloon."[54] The city government barely exercised authority over the working-class neighborhoods of Chicago, and employers exercised no authority over their workers' leisure time, which for men was largely spent in saloons. Temperance gave them an opportunity to do so.

Yet temperance was a deeply divisive issue, holding little attraction for even the wealthiest Germans or other Chicagoans who liked to drink. As a result, the Committee of Seventy was itself divided over what to do about temperance. Echoing the temperance sentiments of the day, one leading citizen argued that the root of crime was drunkenness, and that all the murders and major crimes seemed to happen on Sunday. He therefore suggested vigorously enforcing the (previously unenforced) Sunday closing laws. The same Anton Hesing who owned the *Illinois Staats Zeitung* and had helped organize the crowd to protest Medill's fire limits was a member of the committee, and he objected. Drinking did contribute to social problems and caused men to beat their wives, but it had nothing to do with murders. "Burglars, pickpockets and gamblers—such men as carried concealed weapons and committed the murders were not drunkards," insisted Hesing. He proposed instead that the liquor business be regulated and that the fees for saloon licenses be raised. This would have helped his associates, the established saloonkeepers, who suffered from too much competition from small, newer saloons. The conflict within this meeting portended a deep division between the native-born elite and the immigrant elite over drinking in the months to come. It also illustrates the radically different opinions on the roots of disorder and crime. In the end, the committee appointed an official subcommittee to deal with the problem, and this committee took a decidedly protemperance stance. Because Washburn was politically dependent on the Committee of Seventy, this subcommittee was to have as much control over his policies as the police board or the city council.[55]

Over the next few months, the Committee of Seventy exerted more and more pressure on Medill and Washburn to enforce the Sunday closing law. They held gatherings and sent delegates to meet with the mayor and police commissioners, and even accused Medill of being beholden to liquor interests.[56] Medill was no temperance man. He could see that enforcing the Sunday closing laws was a fool's errand on two fronts: he did not believe that drinking was the basic cause of crime, and he recognized that it would be impossible to force people to stop drinking on Sundays. "It would require one policeman for each drinking place to see that the law was enforced," he wrote, "or say, three thousand altogether, whereas the taxfighters [many on the Committee of Seventy regularly objected to taxes] made it hard to support a force of four hundred and fifty policeman."[57]

Medill was right about the political difficulty of increasing the force. This was because the same members of the Committee of Seventy who were concerned with order were also highly resistant to taxation. On November 15, 1872, in a discussion on fire safety with the city council, Medill suggested that, since the police initiated most of the fire alarms, their number should be increased. There had not been an increase in the force for two years, he reported, and the beats were so large that most patrolmen could only walk their beats once or twice in a night, and this encouraged crime. He argued that "all sorts of expedients had been tried—private watchmen, burglar alarms, bull dogs, and other humbug contrivances, and it was evident that more policemen were needed." A number of alderman agreed with this, but when actually hiring more officers was discussed, the city council objected that money was already tight. It finally recommended that seventy additional men be hired and paid out of the State Police Fund. The disbursement was up to the city council's committee in charge of that fund, and the extra men were never hired.[58] Under the act establishing the police board, members of the force were appointed "for life," so an increase in the force meant a perennial tax increase. The corporation counsel (the lawyer responsible for reviewing the legality of municipal policy) declared that, because of the tax issue, the city council lacked the authority to increase the force except within its annual appropriation.[59] At that same meeting, even while they were lamenting the shorthandedness of the police force, the city council ordered the police commissioners to appoint policemen to inspect the fire safety of every building in the city. This would have taken many thousands of man-hours. As with Sunday closing, the legal powers of the city government were not matched by their powers of enforcement. And these powers of enforcement were limited by the elite's willingness to tax themselves.[60]

The men most responsible for the force—Superintendent Washburn, Medill, and the police commissioners—knew all of this and tried to resist the Committee of Seventy because they knew it would be nearly impossible to enforce the Sunday closing law. When Mayor Medill expressed his doubts about the police, the Committee of Seventy (actually the subcommittee of fifteen appointed to deal with law and order) began to pressure Medill, Washburn, and the board of police commissioners to attempt to close saloons

on Sundays, anyway. Finally, they convinced both the mayor and the board
that they had best go along with the committee's decision.[61] Consequently,
on October 11, 1872, the police commissioners ordered Washburn to enforce
the Sunday closing law "as far as practicable."[62]

Knowing the problems this enforcement would cause, the police themselves
initially resisted this order. Two weeks after the order went into effect, however,
the police bowed to the inevitable and began forcing saloons to close, though
even then they made few arrests. When the news was first publicized, some
of the more reputable saloons closed their doors voluntarily, and one even
offered to pay the $100 fine every Monday if he could be allowed to stay open
on Sundays.[63] Liquor could still be obtained legally outside the city limits, and
within the city through apothecaries or physicians' prescriptions. In fact, many
saloons remained open illegally, but with shades drawn and curtains covering
the front doors so they would give churchgoers no cause for complaint.[64]

The attempted enforcement of this law immediately divided the city between supporters of temperance and those who saw Sunday closing laws as
a violation of their rights. This rift correlated imperfectly with the class and
ethnic makeup of the city: as elsewhere, native-born Protestants were more
likely to support temperance, while immigrants and workers were more
likely to oppose it. The city's Germans in particular felt that they were being
unfairly blamed for a crime wave that had little to do with them. However,
the Germans were not the only group to oppose temperance. Many native-
born Protestants of all classes enjoyed drinking or participated in one way or
another in the liquor trade and resented the equation of alcohol with crime
and disorder. Others objected to the interference with their personal liberty.
On a deeper level, this division portended a serious divide over what role
government should play in the city's daily life. The advocates of temperance
were no longer just handing out tracts, like they had in the early 1850s. Now, as
in 1855, they were attempting to use armed force to control what Chicagoans
did on what was, for most workers, their only day off.

In the immediate aftermath of this attempt at liquor control, German
politicians organized a mass meeting and elected a delegation to meet with
the mayor and argue that Sunday closing laws should once again be ignored,
but to no avail. In the short term, they forced the resignation of Sunday closing law advocate Mancel Talcott from the board of police commissioners,
though this did not settle the matter. Talcott was replaced by C. A. Reno, who
was more amenable to the city's Germans but was not yet ready to provoke
a fight with the Committee of Seventy.

The city's supporters of the freedom to drink then began to organize in a
"Personal Liberty League." On December 23, 1872, this group presented the

city council with a petition signed by twenty-five thousand Chicagoans of all ethnicities advocating a new liquor law. Their proposed law would ban saloonkeepers from selling liquor to a man whose wife asked them not to, would ban noise in saloons, and would ban saloons from selling liquor on Sundays "with their doors open." A Special Committee of Nine investigated the matter and urged a compromise that would allow saloons to open after 1 P.M. on Sundays, well after church was over. But the Committee of Seventy was unwilling to compromise, so the old laws against selling liquor on Sunday stayed on the books.[65] In fact, between October 1872 and April 1873, Sunday drinking appears to have continued more or less unimpeded, if somewhat more covertly than before. The main effect of this attempt to enforce the law was to drive prodrinking rights Chicagoans, especially Germans, away from the elite political grouping dominated by the Committee of Seventy.

Superintendent Washburn then redoubled his efforts to remake the police department according to the Committee of Seventy's program, at least in part to build a force that could enforce the Sunday closing laws. This attempt, however, met serious resistance from within the department and led to a substantial weakening of Washburn's authority. First, he prohibited the police from accepting fines or bail from those they arrested.[66] This had been common practice in the city, and allowed the police to treat "respectable" and "unrespectable" citizens differently, and to differentiate between people who committed petty and major offenses. But it left the police open to accusations of corruption, since individual patrolmen could accept money on the spot for fines. The enforcement of this new order was both difficult and inconsistent. Sergeant Rehm was forced to resign for releasing a prisoner, while Commissioners Talcott and Klokke fought over whether or not even they had the right to release anyone.[67] Washburn accused Captain Michael C. Hickey of releasing prisoners and holding recovered stolen goods, and brought him up on charges before the board of police commissioners. The case fell apart during two days of testimony, and Hickey had his star restored though at the lesser rank of sergeant. This incident weakened Washburn considerably and cost him whatever respect he still had among his subordinates, especially since Captain Hickey was a highly respected officer.[68]

This defeat led to a power struggle in the department that would continue through 1873. First, the police commissioners challenged Superintendent Washburn's right to change patrol duty or even order a raid on the city's gambling dens. They attempted to force Washburn to resign, but he retained enough support from the mayor and the Committee of Seventy to keep his job.[69] In January 1873, however, the city council passed an ordinance that anyone arrested could secure his or her release by posting a special bail double the amount of the highest fine that they could face. This money could be deposited with the officer in charge of whatever station they were taken to, exactly the practice Washburn had objected to in the first place.[70] The upshot of this whole affair was that Washburn kept his job but was unable to implement the reform he desired, losing credit with the department as a result. At the same time, the city government was beginning to divide between those willing to do the bidding of the Committee of Seventy, including Medill and Washburn, and those who were not, including the police commissioners and many members of the police hierarchy.

Medill did not help Washburn's standing with the police. Patrolmen constantly complained that the city made them pay for their own belts and clubs. In part to reinforce the morale of the police, the city council passed an ordinance that the council should refund the amount patrolmen paid the city treasury for these items, since they were necessary for police duty. But Medill vetoed the measure. He insisted that it would prevent policemen from being liable for keeping proper care of their equipment. He said he would only sign the ordinance if it included a provision that policemen had to return their clubs and belts in good condition or pay for them. The ordinance was eventually passed with this amendment, but Medill's insistence on this point of economy negated any possible morale boost that the force might have received from the measure, and encouraged resentment against Medill, Washburn, and by extension the Committee of Seventy among many ordinary patrolmen.[71]

Washburn received another black eye when the owners of the gambling establishments he had raided sued him to secure the return of their faro table and other gambling implements. The courts ruled in favor of the gamblers: Washburn had the right to restrict gambling and arrest people for practicing it, but he did not have the right to seize property without due process.[72] Not only did this ruling set back Washburn himself, it marked yet another defeat for the Committee of Seventy's attempt to control vice in the city.

The struggle within the police department came to a head when Washburn attempted to make policemen work twelve-hour patrols. In fact, they already spent much of their time on the streets. Before Washburn's order, patrolmen were required to work six hours during the day, six hours at night, and spend six hours on duty at the station in a given twenty-four-hour period, leaving only six hours of actual off-time, though they could nap at the station. Washburn's proposal would have made them patrol for twelve straight hours, following which they would have had to handle any cases they brought before the police court. Then they still would have been required to spend six hours on duty at the station house. In response, the police organized a petition drive against

Washburn's order, and presented their petition to the city council, signed by the entire force of 450 officers and men.[73] The council did not have authority over police work rules, so it referred the petition to the board of police. The board was already incensed at Washburn. They cited the Rules and Regulations for Patrol Duty established by the City Charter of 1866, which established a rotation of six-hour shifts, and which stated clearly that only the board had the authority to change patrol duty. "Upon thorough investigation," they declared, "it is the *unanimous* conviction of the Board supported by the individual testimony and judgement of the Captains and Sergeants of Police . . . that the enforcement of the order issued by the Superintendent of Police requiring men to patrol their beats for twelve (12) consecutive hours would work to the utter physical prostration of the men."[74] Not only did the board overrule Washburn, but they did so publicly and emphatically.

The entire police department, including its commissioners, was now in open revolt against Washburn and, by extension, the Committee of Seventy. Even Police Commissioner Klokke, who had been appointed by Mayor Medill, joined the rebellion. But Washburn refused to give in. He would not rescind his order directing the men to work twelve-hour shifts. In response, on January 27, 1873, the three police commissioners unanimously charged him with "neglect of duty, incompetency, disobedience of the orders of the Board of Police; violations of the rules and regulations of the Board by enforcing orders unauthorized by the Board of Police . . . and conduct unbecoming a police officer."[75] They moved to suspend Washburn pending a trial on these charges and appointed Police Secretary Ward as acting superintendent.

Mayor Medill sided strongly with Superintendent Washburn. He and his corporation counsel claimed that the state law giving the mayor power to remove any member of the force also gave him the right to retain the officers of the force against the wishes of the board. In other words, Medill insisted that only he had the right to remove Washburn. The board, of course, objected. They argued that, even if the mayor had the right to remove police officers, which they disputed, that did not prevent the board of police from disciplining the police force under the regulations of the City Charter. Medill then moved against the board itself, and on January 29, he ordered the removal of Commissioner Klokke. The commissioner would not go quietly. He issued his own statement, replying that, since he had been elected in November, he refused to recognize the mayor's right to remove him and insisted that he would stay at his post. In response, Medill ordered the removal of Commissioner Reno as well.[76]

Medill then tried to undercut the powers of the board by going directly to the officers of the police force. He issued a general statement "To the Officers and Patrolmen" of the city, ordering them to continue to obey Washburn as superintendent, and he ordered Washburn himself to resume his duties. The next day, Medill summoned all the captains of the force to his office and made them declare that they would obey him and Washburn. Captains Hickey and Fred Gund refused, and as a result, Medill promptly dismissed them from the force.[77]

This caused a rift in the force. In the First District, on the South Side, Washburn appointed a new captain, Simon O'Donnell, to replace Hickey. But the sergeants at the First District station refused to obey him. O'Donnell appealed to Hickey to support his new authority, but Hickey refused. The new captain had to return to Washburn and report that the sergeants would not obey. Meanwhile, Captain French, who had sided with Washburn and the mayor, expressed the fear that his men would not obey him as a result. At least for the moment, then, the police department was headless and paralyzed. Or more accurately, it had two conflicting heads at odds with each other: Medill and Washburn versus the police board.[78]

A large segment of the city's businessmen remained committed to Washburn's policies and continued to throw their support to the mayor. The board of underwriters and the wholesale merchants of the city sent official communications to Medill saying that they backed him. The wholesale merchants' petition also called for the state legislature to abolish the board of police all together. A large number of aldermen visited the mayor's office and assured him of their support. More crucially, the Committee of Seventy called for a mass meeting at the board of trade building on February 4 "for the purpose of endorsing and sustaining the Mayor in his course."[79] That mass meeting was well attended, and many prominent speakers defended Medill's right to control the force. Even former mayor "Long John" Wentworth, against whom the original police board was created, spoke up in favor of Medill.[80]

These men still possessed sufficient strength to regain control over the department. While Klokke and Reno continued the fight into April, the police officers themselves gradually submitted to Washburn again. The city council backed Medill and the superintendent, and upheld Medill's appointment of new commissioners to replace Reno and Klokke on the board.[81] Commissioner Sheridan continued to insist that Klokke and Reno were correct, and that the mayor did not have the legal right to remove them, but he agreed to work with the new board members in the interests of the city and the police department. This new board dismissed the charges against Washburn.[82] It also upheld his firing of Sergeants Rehm, Bishoff, Douglass, and Macauley, who had obeyed the old board of police commissioners and Acting Superintendent Ward instead of the mayor and superintendent. Captains Hickey and Gund got their jobs back once they agreed to obey Superintendent Washburn.[83] That same month, the city council also shelved the formal complaint issued by Klokke and Reno.[84] Nonetheless, Washburn backed off on the idea of twelve-hour shifts. The battle had ended in a draw—the superintendent retained his overall authority and got rid of those officers who had resisted him most forcefully, but his power to reorganize the force had been checked.

This conflict revealed two obstacles to creating a strong police force. First, professional police officials—including Hickey and the police board, which identified with the department and viewed policemen as professionals—confronted elite reformers who believed the police department could be run like a business. Second, the patrolmen themselves came under pressure as wage workers. Washburn, Medill, and the majority of the Committee of Seventy believed that patrolmen could be treated like other employees. If they were ordered to work twelve-hour shifts, they should do so in a disciplined manner or face the consequences. The patrolmen and their advocates on the police board, however, viewed policing as an important profession and patrolmen as independent free workers who had the right to defend their standards of work. This clash, then, mirrored the clashes over labor discipline that swept many industries in the 1860s and 1870s. Unlike manufacturing workers, however, policemen's work could not be rationalized, subdivided, or mechanized. In addition, the city's employers needed the police to support them if they hoped to retain control over Chicago and enforce their broader program.

This clash also revealed that the language of professionalism and reform could cut both ways. In 1860, Illinois Republicans deployed the ideology of professionalism to remake Mayor Wentworth's police department. In general, these reformers had wanted what the Committee of Seventy wanted—an efficient force that could extend its authority over the entire city, enforce regulations decided by the municipal government, and ensure order in times of crisis. Yet in 1873, it was the extant police force, with all its accusations of corruption and inefficiency, that used the ideology of professionalism to defend its status. For the rest of the century, the elite would be divided between advocates of "reform" style politics and backers of a more inclusive "machine." The police were the central object of the fights between these two groups. Yet the police themselves could turn either way. The permanent police leadership of men such as Michael Hickey and Jacob Rehm sought funding and independence to set policy as they saw fit. They used the political division over policy to promote their own interests and autonomy at every turn. In 1873, while they failed to force the removal of Superintendent Washburn or restore their fired compatriots to the force, these men successfully checked the Committee of Seventy's attack on their power.

With this compromise achieved, Superintendent Washburn and the Committee of Seventy once more began an assault on the city's drinkers. This attempt would destroy the Committee of Seventy. Washburn again sought to strictly enforce the Sunday closing law, and commanded the police to investigate every saloon in the city on Sundays.[85] Commissioner Sheridan submitted a public condemnation of the order, stating that he considered it "unnecessary, odious and oppressive." He also thought that the order violated the Fourth Amendment, which protected from unreasonable searches and seizures, but the police were ordered to carry it out anyway.[86] Washburn and ex-Commissioner Talcott also persuaded the city council to pass an ordinance ordering all saloons to close at 11 P.M. every night. By this time, Mayor Medill was firmly committed to the Committee of Seventy's reasoning about liquor. "Nearly all the riots and tumults which disturb the peace, disgrace the city, and cause injury to person or loss of life," he wrote in his official recommendation to the council, "proceed from the vending of intoxicating liquors" at night.[87] On May 7, Washburn issued "Order Number 21," which required patrolmen to enter into all saloons on Sundays to ensure they were observing the new law.[88]

This was simply too much for the city's drinkers. About three hundred men, including a number of aldermen, deliberately assembled at the famously elegant Chapin and Gore saloon on Monroe Street to publicly violate the new ordinance. The police came in a little after eleven o'clock and arrested Mr. Gore and six bartenders.[89] The saloonkeepers then challenged the legality of the law and applied for an injunction prohibiting the police from enforcing it.[90] By this point, the opposition to Medill and Washburn included increasing numbers of "respectable" businessmen, who considered the continued attempts to crack down on drinking a violation of their basic rights.

A group in the middle still stood for compromise. Alderman Cullerton submitted an ordinance that saloons be allowed to stay open until midnight. This ordinance was eventually passed, but it could not paper over the rift between the advocates of temperance and those who favored less-stringent regulations.[91]

Indeed, the mayor then took further actions to alienate the city's saloonkeepers and their supporters. He revoked the liquor licenses of saloons that continued to sell on Sundays, and some aldermen accused him of ordering the city clerk not to renew liquor licenses to anyone doing business in those buildings. This led the city council to pass a resolution that amounted to a censure of the mayor, demanding that the Corporation Counsel report under what authority the mayor could revoke saloon licenses. Medill vetoed this resolution and cited the passages in the city charter that gave him the right to regulate liquor licensing. A series of later resolutions supported the mayor against the councilmen.[92] Medill retained control over liquor licensing, but his actions were generating increasing resistance.

The liquor question, however, was only the most important example of the deeper clash over order that was thoroughly dividing the city. Chicago was split between the supporters of the Committee of Seventy, notably the mayor and Washburn, and those who opposed harsh regulation of drinking, including the Personal Liberty League and its supporters, but these divisions correlated with a deeper conflict over how to maintain order more generally. Would the city be governed by a powerful municipal government led by the native-born, Protestant elite that disposed of a disciplined police force to enforce its will, or would Chicagoans be free to carry out their daily lives largely outside the surveillance and control of the authorities? This conflict was as much about the power of the police as it was about drinking.

In addition to enforcing unpopular liquor regulation, during Washburn's superintendency the police fueled the population's distrust and anger by pursuing all perceived lawbreakers overzealously. The Committee of Seventy wanted to see action on the streets, and that meant arrests. After Medill replaced the board of police commissioners, the new board offered prizes to the three patrolmen who made the most arrests, no matter what they were for.[93] This induced everyone on the force to arrest as many people as possible, regardless of whether or not a crime had been committed. It encouraged patrolmen to view the population of the city as potential targets for arrest. It also increased policemen's power over ordinary citizens because their superiors promised to back them against any complaints their zealous behavior elicited. This illustrates the contradictory nature of the patrolmen's status as wage workers. While they resented attempts to control their labor, they could also be pushed to treat the rest of the city's working class and poor population with disdain.

The case of Ann English illustrates the results of encouraging this attitude among patrolmen. English was a fifty-year-old native-born washerwoman and house cleaner who had lived in the city for five years. On October 21, 1872, at about six in the morning she was "observed" by an intoxicated policeman named Gustav Bustar while on her way to church. English claimed that the drunken patrolman pursued her, took hold of her, and commenced to beat her. He "struck her with his fist several times," English testified, "and greatly abused and maltreated her." After this attack, Patrolman Bustar took her to the Madison Street Station and charged her with drunkenness and disorderly conduct. The police magistrate fined her five dollars and costs. She was held at the station until noon, when she managed to obtain the five dollars, presumably from a relative. On her way home, English claimed that the money was returned to her "with the injunction to say nothing about the treatment that she had received at the hands of said officer and the police court."[94]

But English did not keep quiet. On November 16 she lodged a formal complaint. Ann English swore that she could no longer work as a result of the abuse and asked the city for $1,000 for her support. She submitted testimony from a witness and from her employer to the fact that she had been a good worker but was unable to perform her duties since the incident. Patrolman Bustar was fined fifteen dollars and forced to resign, but the city insisted that, since she had already been refunded the five dollars and since Bustar was off the force, there was nothing more they could do.[95]

The Ann English case was somewhat extreme, but many other cases of overzealous policing came to light in late 1872 and early 1873. Catherine Garrigan, a widow and mother of five, requested the remission of a fine of $24.50 imposed on her twelve-year-old son for disorderly conduct, when he had never before been charged with any crime and the neighbors testified that he was a well-behaved child. The finance committee decided "adverse to the prayer of the petitioner," and Garrigan never received her money back.[96] Saloonkeeper Abraham Bernstein reported that Patrolmen Andrew Jacoby arrested him on June 28, 1873, while he was "not in the commission of any act whatever against any law of the State of Illinois or against any ordinance of the City of Chicago." He was at first charged with disorderly conduct and fined $10, then he was also charged with selling liquor after midnight and fined another $22. Like Ann English, Bernstein submitted a formal charge against the patrolman, and Patrolman Jacoby resigned from the force before a trial could be convened. Yet again, the finance committee recommended against Bernstein's petition, and the city kept his money.[97]

This overzealousness created increasing anger at Washburn and the Committee of Seventy's police policy both within the city government and in the media. In a meeting of the police board, Commissioner Sheridan, who remained opposed to Washburn, accused Sergeant Hood of calling his men "dirty dogs" for not bringing in more prisoners.[98] This arrest policy was too much even for the *Tribune*, which was generally a staunch defender of Medill, Washburn, and the Committee of Seventy. "If real lawbreakers do not come their way," the *Tribune* commented about policemen trying to win the prizes, "they have to manufacture them." Because of the malleable definition of disorderly conduct, which was the most common charge by far throughout the nineteenth century, the police could more or less arrest whomever they chose. After its initial article criticizing the police for arresting innocent people, the *Tribune* received letter after letter testifying to the "misery and unhappiness . . . desolated homes, domestic strife, [and] divorce suits" that resulted from "the misguided zeal of these preservers of the peace."[99]

The fight over police policy culminated in the organization of a People's Party in 1873. This party united everyone opposed to the Committee of Seventy, Washburn, and Medill, especially the Germans. Chicago's Germans, led by Anton Hesing, had traditionally been a bulwark of the Republican Party. Except for the interlude of the Lager Beer Riot, the Republican Germans were usually politically opposed to the Democratic Irish. This division between immigrant groups helped the native-born elite retain control of the city government by playing the two groups against each other. But the Committee of Seventy's crackdown on their leisure activities pushed the Germans and Irish together in the new People's Party. This party denounced the enforcement of the Sunday closing law as a revival of Know-Nothingism and a "nauseating" mixing of religion and politics.[100] It opposed the Committee of Seventy and Mayor Medill, of course, but it was particularly energized against Superintendent Washburn. In addition to Irish and German immigrants, the People's Party attracted many native-born Chicagoans who were disgusted by the behavior of the police. The movement tried to unite "all liberal elements of all parties and nationalities prone to combat an attempt to destroy personal liberty."[101] The People's Party was not opposed to law and order or to the police generally. In fact, one of its greatest complaints was that Washburn's lack of experience, his incompetence, and his insistence on enforcing the Sunday closing law had rendered the police even less effective. Rather, the People's Party objected to the idea that law and order meant that the teetotaling native-born elite organized in the Committee of Seventy could deploy the police to do whatever it wanted.

Continual disputes and scandals within the police department strengthened the People's Party movement leading up to the fall elections in 1873. Commissioner Sheridan and Superintendent Washburn fought throughout the summer, at one point even swearing at each other in a meeting of the board of police. In a turn of events more reminiscent of a family fight than discord within city government, Medill tried to get them to apologize to each other. Washburn agreed to apologize for his use of profanity in front of the board, but Sheridan refused.[102] Less than a week later, Milwaukee newspapers accused Washburn of forcing a Wisconsin businessman named Wheeler to pay the Chicago police $200 for the return of stolen goods. Washburn was eventually cleared of any criminal wrongdoing, but a select committee of the city council recommended that he be censured for asking for this money and for "the discourteous manner in which he treated Mr. Wheeler and Mr. Ludington, Mayor of Milwaukee."[103]

This scandal was the final nail in Medill's coffin, although he was probably doomed in the ensuing elections in any case. The city's Republicans, minus their departed German allies, attempted to boast of Washburn's successes in taming gambling and other vice operations in the city. The *Tribune*, for instance, reported that the notorious gambling boss, Mike McDonald, had been dethroned, and that his princes and noblemen were at each other's throats over the dwindling business.[104] This success might have rallied some native-born reformers and the Committee of Seventy to the new Law and Order Party formed to oppose the People's Party, but it was not enough to appeal to those Chicagoans against whom the mayor and his superintendent deployed the police regularly. Medill could see which way the wind was blowing, and before his term was over, he decamped for Europe and turned the mayoralty over to former Illinois legislator Lester Bond.

The People's Party won in a landslide in the municipal elections. Every single candidate on its ticket gained office. Its mayoral candidate, Harvey Doolittle Colvin, defeated his Law and Order Party opponent, the acting mayor Lester Bond, by a vote of 28,791 to 18,540. Colvin was supported by a new majority on the city council, along with every other elected municipal official.[105] As John Jentz, Karen Sawislak, Richard Schneirov, and other historians have pointed out, this election was about immigration, ethnicity, class, and civil liberties.[106] However, it directly turned on the appropriate activities of the police. The central questions did not revolve around the law, since the Sunday closing law was on the books before Washburn's appointment and no one had either enforced it or objected to its existence. Neither did the conflict involve simply questions of class or status, since Anton Hesing, the most prominent figure in the People's Party, had been a member of the Committee of Seventy and was unquestionably a member of the economic and political elite of the city. The city's workers were generally on the side of the People's Party, but the People's Party was not antibusiness. The election did divide the city on ethnic lines, but the People's Party had considerable support from native-born Chicagoans opposing temperance. The central issue in the election was temperance, but beneath that loomed the question of what role the police should play in the city, what activities the department should seek to curtail, and how the force should be organized.

In his inaugural address, Colvin made the centrality of policing to the People's Party clear. "Our police system should be conducted upon the principle of the prevention rather than the punishment of crime," he said. He criticized the policy of making arrests and imposing fines in order to secure funds. He also denounced police brutality. "In no case should a person be inhumanly treated," he announced, "simply because he has been arrested for some petty offense or misdemeanor." He condemned police who received rewards for their services, an explicit reference to Washburn's Milwaukee scandal, but also a common issue for police reformers. Colvin immediately removed Washburn and replaced him as superintendent with the more experienced Jacob Rehm, who had become Chicago's first deputy superintendent in 1855.[107] Colvin also reinstated Klokke as a police commissioner and restored now-sergeant Hickey to the rank of captain.[108] Thus, the victory of the People's Party was in many ways a victory for the old police board against Washburn and Medill. Mayor Colvin did not intend to revolutionize the force. By his actions, he indicated that he preferred to return to the status quo ante. In fact, over the next two years, People's Party officials gave control of the department back to the older generation of professional policemen and meddled only minimally in police management.

Over the next two years, the continuity in leadership was maintained. After Superintendent Rehm retired in yet another scandal in 1875, he was succeeded by Michael Hickey, one of the captains who had stood up to Medill and Washburn. This represented the ultimate victory for the old police board against the unpopular former superintendent. That same year, voters abolished the police board itself, further strengthening the independent power of the police hierarchy against interference from elected officials. Thus, even in its weak, oft-derided form, the police proved stronger in the long run than the reformers organized around Medill and the Committee of Seventy.[109]

While Washburn's attempts at reform had disrupted rather than strengthened the department, a return to the pre-Washburn days meant a return to a generally weak, untrusted, and ineffective department. The most obvious way to fix this problem was to increase the number of men on the force, and this the People's Party tried to do. While the city council refused to increase the force to the numbers the superintendent requested, it nevertheless grew to 565 patrolmen, twenty sergeants, four captains, a deputy superintendent and a superintendent by mid-1876.[110] The department added a fourth captain for a precinct it created on the Northwest Side. But the People's Party took office just as a national economic depression was setting in following the panic of 1873. City revenues declined as more and more Chicagoans demanded relief, the specter of crime motivated by desperation increased, and rumblings of disorder began to shake the city. The depression crippled the People's Party itself, since it had neither the means nor the policies available to alleviate the problems caused by the depression, but it also meant retrenchment for the police department. In July 1876, the city council refused Superintendent Hickey's request for an increase in the force, and instead demanded that the department cut its expenditures by 25 percent. This meant laying off seventy-five men, when the city, and indeed the whole country, was about to explode.[111]

The Committee of Seventy was the first organization formed by a wide cross section of Chicago's elite with the express purpose of increasing their control over the lawless poor. The Committee succeeded in forcing the city government to accede to their demands. It put its man in charge of the police department. But, for a number of reasons, the Committee of Seventy failed to accomplish its goals. First, in order to create a police department capable of accomplishing all that the committee demanded, the city would have had to increase taxes dramatically. As Medill pointed out, many members of the committee refused to pay the relatively low taxes they already owed, let alone advocate a sufficient increase in taxes to hire many more police.

Second, despite their claim to represent all citizens of Chicago, their denunciations against Know-Nothingism of all sorts, and their attempts to include some prominent immigrants, such as Anton Hesing, the committee's temperance program put them at odds with the city's immigrant population and with native-born businessmen who liked to drink.[112] On top of this, the extreme police policy carried out under their direction allowed the People's Party to win over Chicagoans opposed to arbitrary arrest and police brutality, even if they might be friendly to temperance.

Finally, by attempting to radically reorganize the police department against the wishes of its men, the Committee of Seventy alienated precisely the people it needed to carry out its policies. Even though they won the short-term battle for control of the department, the city's elite needed the experienced leadership of the force on their side if they hoped to use the police department to check the disorder they so feared.

Despite the failure of this first attempt, the city's elite learned from its mistakes. For the rest of the century, it would refrain from following Protestant religious leaders' insistence on temperance. From this point forward, the new elite organizations made themselves the best friends of the police department, rather than its enemies. And while they continued to resist taxation, the elite formed new organizations that succeeded in raising considerable funds to support law and order.

Working-class leisure: W. W. Chambers Saloon and Boarding House. Source: Chicago History Museum

Homes of the wealthy: Prairie Avenue, ca. 1887. Source: Chicago History Museum

Upper-class leisure: A roller-skating rink. Source: *Harpers Weekly*, April 24, 1875

Harrison Street Police Station, 1870s, showing the solid physical presence of the
new institution. Source: Chicago History Museum

DRIVING THE RIOTERS FROM TURNER HALL.

Police violence in 1877: The assault on Turner Hall. Source: *Harpers Weekly*, August 18, 1877

PATROL BOX — OPEN.

New capabilities: Police Telegraph Call Box, erected all over Chicago in the 1880s. Source: Flinn, *History of the Chicago Police*

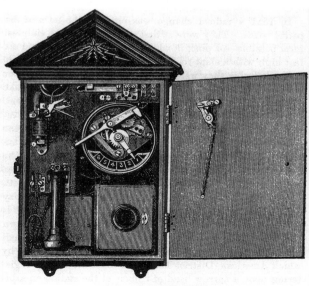

SIGNAL INSIDE BOX—OPEN.

New capabilities : Police wagon with five patrolmen in the 1880s. Source: Flinn, *History of the Chicago Police*

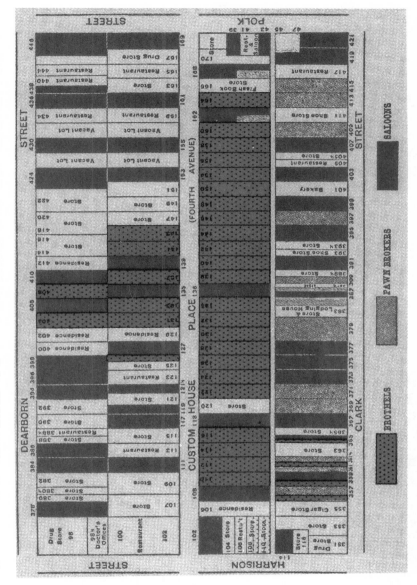

Prostitution off the streets and into brothels: A map of the Levee District showing brothels. Source: William Stead, *If Christ Should Come to Chicago*

ANARCHIST BANNERS CARRIED BY THE ANARCHISTS IN THEIR
NUMEROUS PROCESSIONS IN CHICAGO.

Anarchist banners critiquing the police. Source: Flinn, *History of the Chicago Police*

UNDERGROUND RIFLE PRACTICE. A MEETING OF THE LEHR UND WEHR VEREIN.

Representation of the anarchist militias meant to justify repression after Haymarket. Source: Schaack, *Anarchy and Anarchists*

JOHN BONFIELD,

Inspector of Police.

Inspector John Bonfield, the antihero (or hero) of Haymarket. Source: Flinn, *History of the Chicago Police*

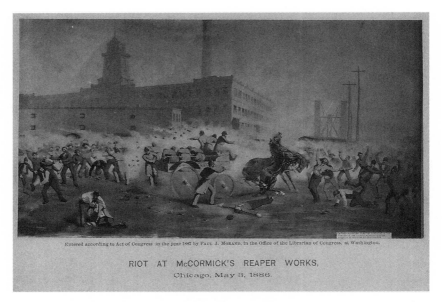

Representation of police fighting "rioters" during eight-hour-workday strikes of 1886. Source: Chicago History Museum

Representation of police as victims of violence after Haymarket. Source: Chicago History Museum

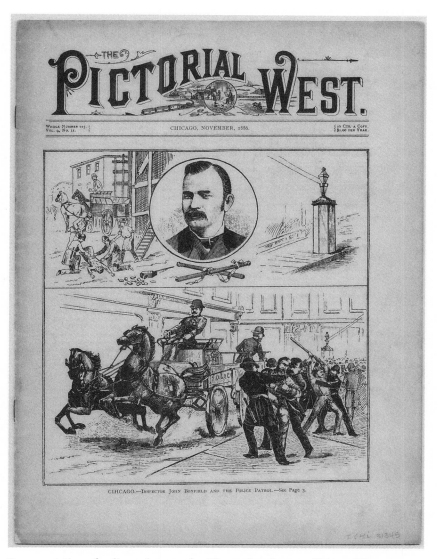

Representation of police as heroes after Haymarket. Source: Chicago History Museum

CHAPTER 5

1877 and the Formation
of a Law-and-Order Consensus

The massive strikes that erupted in 1877 marked a turning point for the Chicago Police Department. The department's role in putting down these strikes illustrates most clearly how the Chicago police reconciled democratic politics with the industrial capitalist order through violence. In these strikes, the most dramatic and disorderly they had yet to confront, the police appeared most starkly as little more than hired thugs of the city's businessmen.

In part, the police played this role because Chicago's businessmen organized themselves as never before. As the economic crisis that began in 1873 deepened and the workers' movement gained strength, businessmen were not content to sit back and let democratic politics run their course. Rather, these businessmen increasingly organized themselves in more permanent, politically inclusive, and effective organizations than the Committee of Seventy from the beginning of the decade. These businessmen's groups were involved with many issues beyond policing, and they in no means represented unanimity of opinion among businessmen. Chicago's elite remained divided politically, socially, and in its economic interests on a range of important issues, including what police policy to promote. But once workers and the unemployed erupted in anger across the country, maintaining order moved to the fore and overrode all other concerns and divisions.

The police faced an increasingly difficult task as the depression deepened. They were the main institution charged with maintaining order in the face of increasing misery, unemployment, and anger. Yet violence was the only tool at their disposal. Thus, in the period immediately before the strike, police attempts to keep order served as much to engender anger among workers and the unemployed as to keep those groups orderly. The city council also heaped increasing responsibilities on the police, at the same time that it began severely cutting police funding. As a result, the police were unable to perform their assigned tasks efficiently and came under renewed criticism from even their elite backers as corrupt and inefficient. As the strikes began, then, the police force was undermanned and disliked by rich and poor alike. Their performance during the strikes helped cement elite support for the department, but it only increased the anger of the rest of the population.

Elite contemporary observers and historians alike have often portrayed the strikes of 1877 as spontaneous explosions of violence stemming from the economic depression that began in 1873.[1] According to this interpretation, the strikes spread spontaneously up and down the railroad lines, feeding off the resentment caused by poverty, unemployment, and employer attacks on pay and working conditions. Allan Pinkerton and other observers even blamed outside agitators for inciting otherwise peaceful workers to rebel.[2]

This approach, however, fails to locate 1877 in the context of its prehistory. As historian Sheldon Stromquist points out for Upstate New York, workers had militant traditions that necessarily informed their activity in 1877, and this was equally true in Chicago.[3] The flip side of this standard interpretation is that the strikes took employers completely by surprise. However, Chicago's businessmen also had a reservoir of experience in dealing with militant labor activity. The experience of the postwar strikes ten years earlier gave Chicago's law-and-order advocates a crucial advantage compared to Baltimore and Pittsburgh when the strikes of 1877 reached the city. In fact, all of those cities that had relatively well-established police forces, such as Boston, New York, Chicago, and Philadelphia, managed to avoid losing control to the strikers, while cities in which the strike reached its most powerful crescendo, among them Pittsburgh, Baltimore, and St. Louis, relied on state militia to retain (or regain) order.

At the same time, in the first half of the 1870s, Chicago appeared more starkly divided along ethnic lines than along those of class. But the depression that began in earnest in 1873 and then the strike of 1877 broke the relative ethnic solidarity that had dominated Chicago politics since the 1850s. Chicago's Germans, long the largest group of immigrants in the city, divided along class lines. Germans led increasingly militant working-class organizations against a German-dominated city government. The Irish, Chicago's second largest immigrant group, also divided between the workers and unemployed who fought the police and the Irish American militia that helped put down the strike. In a strike that again began among railroad workers and included many skilled native-born whites, the city's native born also divided. German, Irish, and native-born workers did not

unite in 1877 around a common political program or within a single organization. Nor did they come to see their interests as entirely congruent.
Nonetheless, they were united in their anger with the employers and their
willingness to do something about it.

The breakdown of ethnic solidarity and the beginnings of relatively co-
ordinated working-class action eventually pushed the city's businessmen
to consolidate around a law-and-order program as never before. This was
accomplished by a retreat from ethnically divisive issues and the creation of
multiethnic elite organizations. Businessmen did not unite around all issues,
nor did they form a unanimous front even on police policy. However, they
did form new powerful organizations, including the Citizens' Association of
Chicago and the Commercial Club of the City of Chicago, that solidly supported law and order. These elite organizations would prove more powerful,
more permanent, and more momentous for the future of Chicago and indeed
the nation than any local political coalition since the Civil War. As Richard
Schneirov, the leading historian of Chicago's late-nineteenth-century labor
and politics points out, the city's class polarization "created a major problem
for democratic politics: could majority rule exercised by professional politicians, who were responsive to those who had no income-producing property
to protect, be reconciled with the existence of an industrial capitalist order?"[4]
The new elite organizations sought to protect the industrial capitalist order
from both democratic politics and the militant mass action of workers and
their allies by ensuring that the key institutions responsible for maintaining
that order, the state militia and the city police, were run by "reliable" men
tied directly to the businessmen.

The depression of the 1870s caused an unprecedentedly deep crisis in the
city's wage labor political economy. With thousands of Chicagoans dependent on wage work, the economic collapse sparked a wave of job cuts and
a dramatic increase in unemployment. By 1877, about thirty thousand men
were unemployed in the city.[5] In addition, thousands of people flooded into
the city seeking work. Those workers that kept their jobs faced increasing
pressure to do more with fewer workers and to accept pay cuts. Many small
businesses shut their doors, increasing the ranks of the unemployed still
further and accelerating the concentration of capital. Many large employers
also faced reduced profits.

Chicagoans soon divided over what to do about the large numbers of
hungry people roaming the streets as some of these unemployed began to
organize and demand relief. As early as the winter of 1872, Captain Hickey
helped subdue a bread riot outside the Chicago Relief and Aid Society. The

economic situation only got worse from that point on.[6] Right after the People's Party took office in 1873, the unemployed held a mass meeting at Turner's Hall on the West Side demanding relief, and demanding that relief be distributed under the direction of the workers themselves. In response, the city council requested that the Relief and Aid Society "expand and distribute the funds in their hands liberally to all worthy persons needing aid." The city council also appointed three aldermen from each division of the city (North, South, and West) to help the Chicago Relief and Aid Society determine "the proper distribution" of funds and it appointed a commission of five aldermen to approach the organization with their proposals and demands.[7] But the relief society was controlled by men allied to the Committee of Seventy and it refused to accede to the demands of council. The society insisted on maintaining its system of distinguishing "worthy" from "unworthy" recipients of aid.[8] Thus at the beginning of the worst depression of the nineteenth century, Chicago's elite was starkly divided over the proper response to increasing poverty.

The dispute over poor relief also led to increasing political divisions within the city's German population. In January 1874, a group of mostly German-born radicals founded a new Workingmen's Party of Illinois to challenge the People's Party for control of city and state government, claiming that the People's Party did nothing to help the poor. This new party failed to dislodge the majority of Germans from their support for the People's Party, but its defeat at the polls pushed many Chicago radicals further to the left. They began to abandon electoral politics and tried to build up organizations within the working class that could confront their employers directly. The split within the German population between the leftists and the probusiness supporters of the People's Party deepened from this point forward. In December 1874, the radicals proposed turning their organ, the *Verbote*, into a German daily newspaper for the Workingmen's Party that would compete with Anton Hesing's *Illinois Staats Zeitung*.[9] Thus, by the beginning of 1875, German Chicagoans were divided between the supporters of law and order organized around the *Staats Zeitung* and a group of increasingly radical activists who were forming their own political organizations under the banner of the working class.

Meanwhile, the threat of the Workingmen's Party and the People's Party's actual control of city government revealed the extent of the crisis facing the native-born elite. The root of the problem was that, in the rapidly growing city filled with foreign-born wage workers, the native-born elite simply could not sustain an electoral majority. As historian John Jentz points out, this pushed Chicago's elite to question the wisdom of universal suffrage and to contemplate extreme measures, even before the strike of 1877. "The way to prevent the spread of communism here," the *Times* proposed, "is to close our seaports against the further ingress of European vagabondage." The paper called for a law requiring each immigrant to show credentials proving he or she had not been "a thief, a pauper, or a vagabond in the country from which he comes."[10] Horace White, editor of the *Tribune*, proposed more forceful policies to deal with Chicago's poor: "Cure the elders with club and bayonet, and force the young into schools. Drain their sewage-soaked streets. Cleanse the tenements reeking with disease, in which their minds and bodies rot. Do, in a word, what can be done to give them a fair chance at life, and then, if they still cling to their false gods of misrule and crime, let justice be swift and sharp."[11] Here is the clearest expression of elite reaction to the failure of the free-labor ideology in postbellum Chicago: the poor should be given a chance to become free laborers, but it was fundamentally their fault if they failed to take that chance, so they couldn't blame the rich. Of course, part of the problem for White and those who thought like him was that there was no force readily available to "cure the elders." When Medill and the Committee of Seventy had tried to assert greater control over the city's population, they had been defeated. But White was not alone in proposing force as a solution to the problem of order.

In July 1874, another fire wiped out a large section of the city. That same month, prominent Chicagoans including merchants, bankers, and manufacturers from throughout the city reprised the Committee of Seventy by forming the Citizens' Association (CA), first to deal with the problem of the flight of fire insurance companies, then to more generally assure elite control over the city.[12] The new CA united hundreds of Chicago's most important businessmen, both native and foreign born. Future Treasury secretary Franklin MacVeagh served as the CA's first president. He earned his initial fortune as a wholesale grocer, then served as director of the Commercial National Bank of Chicago and on the board of government directors of the Union Pacific Railroad. Throughout his adult life, MacVeagh was committed to perfecting and defending the constituted order of the country. In 1888 he even gave a speech critiquing socialism and defending capitalism that was attended by both Lyman Gage, president of the First National Bank, and Lucy Parsons, anarchist widow of the Haymarket martyr Albert Parsons (on Parsons, see chapters 7 and 8).[13] The CA counted among its members department store magnate Marshall Field, meatpacker Philip Armour, agricultural equipment manufacturers Cyrus McCormick and William Deering (after the latter moved to Chicago in 1880), and railroad car manufacturer George Pullman.[14]

The CA tried to avoid the mistakes of the Committee of Seventy. Instead of pushing for a specific policy or slate of candidates, it worked to remake municipal government to ensure that the city would protect the interests of its members. This meant limiting the power of aldermen and elected boards and reinforcing the power of the executive, which they hoped to control. The association also sought to reinforce the power of professional officials, such as those that ran the police department. The police leadership might be corrupt, but the CA believed they could count on that leadership to ensure order. Like the police leadership, the CA consistently favored a strong force. Thus, the association did not organize directly against the People's Party. Rather, it worked to reinforce the institutions responsible for maintaining order, no matter who won elections. This marked a retreat from the aggressive stance of the Committee of Seventy, when the native-born elite tried both to restrict drinking and to directly control municipal appointments and, by extension, the police department. The association hoped to ensure elite order by leaving one area of the field free for politicians and the electorate to wrangle over, while reinforcing the executive power to make sure that men like MacVeagh, Field, Armour, and McCormick retained overall control.

The CA first proposed centralizing municipal power in the hands of the mayor and the appointed heads of the various municipal departments. To do this, they wanted to eliminate the system of boards, like the police board, that limited executive power. Once these boards were eliminated, the mayor and the newly created city marshal would have power to control both municipal expenditures and the various city departments like the police. The association also intended to limit the power of the city council over the permanent institutions of the city, especially the police, by establishing the position of marshal and reinforcing the internal hierarchy of these bodies. This was a continuation of the changes begun by the state with the passage of the "mayor's bill" that Medill had used to challenge the authority of the police board. In fact, the CA's reforms fit with the way the People's Party was already running the police. Both wanted to diminish civilian control over the police department by increasing the power held by the regular police hierarchy. The specific changes contemplated by the association in 1875 and 1876 were the opposite of those demanded by the city's elite in 1860, when it wanted the state to put in place a police board to limit the power of the mayor. But in both cases, the changes represented an increase in power for the stable police hierarchy. The promotion of these reforms marked a retreat by the city's native-born elite from its vigorous attempts to control immigrant leisure activities. The members of the CA now hoped to reinforce the police department so they could trust it to protect their basic economic interests, even if they could not elect one of their own as mayor or control a majority in the city council.[15]

The association achieved some but not all of the reforms it sought. It wanted to establish a bicameral city council, with citywide elections for one branch, to limit the power of ward politics, and this they did not get. But on almost every other proposal, they succeeded. In 1875 voters approved a new charter that was also promoted by the People's Party. This charter abolished the separate townships within the city and gave the mayor the sole power to appoint and remove the heads of city departments, including the police. The police board was eliminated and replaced with the strange and short-lived position of city marshal, who was appointed by the mayor and whose duties were unclear.[16] This was actually a contradictory victory for the CA, since the police board was abolished while the People's Party still controlled the city government. Police Commissioner Sheridan also objected to the abolition of the board and led an ultimately futile legal fight against the new rules.[17] But the fact that the People's Party controlled city government actually made it easier to get the new charter passed. Also, by this time the People's Party had firmly demonstrated that it did not represent any kind of threat to order. Since Jacob Rehm remained superintendent at that time, the force was in the hands of a trusted, long-time police officer, who was loyal to the institution rather than to the new party. More importantly, the concentration of political power in the executive branch long outlasted the People's Party itself and reinforced officials, such as Rehm, who would act to enforce order no matter who was mayor or what party had control over the city council. In short, the CA succeeded in assuring that the police department would remain under the control of responsible, experienced police officials regardless of the outcome of the electoral battles of the day.

As the depression deepened in 1875, the CA and the city's elite in general turned their attention more directly to the problem of armed force. In August 1874, the association provided $17,000 for uniforms and equipment to form a new businessmen's militia, the First Regiment.[18] This militia, along with the police, confronted an increasingly angry population. In early 1875, the city's socialists again proposed a demonstration against the Relief and Aid Society. They accused that society of refusing to help and referring the poor to county relief, which was woefully inadequate since "the capitalists are paying few or no taxes; preferring to fight the city claims in court."[19] The *Times* headline reporting on these events read "Load Your Guns, They Will Be Needed Tomorrow to Shoot Communists." This article promised that "the

Authorities will make it warm for the malcontents."[20] In fact, the proposed demonstration never took place, but throughout 1875, Chicago's left, now calling themselves alternately socialists, communists, and anarchists, continued to meet at Turner's Hall, protest the inactivity of the Relief and Aid Society, and invoke the memory of the Paris Commune.[21]

The following year, the radical workers' organizations went a step further and established their own militias, first the German Lehr und Wehr Verein, then the Bohemian Sharpshooters, the Jaeger Werein, and the Irish Labor Guard. "The underlying idea for the formation of the Armed Organization of the proletarians of Chicago," the anarchist leader, Albert Parsons, announced "has been to give battle to the present system of industry oppressing the workman."[22] The Lehr und Wehr Verein probably had over six hundred members at its peak.[23] In response, the CA launched a legal attack on these militias. It urged the state legislature to prohibit private militia companies and to ban armed drilling without the governor's consent. The state legislature passed this law in 1879. Richard Schneirov called this "perhaps the most stunning triumph of Chicago's top citizens in creating a new state administrative apparatus and centralizing political power."[24] The *Illinois Staats Zeitung* crowed that "the Socialists need not be surprised if, henceforth, the people's delegates are unwilling to tolerate independent, fully equipped communist troops."[25] The radicals mounted a legal challenge to this ban. The day the law went into effect, July 1, 1879, both the Lehr und Wehr Verein and the Bohemian Sharpshooters marched fully armed through the streets to challenge the law. The police arrested the leaders of each company, but the socialists asserted in court that the Second Amendment afforded them the right to carry weapons.[26] Eventually, the case went all the way to the United States Supreme Court, where, in Albert Parsons's words, "it was decided by the highest tribunal that the State legislatures of the various states had a constitutional right to disarm the workingmen."[27] This had not yet been decided in 1877, however, and throughout 1876 and early 1877, both sides continued to try to strengthen their nonpolice forces in advance of the feared and coming battle between workers and their employers.

In 1876, the People's Party administration collapsed. During the depression, increasing numbers of property owners refused to pay taxes. Even some property owners who were in the CA and favored increasing the powers of the municipal government did not pay. Yet the city did not force them to. The city explored the option of denying police and fire coverage to citizens who did not pay their taxes, but this was not entirely legal or practical.[28] Instead, the city borrowed heavily and then came under attack for running up debt.

"The so-called respectable element has fought against the payment of their just indebtedness to the city year after year," Mayor Colvin complained, "and at the same time were insisting upon and demanding increasing privileges and new improvements," such as the increase in the police force.[29] At the same time, the city's press howled ever louder over the People's Party use of patronage to fill any number of municipal posts. Then, Anton Hesing was caught up in a whiskey ring trial that also engulfed police superintendent Jacob Rehm. Rehm secured his acquittal, though he was accused of having paid off a judge, but Hesing was actually imprisoned and his political career ended with the scandal.[30] The last straw against the People's Party was a charge of ballot box fraud. The city's elite responded to this collapse by mobilizing a ticket of Democrats and Republicans in favor of fiscal retrenchment that swept to power Republican mayor Monroe Heath and a majority of "respectable" men on the city council.

Mayor Heath had learned from the Committee of Seventy and Mayor Medill that he should not introduce the temperance issue so that he might win back the support of the city's respectable Germans, but he had no solution for the lingering problem of defining and maintaining order. The whole experience of the temperance fight in the first years of the 1870s, the reign of the People's Party, and the traditional elite's recapturing of the mayoralty served to reshuffle Chicago's political alliances. The business leaders of both Germans and the native-born purposely downplayed their differences in order to maintain businessmen's control over the city. However, this reinforced the class divisions that were sharply revealed by the depression. This class tension was increasing daily—but the police were in no better shape to handle the crisis than they had been at the beginning of the decade. In fact, Heath and the city council cut the department's funding just months before the explosion of 1877 began.

The police were doing their utmost to prevent the conditions that might lead to a riot, and they were aware that the economic depression made order very difficult to maintain. In his annual report for 1876, Superintendent Hickey reported that the police had housed 7,467 different homeless men in the police stations that year. According to Hickey, some of these men were real vagrants or even criminals, but "many . . . would gladly make an honest living, but are out of employment by reason of the general depression in business which now affects all sections of the country. These are entitled to more humane treatment, and should be rendered facilities for bettering their condition and preventing them from becoming criminals."[31] Hickey suggested that trouble was likely if the city did not act to help the unemployed.

In fact, Hickey urged the city council to do exactly the same thing that the socialists wanted: force the Relief and Aid Society to provide succor for the unemployed. Here was revealed in its clearest terms the fundamental problem that would haunt the criminal justice system into the twenty-first century: the police were charged with solving social problems caused by modern society, but the only tool open to them was force, which could not address the cause of these problems. Hickey did not have any authority over the relief society, so from 1873 to 1877, the city's patrolmen spent a considerable share of their patrol time encouraging "tramps" to leave Chicago.

Even as the depression was deepening and the city was cutting funding for the police department, it charged the police with addressing a new series of social problems. Some of these problems had nothing to do with the depression, but still exacerbated the gap between the department's responsibilities and its capabilities. For instance, the city council ordered the police and the city's law department to "prosecute all parties responsible for stenches arising from various establishments in the city."[32] Given the numerous slaughter-houses that dumped animal offal into the river, along with Chicago's other nausea-inducing industrial processes, this was a serious concern in the 1870s. But short of widespread government regulation, there was no way the police force could effectively deal with this problem.

The police were also expected to control stray dogs. These dogs became increasingly numerous during the depression and roamed the streets, threat-ening passersby. They became such a problem that Mayor Heath ordered the police to kill any unmuzzled dogs on the streets.[33] As with controlling stenches, vagrancy, and the problems caused by unemployment, this was not an easy task for the already-stretched police force to carry out. There was no humane society or separate animal control department. A policeman might shoot a stray dog from time to time, but the force could not solve the problem as a whole.

And as if the police were not already expected to perform enough duties, on June 4, 1877, the city ordered the police to enforce yet another ordinance. "It shall be unlawful for any person," the city declared, "to bathe in Lake Michigan, the Chicago river or any of its branches . . . in a naked state, or with the person so much undressed as that there is an indecent exposure of the body publicly or where such person may be publicly seen during the hours between 6 AM and 8 PM."[34] This ordinance also demanded more of the police than could reasonably have been expected. If a patrolman happened to see someone skinny-dipping, he could intervene, but for young Chicagoans the enactment of the ordinance may have provided a new entertainment: the thrill of evading the police, since swimming in the foul waters surrounding the city could in itself provide little pleasure.

These increasing demands put Chicago's patrolmen in a situation similar to that of many other workers in the city. They were expected to carry out more tasks with fewer workers, under harsher conditions. Yet the police did not respond like other workers, and there was never a threat that they would. This is in part because the daily actions that the police carried out put them at odds with those they interacted with. Arresting people for drunkenness and disorderly conduct and imposing fines on those who could ill afford to pay; housing foul-smelling, dirty unemployed people in cold, hard-floored police stations; harassing prostitutes, pushing vagrants out of the city, shooting stray dogs; and even trying to stop young people from skinny dipping all desensitized patrolmen to the humanity of those they interacted with. In addition, by this time, while the force had some Irish and German recruits, it was still largely dominated by native-born men patrolling an immigrant city. The police who remained on the force after the upheaval of the Medill administration had proven their willingness to attempt to enforce unpopular temperance laws. The city's new demands certainly stretched the department's resources, but they continued to set the police against the people whose neighborhoods they patrolled.

At the same time the city government was imposing more and more demands on the department while cutting its funding, the police force leadership was itself divided. In May 1877, a grand jury indicted Superintendent Hickey after fired Captain William Buckley sent a letter to the city council accusing Hickey of corruption. According to this letter, Hickey forced prostitute Lizzie Moore to pay him $430 in 1873 in order to get some stolen property returned to her, and then had sex with her and urged her to leave town to avoid prosecution. Buckley also accused Hickey of owning property that was used as a brothel, gaming house and fence, and of lying about it. In addition, Buckley charged that the superintendent was often drunk on the job, that he countermanded the orders of his captains when they tried to crack down on gambling, that he tolerated drunkenness and brutality on the part of his men, that he slept with prostitutes and spent the night in brothels when drunk, that he stole money from the police association to pay lawyers who defended him against earlier indictments, that he secured the pardon of a criminal from the penitentiary at Joliet for $3,000 in cash, and that during earlier riots arising out of a lumbermen's strike he feigned sickness and "sat on his back stoop, at home, smoking a cigar, when he should have been directing the Police in quelling the riots."[35] On June 18, some aldermen proposed suspending Hickey as superintendent since he was under investigation, but the council did not act because only the mayor had the power to remove Hickey unless a grand jury brought him to trial.[36] Hickey survived the attack largely because Buckley had little proof and most of his accusations were not actually crimes, but the scandal certainly did nothing to improve anyone's opinion of the police or its leadership.

Two months later, a railroad strike began in Martinsburg, West Virginia. By the time the strike launched full-scale riots in Pittsburgh and Baltimore, Chicago workers were ready to join in. The news from the East was the spark, and everyone knew it. Marshall Field's partner, Levi Leiter, even asked the editor of the *Daily News* to suspend publication of his paper because the news was so inflammatory. On the night of Monday, July 23, Chicago's Working-men's Party held a mass meeting on Madison Street.[37] Some newspapers urged Mayor Heath to disperse the meeting, but he chose not to, in part perhaps because he feared the police were not strong enough for the job. At this meeting, journalist John Flinn reported that speakers scorned the "'cowardly police.' Would the police, the well-fed, idling, lazy police dare interfere with the rights of honest workingmen? No! Would they dare attempt to prevent such gatherings as this? No! If they did attempt to interfere with men who were exercising the right of free speech, what then? Why, my fellow citizens, they would be swept away like chaff before the wind. [Loud and continued cheering]."[38]

Historian Richard Schneirov argues that Chicago's socialists played an important role in the strike because the CA had succeeded in destroying the basis for machine politics with the reforms they had enacted in the previous years. The Workingmen's Party was able to attract considerable numbers of Chicagoans to its meetings. It also received a lot of attention from the police and the city's businessmen, who blamed it for the strike. Also, given the successful attempts of many different strikers to spread their actions, the socialists' calls for labor unity appear to have been taken up more broadly within the city's working class. Thus, the police had a clear target for their ire from the outset.[39]

The strike began in Chicago on Tuesday, July 24, with railroad workers, but quickly spread to lumbershovers on the Southwest Side. The lumber workers marched through the area, calling on or compelling (depending on whose account you believe) all the workers in their path to quit work and join them. This group was actually dispersed by a detachment of just twenty-five police. But that was not the end of it. Throughout the day, the strike expanded to include the sawmill and planing mill men, ironworkers, brass finishers, carpenters, brickmakers, bricklayers, stonemasons, furniture makers, polishers, shoemakers, tailors, painters, glaziers, butchers, and others, and their crowds were joined by thousands of the unemployed. All day, the police marched from one place to another to confront bands of strikers. They did not have horses or patrol wagons; instead they walked or took the streetcars. The stationhouses were connected by telegraph, but there was no easy means of communication with men in the field, so messages had to be conveyed on foot. By the end of the day, many individual officers had fought in numerous battles and had marched many miles from one part of the city to another. The mayor was afraid that the conflict would escalate, so he ordered the police to try to stop the crowds without bloodshed. This restrained the police from firing their pistols, but it was hard for a few police to overawe hundreds or thousands of strikers with their clubs alone. Under the circumstances, however, the police were effective in containing the disturbances.[40]

The success of the police and the growth of the strike pushed the mayor to adopt a more aggressive policy. The police arrested and threatened two important leaders of the socialist movement, Albert Parsons and Phillip Van Patten (discussed further in chapter 7). This succeeded in overawing the socialists, whose leaders were largely absent from the subsequent battles. The socialists also insisted on calling for the strikers to desist until a more orderly movement could be organized. Still, the night after the strike began, the Workingmen's Party called for another mass meeting, which was even better attended than the previous night's, though not by the main socialist leadership. This time, the mayor ordered the police to break it up. Lieutenants Baus and Gerbing approached with seventy-five men and fired round after round of blank cartridges at the group. This provoked a panic and the crowd fled, trampling one another. Rumors started in the South and West Sides that the police had killed hundreds of strikers. But once the strikers realized that the police had only fired blanks, they were more disdainful than ever of the ability of the police force to defeat them.

On Wednesday, July 25, the mayor called upon the "respectable" citizens of the city to volunteer, mobilizing the city's militia units. He put all these forces under the command of General Joseph Torrence. The city's businessmen rushed to volunteer with their weapons. But despite these additional armed forces, the police still formed the shock troops against the strikers. The 322 volunteers sworn in as special policemen that day mainly patrolled the regular police beats, with the regular force occupied in quelling the riot. Lieutenants Vesey and Callahan broke up a crowd of strikers assembled in front of the McCormick Reaper Works on Blue Island Avenue, and only needed the "specials" to patrol the area after they defeated the crowd. Lieutenant Ebersold with thirty-five men broke up another crowd on the East side of the Polk Street Bridge. Lieutenants Bell and Baus confronted additional strikers at the Illinois Central grain elevators and at Fifteenth Street and Dearborn Avenue.

That night the Workingmen's Party had called yet another mass meeting, which attracted two thousand people. The Workingmen's Party had actually requested police protection for a peaceful meeting, but the police refused and warned them that they would be attacked if they disobeyed. True to the department's word, Lieutenant Gerbing arrived with fifty patrolmen before the meeting could get under way and assaulted the crowd with clubs flying. The police then threw the speaker's platform into the river. Once the police broke up the initial meeting, reinforcements for the Workingmen's Party began marching to the location with fife and drum, but without weapons. The police in turn called up their own reinforcements, so that two hundred police confronted another crowd and fought it out, club against stone. Superintendent Hickey later reported that the police did not fire into the crowd only because about 150 small boys and girls had gathered to watch the fight, and the police were afraid of killing them if they unleashed a fusillade. The police finally drove the crowd away by firing live rounds repeatedly over their opponents' heads.

That same night, Captain Seavey and Lieutenant Callahan confronted another crowd at the Chicago, Burlington and Quincy roundhouse. As had happened in Pittsburgh, the men were destroying railroad property. The small number of police attacked the crowd and engaged in a full-scale battle with perhaps three thousand rioters. This time the police fired into the crowd, which responded with stones and perhaps even bullets. At least seven rioters were killed in the exchange of gunfire. The police finally succeeded in driving the crowd away from the roundhouse toward Halsted Street. The police were holding their own, but barely.

While Captain Seavey and Lieutenants Gerbing and Callahan were fighting Chicago's strikers, a huge crowd of businessmen was meeting at the Tabernacle building to form a defense organization. Reverend Robert Colyer, a favorite of the city's elite and a frequent speaker at "lyceum" meetings throughout the country where he charged $100 per speech, chaired the meeting and assured the crowd that he was willing to give his life "in defense of order."[41] Congressman and future mayor Carter Harrison insisted that the police could control the mobs, since even the rioters had a strong "feeling of law-abiding reverence for those who are the officers of the law." He called on the city's factories and shops to open for business the next morning, claiming that the strike was carried on by "idlers, thieves and ruffians," rather than the city's honest workmen.[42] Former mayor Levi Boone agreed with Harrison that the police could handle it, but only if they were better armed. Others at the meeting called for the mayor to request that the military be sent in to completely occupy the city. In the end, the meeting resolved to call for volunteers. Allan Pinkerton asserted that a total of fifty thousand volunteers joined the newly formed force of deputies during the course of the strike, while Superintendent Hickey claimed there were twenty thousand.[43]

The city government also tried to appease the unemployed who formed the shock troops of the riot. That same night, the city council held an emergency meeting and resolved to borrow $500,000 to build a new courthouse and to complete the sewers. This would provide employment for a large number of the unemployed. Since it would take time for such an undertaking to get under way, it could not halt the upheaval. Still, it indicates that, despite their eventual defeat, the unemployed who participated in the strike did ultimately gain something from their actions. The council also passed a resolution authorizing the mayor to "incur any and all expenses which he shall deem necessary or proper to enforce law and protect lives and property."[44] This was a remarkable statement in view of the government's general insistence on thriftiness in all matters.

In order to put down the riot, the police wanted "to get the rioters together at some given point that there might be an opportunity of settling the matter at once." The problem was that, "with mobs collecting here and there at the same time and not sufficiently resisting the police to justify indiscriminate shooting into them by any means," the police had been forced to race from place to place.[45] By this time, wealthy men and firms, including Field, Leiter and Company of Marshall Field fame, had furnished teams and wagons to move the police where the mobs appeared, but the police still wanted to confront the entire crowd at once because up to that point, once the crowds were dispersed from one place, they simply reappeared at another.

On July 26, the police finally got their chance. Early in the morning, a large crowd of rioters confronted about fifty police at the Halsted viaduct and exchanged gunfire and stones. Both sides soon received reinforcements. Deputy Superintendent Dixon soon arrived along with 125 additional patrolmen. Dixon was determined to fight the decisive battle at that spot. "'There must be no firing over the heads of the mob today,' he cried, 'we've got to crush out the riot today or the riot will crush us out tomorrow.'"[46] Not long after, Superintendent Hickey joined the police at the viaduct with more reinforcements, bringing the total to 350 police engaged against the rioters, firing into the crowd and clubbing those who remained. Soon, the state militia in the form of two cavalry companies and the second regiment of Irish Americans arrived as backup, bringing with them two ten-pound guns armed with grape and canister. These militiamen did not enter the fray, but waited in case the police were pushed back. The battle raged up and down Halsted Street all day, with the police giving much better than they got. They killed an untold number of rioters and clubbed down hundreds. Many more were imprisoned at the Twelfth Street Station, where, in the aftermath of the battle, one dead man lay on the floor, another lay dying, and "the streets thronged with people evidently in sympathy with the prisoners and rioters."[47] In fact, the police did almost all the fighting themselves, even if the presence of the militia might have helped overawe the strikers.

The police offensive extended beyond the strikers on the street to include the more orderly working class organizations. The same day as the battle of the Halsted viaduct, the police also attacked a meeting of the cabinetmakers' Harmonia union at Vorwarts Turnehalle (Turner Hall) on Twelfth Street. The police claimed that the hall was actually hosting a meeting of communists and that the mob inside attacked them with stones. Some observers later claimed that rioters might have fled into the hall. But many members of the Harmonia union, the lessee of the hall, and even an alderman later testified that there was no apparent reason for the police to raid the hall. According to the financial secretary of the union, the windows of the hall were shut, so no one could have thrown stones, and the door was ajar, so that the police could have entered peacefully had they wished to. In any case, as reported later, about twenty-five police rushed into the hall, shouting "Get out, you ___ ___ ___ [expletive excised in original]" and began clubbing and shooting everyone within. Policemen guarded the doors and beat all the participants in the meeting as they tried to obey the order to leave. The owner of a cabinet factory employing two hundred men testified that he even saw the police attack an old man passing by on the street. The police killed cabinetmaker Karl Tessman and badly wounded many other people. The Harmonia union later sued Superintendent Hickey, Sergeant Brennan who led the raid, and a number of individual patrolmen for damages. Two years later, it won the suit against Brennan and Policeman Householder, the only individual policeman they could positively identify, though the other defendants were found not guilty. Judge McAllister's decision strongly criticized the police for violating the free-speech rights of the union members, but his final award for damages was just six cents. This raid and the subsequent decision in June 1879 raised the ire of some workers in a way that the suppression of the 1877 riot had not. Many skilled workers were opposed to the rioters, but they strongly resented the police raid on the meeting and the contemptuous award for damages.[48]

Across the nation, the police were not very effective in controlling the upheaval of 1877, and writers from outside the city assumed the Chicago police had done no better. In his book on the events of 1877, Allan Pinkerton devotes a few pages to Chicago's preparations for the conflict. He mentions that the city deployed two militia regiments, a local artillery battery, and a cavalry unit. It also had several companies of federal troops brought to the city from the Indian Wars, and he mentions that it eventually assembled a large force of volunteers. Pinkerton considered Chicago much better prepared for the disturbances than Eastern cities, where the strike arrived earlier and the authorities were overwhelmed. Although his narrative shows that the police played the leading role in the actual fighting, Pinkerton does not mention them as even a part of the city's forces ready to defend order.[49] This was not due to jealousy between Pinkerton's detectives and the police. The two would become rivals in the future, but in 1877 they were on the same side and the police were no real competition for Pinkerton. Instead, Pinkerton's view reflected businessmen's general lack of trust in local police forces. Tens of thousands of armed businessmen, a few militia companies and small numbers of federal troops seemed more powerful in retrospect than the 481 patrolmen who actually did the bloody work that July. In fact, however, the "specials" and militiamen were almost useless.[50]

The Chicago police had, in fact, been quite effective, especially compared to other cities, though they had put down the disturbance so vigorously that most of the violence of the events was due directly or indirectly to the police.[51] In both Baltimore and Pittsburgh, strikers had completely overwhelmed local authorities, and were finally put down only by the army. In Chicago, where the number of potential recruits for the strikers was at least as large as in those other cities, the police had succeeded in suppressing the revolt. The city as a whole never passed into the hands of the rioters, and the destruction of property was comparatively small. This may have been partly due to police actions against the socialists and the Workingmen's Party's failure to gain control of the strike. It may also have been due to the viciousness of police violence. The police themselves reported killing ten rioters and severely wounding forty-five. Seventeen policemen were wounded in the fighting, though none were killed. The police arrested three hundred rioters who were held on bonds ranging between $500 and $3,000. Although the fighting hung in the balance at times, the police had emerged victorious.[52]

Many in Chicago and across the country recognized that the rioters had almost overwhelmed the combined forces of order. This recognition prompted a demand among wealthy people across the nation to increase the armed forces that could be deployed against future strikers and rioters. From the end of the Civil War until 1877, the Democratic Party had called for the disbandment or at least a great reduction in the army, but the upheaval of 1877 changed that. In Baltimore, for instance, the Democratic city government that had been overwhelmed by strikers now called for an increase in the army to handle domestic disturbances. Many people involved in Chicago politics felt the same way.[53] The city council tried to facilitate the coordination of all the various forces that had been called upon to put down the disturbance. They called for a clearer chain of command over the volunteer militia units with the aim of putting all armed forces under the control of the mayor in times of emergency.[54]

The suppression of the riot had also been expensive. The city council received a number of petitions from citizens asking to be remunerated for damages they sustained at the hands of the rioters. A hardware storekeeper, Ferdinand Goppehwading, for instance, reported that on the Thursday of the battle of the Halsted viaduct, some rioters burst into his store and demanded arms and ammunition.[55] Goppehwading had already removed his weapons at the request of the authorities. When their aims were thwarted, the rioters smashed up his shop. Goppehwading requested $500 reimbursement for these damages, but the council decided that "the City of Chicago is in no way liable for property of individuals, destroyed or stolen by mobs or riotous assemblages."[56] They were responsible, however, for the expenses incurred in suppressing the riot. This included $4,580 for the Special Police Pay Roll, $1,788 for the volunteer veteran battalions, plus an additional $15,073 to reimburse the 131 wealthy Chicagoans, businesses, and clubs who had contributed money and material to the effort. The list of individuals and organizations that the city reimbursed included many of the most prominent people and institutions in the city, including the Fields and Leiters, the McCormicks, and ten hotels.[57] At first the city refused to reimburse the militias, since they had volunteered for such duty. But a few months later, the city reversed itself and paid out $8,000 in wages to the militias out of fear that without the payment no one would sign up for militia duty in the future. All told, the city spent at least $29,910.30 suppressing the riot, in addition to the normal expenses of the police.[58] This was quite a sum, when the total budget for the police department in 1877 was $534,842.80.[59]

In Chicago, the suppression of the riot improved the elite's opinion of the police force. The *Tribune*, for instance, wrote the day after the battle of the

Halsted viaduct that "the police, supported by the presence of the military and aided by a handful of volunteer cavalry, were efficient at all times for any purpose." At the same time, however, the paper downplayed the danger and insisted that "the whole riot was but a series of puerile charges by a variety of timid mobs, easily met and readily suppressed by the quick though temperate action of a small but determined force." According to the *Tribune*, the rioters had met their match and Chicago had proven that it would not be the "camping ground" for a mob.[60] Soon afterward, the city council passed a resolution praising the "valorous conduct of the police force" and tendering them "a vote of thanks as an expression of its appreciation."[61] The council then appointed a board of trustees for a newly created "Police and Firemen's Relief Fund." This fund would provide financial aid to police officers or firemen wounded in the line of duty, or their families if they were killed. The first recipient of such an award was the widow of fireman Daniel Harknett, killed in an accident while on his way to a fire on July 14, 1877. The suppression of the riot by the police helped make the creation of such a fund possible.[62]

The upheaval of 1877 marked a turning point in the development of the Chicago Police Department. Up to that point, the city's elite had been as likely to blame and attack the police for corruption and inefficiency as it was to praise them. This was no longer the case afterward. Even Superintendent Hickey, who entered the violent days of July under the cloud of former Captain Buckley's accusations that he was a drunken thief who protected criminals and had sex with prostitutes, became a minor hero to the city's elite after his successful direction of the police against the rioters. As John Flinn points out, before the riot the "public" saw the "average blue-coat as a barnacle and a nuisance. He was only tolerated because there still remained a doubt as to the wisdom of trying to get on without him."[63] Before the riot, the persistence of gambling, prostitution, Sunday drinking, vagrancy, and unions seemed to prove that the police were ineffective. Afterward, the elite never again questioned the necessity of the police, even if it did not yet regard them as heroes.

It is important to recognize the limits of the city's newfound love for its police force. In fact, Mayor Heath cut the police force so that by the end of 1878 there were only 409 men on the police payroll.[64] This cut was part of Heath's extreme program of fiscal retrenchment, rather than any specific attack on the department. Cutting the force was not novel or particularly remarkable, but what had changed after 1877 was that this cut met with real opposition. In response to a petition from businessmen on the Southwest Side, the city council even passed a resolution urging the mayor to refrain from cutting the police or fire departments.[65] But the improved opinion that the city council held of its police force only went so far. When Patrolman Michael Meyer requested payment for the month of October 1877, when he was unable to work due to an illness contracted on the job, the council refused to grant his request.[66] The successful suppression of the riot did not lead to the immediate transformation of the force, but it laid the groundwork for the far-reaching reform of the institution that Carter Harrison would carry out in the decade to come.

Most important, the riot pushed the city's elite to organize itself even more fully than it had up to that point. First, the CA raised funds for weapons that could be used by the police or the militia in the case of another riot. Over the next year, it raised $28,115 for the purchase of weapons. This money came from a broad cross section of Chicago's businesses: $10,650 came from banks, railroads, insurance, and other corporations, $6,400 from merchants, $4,070 from the city's manufacturers, $3,700 from the Chicago Board of Trade, and $3,295 from the lumber interests.[67] The CA used this money to purchase 599 breach-loading Springfield rifles plus ammunition, four 12-pounder Napoleon cannons with 250 rounds of canister and 125 rounds of case shot, full equipment for a cavalry battalion, and one Gatling gun plus ammunition. It also paid the debts of the First and Second Regiments of the state militia.[68] On June 17, 1878, the CA resolved that "The arms and ammunition purchased by the Committee . . . are held by this Association for the maintenance of public order."[69] It distributed 303 of the guns and the cavalry equipment to the militia and the rest to the police department. The guns and equipment were marked with the letters "C.A." and described as being "held by the Police Department as the property of the CA to be returned to them on demand and not to be used outside of police jurisdiction."[70] "Prominent citizens and business men" donated an additional 102 muzzle-loading Springfields to the department during 1878.[71]

Over the next few years, the CA expanded to virtually shadow the elected government. And it aimed to pressure the government to carry out its program. For instance, the association was not content to pay for arming the police and the militia. On October 1, 1878, it resolved "that a well organized and equipped militia force competent to deal with any emergency is of vital importance to a community such as Chicago will be recognized by all . . . it is the duty of the State to maintain such a force from general taxation."[72] In order to get the city and state governments to carry out its wishes, the CA expanded its reach and focus to address virtually every aspect of government. By 1881, in addition to its executive committee, the association had

committees on finance, city and county legislation and administration, police, river and harbor, state legislation, judiciary, street obstructions, street
pavements, education, public buildings, bridges and street railways, taxation,
civil service reform, smoke, bankruptcy law, stenches, the water supply, the
military, sewerage, drainage, charities, and corrections and elections.[73] These
committees were manned by the big names of Chicago business, among them
Marshall Field (on the executive committee) and Philip D. Armour (on the
police committee), as well as many small businessmen who adopted the elite
viewpoint.

The following year, Chicago's elite formed a much more exclusive organization limited to the sixty most important men in the city: the Chicago
Commercial Club. The original sixty members were a cross section of the
most important businesses in the city, with Levi Leiter serving as the club's
first president. The organization's other members included William Chisolm,
president of the Union Rolling Mills; John Drake, proprietor of the Grand
Pacific Hotel; Charles Fargo of the American Express Company; Marshall
Field; J. Russell Jones, president of the West Chicago Railroad Company;
Franklin MacVeagh; E. M. Phelps of the Phelps Dodge Corporation; George
Pullman; and Anson Stager, vice president of Western Union. New members
could enter the organization only upon the death or resignation of an old
member.[74]

The club organized regular meetings at which the city's most powerful
businessmen discussed the issues of the day and tried to reach consensus.
These meetings were closed, but important figures like the mayor might attend by invitation. Some of the topics were broad, such as the April 27, 1878,
meeting: "The situation in our municipal affairs."[75] Others were more pointed:
"The military as protector of property, local and national."[76] Over the next
six years, the Commercial Club meetings included discussion of Sunday
blue laws, bankruptcy regulation, municipal revenue, the "nuisances such
as smoke, whistles and blocked streets that afflict Chicago," saloon licenses,
and the right of the state to interfere in public corporations. Its topics also
included: "the increase in immorality in the city—can anything be done to
lessen it?" "What are the causes of the present depression in commercial
and industrial interests and what the remedy?" "Is speculation an infamy
or a benefit to the general business interests of the country?" "Unemployed
laborers—what obligations rest upon our citizens for their maintenance?"
Like the CA, the Commercial Club was capable of raising considerable funds,
of pressuring politicians to accede to its demands, and of helping achieve
consensus among the city's elite.[77]

The official history of the Commercial Club insists that it was founded originally to entertain important potential investors from Boston.[78] Nevertheless, its founding one year after the upheaval of 1877 was not a coincidence. Chicago's elite was increasingly organizing itself to make sure the state and municipal governments met its needs. And the single-most important of those needs was the maintenance of order.

Historians have long argued that the events of 1877 marked a decisive shift in the national attention from the problems arising from the sectional crisis to those arising from the nation's industrialization. Not only did the year mark a shift in the national attention from the sectional crisis to the labor crisis, but it also marked a shift in the focus of the nation's armed forces. From 1861 to 1876, thousands of armed men in blue uniforms had striven to protect the system of "free labor" from the threat posed by the slave masters. Many of them were farmers motivated by their desire to save their children from the "wage slavery" they would be reduced to if new land for farms could not be secured. From 1877 onward, thousands of men in blue uniforms in cities throughout the North fought to protect the wage labor system from the threat posed by its own wage slaves. This army of blue-coated men is a large part of the answer to Schneirov's question of how northern cities reconciled electoral democracy with industrial capitalism.

At the same time, the focused police assault on a mass working class movement created a great deal of antipathy toward the department among a broad swath of urban residents. The Chicago police may have proven their worth to the city's elite, but they had done so by crushing a movement born of workers' poverty, frustration, and class resentment. In the aftermath of the great strike, the police could only expect enmity in Chicago's working-class neighborhoods. This might not matter when there was a serious riot and the police strove simply to protect the basic interests of the city's businessmen. It created grave problems, however, for the ability of the police to maintain order daily throughout the sprawling metropolis of immigrant workers. The police had proven that they could and would protect industrial capitalism from the threat its workers presented, but they had yet to prove that they could attain the legitimacy and respect from the city's workers that they needed to enforce everyday order. That would be the central policing problem of the coming decades.

CHAPTER 6

Carter Harrison Remakes the Chicago Police Department

The events of the 1870s set the stage for an unprecedented strengthening of the police department in the first half of the 1880s. At the beginning of that decade, the police force was undermanned and lacked legitimacy among the bulk of Chicago's population. Elite observers continued to excoriate the police for corruption and inefficiency, while working-class Chicagoans had good reason to view the police as little more than servants of the rich. Temperance continued to loom as an issue that could only exacerbate these problems for the department. The city itself was more class divided than ever before, and both sides had created their own armed militias, in part because neither side trusted the police department. During the first half of the 1880s, Mayor Carter Harrison successfully addressed all of these issues by rehabilitating the department's image and pouring resources into the force.

Harrison sought to create a more inclusive version of city politics that would neutralize the threat of worker upheaval, build a cross-class electoral alliance, and ensure order by both reducing class conflict and creating a police department that workers of all ethnicities would consider legitimate and useful. To do this, he pulled the police back from breaking strikes or disrupting anarchist meetings, gave the department a new set of social-service responsibilities, and hired a more ethnically representative group of officers. These measures did not change the basic nature of policing—force remained the main tool that the police could deploy to address the broad range of social problems they confronted. They did, however, make possible a dramatic increase in the policing of Chicagoans' daily lives, especially in areas like unwanted pregnancy, which had previously been the responsibility of the family, rather than the government. His policies also dramatically failed to ensure class peace, as his mayoralty culminated in the massive strikes for the eight-hour workday in 1886, the bombing at Haymarket, and the subsequent extralegal repression of the anarchists. They succeeded, however, in rebuilding the police department into a much more powerful and legitimate force.

In the late 1870s, the police were woefully undermanned. Even after the department's successful suppression of the upheaval of 1877, Mayor Monroe Heath continued with his program of extreme fiscal retrenchment. Heath succeeded in restoring the city's credit but had gutted its public services. There were far too few police still on the payroll to patrol the city effectively. Superintendent V. A. Seavey acknowledged this at the end of 1878, when the force employed a mere 409 men. He reported that each night patrolman had to cover an average of three and a quarter miles of street, while day patrolman were responsible for four and a half miles. As a result, "it should not be surprising if the cry of 'where are the police' is occasionally heard."[1] As the superintendents did each year, Seavey requested an increase in the size of the force. The crises of the 1870s had created a consensus among the city's leaders that the force needed to be increased, but this was only carried out very gradually as business prosperity returned. By the end of 1880, the police force had 473 men on the payroll.[2]

The police also retained a poor reputation even among that class of citizens that had rallied to them during the riots of 1877. The newspapers commonly reported on police officers hanging about in saloons, having sex with prostitutes, and getting in fights.[3] The accusations that Captain Buckley leveled against Superintendent Hickey in 1877 were by no means unique. In mid-1878, for instance, other members of the force accused the Lake Street Squad of being in cahoots with local thieves and gamblers.[4] The newspapers even reported that just a few months before his appointment as superintendent, Captain Seavey, who had been so brutally effective in the 1877 strikes, had been forcibly removed from a saloon after having had too much to drink.[5] Republican newspapers like the *Tribune* regularly complained that the police allowed all manner of vice to flourish in the city. Since police officers were poorly paid in devalued city scrip during the 1870s (when the city lacked sufficient cash to meet its payroll), some officers undoubtedly did take bribes from petty criminals. The force was also so undermanned that it would have been nearly impossible for it to realistically attempt to eliminate vice in any city the size of Chicago. Medill's defeat by the People's Party had forced the elite to pull back from its vigorous program of vice control, but the inability of the police to enforce the elite program had not improved the force's reputation among Chicago's upper class.

Its success in 1877 had only increased hatred of the police among the
unions and many workers and immigrants. The police raid on the cabinetmakers' meeting at Turner Hall remained a live political issue for years as the
cabinetmakers' union, Harmonia, pursued its suit against the department.[6]
Furthermore, large numbers of the city's largely German and Irish immigrant workers voted for the Socialist Labor Party, which openly opposed the
police force. And while the labor movement fought the legal challenge from
the Citizens' Association all the way to the U.S. Supreme Court, it enlarged
its militias.[7] These militias were built explicitly to fight the police and other
forces of order during the next anticipated workers' movement. The Lehr und
Wehr Verein had more than two hundred members in 1878, drilled regularly,
and defended socialist picnics from the police.[8]

As we have seen, the city's elite countered the growth of these militias by
purchasing an extensive arsenal for the police department. Every patrolman
drilled with these weapons in his precinct, and on public occasions they
paraded in platoons with their arms.[9] Thus, in the aftermath of 1877, the city
was deeply divided along class lines, and both sides were armed. For many of
those on the working-class side of the line, the police appeared to be hostile,
organized as a military force to repress them.

The truce between temperance advocates and immigrants remained tenuous into the early 1880s. The police continued to arrest large numbers of
Chicagoans for drinking. In 1878, for instance, the police made 1,688 arrests
for drunkenness, 2,100 for drunk and disorderly conduct, and 8,817 for disorderly conduct, out of a total of 27,208 arrests.[10] Despite their defeats in the
1870s, temperance reformers continued to press for an even more vigorous
crackdown on drinking, for higher license fees for saloons, and for a Sunday
closing law. A letter to the editor in the *Tribune* in May 1878, for instance,
attributed 22,000 of the 28,000 arrests for the previous year to "the rum traffic," and pointed out that liquor license fees only brought in $148,000 to the
city, while the expenses of the police were $534,000.[11] In 1878, the temperance
agitators formed the Citizens' League, an organization dedicated to fighting
underage drinking. The Citizens' League and the policies it proposed no
longer had the support of the majority of the city's elite. The league asked
Mayor Heath to deputize its members as special policemen, with the power
to enforce the underage drinking laws, since they recognized that the regular
police force was too small to do so effectively. Cognizant of the recent failures
of temperance advocates and wary of any move that could incite a repeat of
the People's Party, Mayor Heath refused. But the league continued to agitate
over the issue for months.[12]

Thus, in the late 1870s, between their real ineffectiveness, scandals, class conflict, and the continuing fight over drinking, the police lacked legitimacy among a large section of Chicago's population. The highest levels of Chicago's elite, organized in the Citizens' Association and the Commercial Club, consistently pushed for an increase in the force and for its organization along increasingly military lines, but almost every other group of Chicagoans was at best suspicious and at worst hostile to the police.[13]

The election of 1879 proved to be critical for the future development of the Chicago Police Department. The three major candidates each had widely different views on the police. Abner Wright, the Republican candidate, supported aggressive police policies like those that had failed in the early 1870s. Ernst Schmidt, the Socialist Labor Party candidate, supported the workers' movement against police repression, but had little chance of victory. Carter Harrison, on the other hand, appealed to all comers. He stood aloof from the temperance issue. A respectable businessman with a small fortune of his own, he supported the retrenchment of the city's finances. He had a bachelor's degree from Yale and a law degree from Transylvania College in Kentucky.[14] He rebutted newspaper claims to the contrary, promising not to politicize the police, and he appealed to immigrants by affirming that Chicago was a cosmopolitan city that thrived with the support of different ethnic groups.[15] Harrison attempted to be all things to all people, including the police. Between 1879 and 1885, he almost succeeded.

Carter Harrison won the mayoral election in 1879 and proceeded to strengthen and legitimize the police department as never before. The way he did this drew the ire of the Republican Party (which was already assured since Harrison was a Democrat in what had been a Republican city). It also eventually pushed many employers who had originally backed him, including Cyrus McCormick, to withdraw their support. However, in the long run, Carter Harrison's efforts to make the police department legitimate in the eyes of many immigrants, workers, and even socialists helped him expand and strengthen it so that it was capable of defeating the workers' movement during the mid-1880s.

Harrison began by materially strengthening the police department's ability to do its job. The most important development came in the realm of police technology. Communications were a huge problem for police in the nineteenth century. Most police walked their long beats alone, which left them vulnerable to attack. In fact, police officers were sometimes killed because they confronted criminals alone. On the evening of October 4, 1878, for instance, Officer Albert Race stopped a wagon that he suspected was full of goods looted from a pawnshop. When he accosted the two men in the wagon, one of them shot him in the head with a pistol, killing him. Both men then escaped, at least for a few months.[16] Had Officer Race been able to call for help, it is likely he never would have been killed. In addition, when police officers had to return to their station houses to report often trivial matters, or when they had to bring an arrested person in to jail, their beats were unguarded, sometimes for hours.

Police officials had been aware of this problem for some time and had tried a number of solutions. Since the 1850s, Police officers had been carrying creakers to get the attention of nearby officers.[17] As late as 1860, Superintendent of Police Cyrus Bradley still demanded that the police be equipped with horses.[18] That same year the department introduced height minimums and age maximums to ensure that police officers would be physically strong and imposing enough to deal with all comers.[19] None of these measures, however, solved the basic problem of police communications.

In 1880, the Chicago Police Department introduced a new Police Alarm Telegraph System in the West Twelfth Street District. It was modeled after the fire alarm system already in operation, but was much more extensive. On street corners around the district, the department installed telegraph boxes that were connected to the district station house. Each alarm box was inside a small, enclosed sentry house, about seven feet high, that officers could lock themselves into. The telegraph alarm was equipped with a dial that signaled the station house of a murder, a dead body waiting to be picked up, a robbery, or a riot, among other problems. The department gave keys to these boxes to each patrolman and to certain reputable citizens so they could call for the police, as well.[20]

At the station houses, the police outfitted patrol wagons to respond to the telegraph calls. These wagons were the precursor of the modern police car. They were drawn by two horses and could comfortably carry five officers, including the driver. They were made conspicuous with bright blue bodies, red running gear, and alarm gongs that the drivers could ring while rushing to an emergency, similar to fire department alarms. The wagons were also outfitted with stretchers, handcuffs, ropes, clubs, blankets, and a ring that "obstreperous prisoners" could be tied to.[21]

According to Superintendent McGarigle, who oversaw the development and implementation of the system, the idea was first raised by Police Secretary Austin Doyle in a conversation with Mayor Harrison. Doyle convinced Harrison to use money left in the police appropriation to fund a trial run in the West Twelfth Street District.[22] John Bonfield, who went on to play a major role in later events, was put in charge of the new system.[23] These boxes also allowed the department to offer special services to the wealthy. In December 1880, Superintendent McGarigle wrote an open letter to the public, then reprinted in the *Tribune,* in which the police department offered to install call boxes connected to the Central Police Station at private businesses and residences in the central business district. These private citizens would have to pay $30 to install a box, plus a minimal maintenance fee.[24] This would ensure that wealthy citizens could secure immediate police protection in case of any threat, and ensure their political support for the police department if the system worked.

The police leadership originally saw this system as especially useful in case of riots or major crimes. After the test period in the West Twelfth Street District in 1880, Superintendent McGarigle requested the expansion of the system over the entire city by pointing to just such dangers, which were still fresh in Chicagoans' minds after 1877: "Say a dangerous riot threatened, and it becomes necessary to at once notify all officers," McGarigle wrote, "to look out for [a] criminal, or to rally to resist public violence, how utterly inadequate are the old methods?"[25] In 1877, the police had rushed on foot from one neighborhood to the next, and learned where to go only after a messenger arrived to tell them. The telegraph system would facilitate concentrating forces and moving them where needed. The new system also promised to save the city money, since it meant that one police officer could accomplish more by staying on his beat and covering more ground, rather than going back and forth to the station house for messages and information. With this in mind and with the city revenues increasing due to the improved economic situation of the early 1880s, Harrison and the city council approved funding for a massive, citywide expansion of the system.

By the end of 1883, the alarm system accounted for 30 percent of the arrests made by the police force, though the 84 men working in the alarm system branch of the department accounted for only 22 percent of active-duty officers, compared to the 227 night patrolmen, 80 day patrolmen, and 71 patrolmen in the rest of the department. The police had installed over 350 alarm houses spread throughout the city, and in the densest areas, they were located at every block. In addition, four hundred private citizens had boxes installed in their businesses or homes.[26]

While this massive expansion of police communications capabilities might have meant a greater potential for day-to-day control by the police, in fact the alarm boxes facilitated the police department's assumption of more social service duties. In 1880, Superintendent McGarigle had emphasized that the wagons contained handcuffs and a ring for restraining prisoners, and that the system allowed quick response to riots. By 1883, the new superintendent, Austin Doyle (promoted from secretary), called the vehicles used to respond to alarms "Police Wagon and Ambulance combined."[27] While the wagons still carried handcuffs, they also carried lanterns, a medical chest, and a coil of rope for use at fires. In 1882, the examining surgeon of the police department, Dr. F. Henrotin, began instructing men detailed to the telegraph wagons in first aid.[28] These officers put their new knowledge to use. In 1883, the police alarm telegraph service took 1,058 sick and injured people to the hospital, took 827 to their homes, and treated 328 at the station houses. They also picked up 311 dead bodies and took them to the morgue or the homes of their relatives. They cared for 260 insane persons, and 264 destitute persons. They took 245 lost children to their parents, and also killed mad or crippled animals, overtook and stopped runaway horses, took abandoned children to the Chicago Foundlings' Home, rescued people from drowning, and took "wayward girls" to reform houses. All of these activities were made possible in part by the rapid response capability afforded by the new telegraph system, and together they undoubtedly helped to legitimize the police in the eyes of the population. With the police acting as the main ambulance system, even participants in the 1877 strikes might begin to look on them as a vital municipal service.[29]

Chicago's police alarm telegraph system was a model for the rest of the country. *The Manufacturer and the Builder* gave the system national exposure from its inception in 1881, and *Harpers* even teased the Chicago police for putting rubber tires on its wagons so that "a resident may be restored to his family late at night without attracting the morbid curiosity of the entire neighborhood."[30] Superintendent Doyle reported that the police department had received inquiries from other cities asking about the service, to which he responded with detailed instructions and diagrams. The service was at the nation's cutting edge of communications technology.

The police alarm telegraph system was also at the forefront of telecommunications within Chicago. As a municipally owned system, it could experiment with new protocols before the city obliged private systems to comply. For this reason, its wires were the first to be put underground in the city. In 1884, city electrician John Barrett traveled to New York and Boston to explore the possibility of putting telegraph wires underground, at least in the business district. In February 1884, the city began to invest in burying the wires of both the police and the fire alarm telegraph systems, both to protect them from damage and sabotage and to rid the city of the nuisance of wires strung above ground.[31]

The police also began to publicize their social service activities as part of a general attempt to rehabilitate their image among the city's poor and working-class population. Starting under Austin Doyle, the police began to report to the city council the number of lost children they found, the number of lodgers they accommodated in police station houses, the number of attempted suicides they dealt with, the defective drains, gas pipes, hydrants, culverts, sidewalks, etc. that they reported, and the number of intoxicated people they escorted home. Other than those activities facilitated by the telegraph service, and the general increase in the city's population, there was not a noticeable increase in the police department's performance of social service duties between 1878, the last year before Harrison's election, and 1883, when the city entered a sharp recession. For instance, where they took 922 intoxicated people home in 1878, they took only 673 home in 1883. Where they reported 249 sudden deaths in 1878, they reported 241 in 1883. However, the department's emphasis on these types of activities in their annual reports and their subsequent reporting in the newspapers did mark a major change, and helped the department appear less like just an armed force at the service of the city's elite.[32]

The increased legitimacy of the police and the improvement in the city's fiscal situation also made possible an enormous increase in the size of the force. In 1881, the Citizens' Association Committee on Police carried out a thorough study of the Chicago Police Department in comparison with other cities. This study compared the number of men, their pay, the area they had to patrol, and the ratio of patrolmen to the overall population. They recommended that the city double the force to eight hundred men in part because "foreign capitalists seeking investment want a guarantee that their interests will be protected before making their risks at low rates of interest." The CA estimated that the increase would cost about half a million dollars, and it recommended that the city pay for hiring the new men by increasing the valuation of taxable real estate and personal property.[33] But Harrison had largely been elected by workingmen and immigrants, and he had to relieve their anger at the department before he could politically afford to hire many more men.[34] By 1884, Harrison had achieved this goal. Between 1881 and 1883, the city slowly hired more policemen so that at the end of 1883, the police department employed 637 men, including patrolmen, clerks, detectives, custodians, and bailiffs.[35] In 1884, the department grew by almost 50 percent. By the end of that year, the police department had grown to 924 men.[36] The greatest number of new hires were patrolmen, the number of whom grew from 307 to 576.[37]

At the same time, these newly hired men were required to submit to a physical and "moral" examination and to write out their own histories and applications, meaning they had to be literate. The majority of applicants failed these tests.[38] There were enough applicants that the city could fill the new positions with only the most qualified men. Thus, under Harrison, the police force was not only greatly expanded, but, contrary to what might be expected, the standards for admission to the force had become significantly more demanding.

Carter Harrison also kept the direction of the police department in the hands of highly professional, experienced officers with many years of service. Neither Harrison nor anyone else in the city wanted a repeat of the Washburn fiasco. But Harrison went further than Mayor Colvin, who had simply promoted the most senior officers. Under Harrison, many leading officers had considerable military experience. Dominick Welter, for instance, served as inspector and secretary of police, the second-highest position in the force, from November 1882 until he died of an aneurism on July 9, 1885. In this post, he was responsible for overseeing the training of the newly hired men. He was a military man before joining the police, serving as a private in the U.S. Army Infantry from 1856 to 1857. During the Civil War, he rose to major in the Fourth Ohio Cavalry. As inspector and secretary of police, Colonel Welter used his military experience to design drills for the police officers that helped train and discipline the new officers hired in 1884. Upon his death, the city council passed a memorial crediting him with "the efficiency of our present police."[39]

Carter Harrison also chose a diverse police leadership in terms of nationality and religion, even while he made sure the main leaders of the force had well-established military and police credentials and extensive experience with the city's business community. Colonel Welter was a Luxembourgian immigrant and a member of the Catholic Benevolent Legion. Austin Doyle was born in Chicago of Irish roots. Superintendent Frederick Ebersold immigrated from Bavaria in 1856 when he was fifteen years old. He eventually rose to the rank of first lieutenant in the U.S. Army and served under General Sherman, with whom he fought in the Battle of Shiloh, the Siege of Vicksburg, the Battle of Kennesaw Mountain, and the famous March to the Sea. He joined the police force under Jacob Rehm in 1867 and helped quell the riot of 1877 before rising to the rank of captain in 1879 and serving with then Lieutenant Bonfield. He worked in many different police districts throughout the city before he was promoted to superintendent on the resignation of Austin Doyle in October 1885.[40] The men who led the Chicago police also had experience working with business. Austin Doyle worked for some of the leading mercantile houses of the city before serving as clerk of the Criminal Court, studying law, and passing the bar. Superintendent Mc-Garigle worked at a high level for the United States Express Company and the Chicago, Milwaukee and St. Paul Railroad Company, before becoming a police officer in 1872.[41] Frederick Ebersold worked as a grain merchant in Mendota, Illinois, before the Civil War. Thus, Harrison's police appointments fit a general pattern. He chose people with military experience, made an effort to appoint immigrants from the city's largest ethnic groups, the Germans and Irish, and he also made sure that his appointees were men loyal to the economic system they would be charged with defending.

John Bonfield, portrayed in the standard histories as the brutal cop who put down the 1885 streetcar strike and stormed the crowd at Haymarket Square (see chapter 8), was also a professional policeman with considerable experience on the force.[42] According to John Flinn, a journalist who wrote a history of the police force in the aftermath of Haymarket, Bonfield "belongs to the modern school of police officers—that class of men who have made the police force of Chicago famous for its discipline, efficiency and bravery throughout the nation."[43] While Flinn was a defender of the police department after the repression of 1886–1887, he is closer to the mark than those historians who see Bonfield as a rogue brute acting outside the discipline of the city government.[44] The son of an Irish immigrant father, Bonfield was born in Canada and was brought to Chicago by his parents as a child in 1844. He worked as a machinist, a locomotive engineer on the Chicago and Alton, and a grocery store owner. His brother Joe was a well-known Chicago lawyer who served as corporation counsel under Mayor Heath, while his brother James also became a policeman. After his grocery store failed, John Bonfield was appointed inspector of customs by President Grant, probably because he campaigned for the Republican Party. In 1875, he tried to start a fertilizer manufacturing business, but after the plant was destroyed by a fire, he joined the Chicago police force in 1877. As a police officer, Bonfield rose steadily through the ranks until he reached the rank of inspector when Ebersold was appointed superintendent. He was the man responsible for setting up the first Police Alarm Telegraph System and, as inspector, he was mostly responsible for purchasing supplies, managing the telegraph system, and auditing the expenses of the force. Bonfield rose in the department not because of any brutality but because he was an efficient bureaucrat.[45]

Carter Harrison was mayor at a time when the patronage system was at its peak, when mayors were expected to appoint men of their party to a range of posts. But Harrison did not simply reward Democratic Party activists with jobs in the police department. He kept many Republicans on the force in leadership positions and as rank-and-file patrolmen and detectives. John Ender, for instance, was a black police detective who was committed to the Republican Party. Before the 1881 election, Harrison reportedly asked Ender to vote for him. When Ender refused, Harrison replied, "All right, John, vote as you please, but be a good policeman."[46] Whatever Harrison's motives in carrying out this policy, it cemented the police officers' allegiance to the department rather than a political party or politician as the source of their jobs. The majority of newly hired officers were Democrats, but they had to submit to the same selection process as everyone else.

Harrison's mayoralty also put a definitive end to the policy of excluding immigrants from municipal politics and institutions. This policy had been ineffective from its beginning in the 1850s, but had retained the power to divide the city through the 1870s. After the rise of the People's Party, the growth of multiethnic elite organizations like the CA, and finally Carter Harrison's construction of a multiethnic electoral coalition, it would never again be possible to win major elective office in Chicago without bringing together elements from the city's different ethnic groups. This was reflected in the police department. Since the downfall of Levi Boone, the department had hired some immigrants and their children, but under Carter Harrison, the hiring of immigrants accelerated dramatically. This was partially due to the simple fact that the police force expanded quickly in a largely immigrant city. Also, the new policemen were closely tied to the largely Democratic immigrant neighborhoods, unlike their largely native-born Republican predecessors. By 1887, about 54 percent of the police were foreign born, the majority either Irish or German.[47] Including the children of immigrants like Bonfield raises the percentage even higher.

In addition to expanding the force, implementing the Police Alarm Telegraph System, maintaining an experienced leadership regardless of party affiliation, and instilling the officers with a sense of discipline, Carter Harrison gave the police new incentives for professional behavior, instilling them with the esprit de corps that many observers had found lacking in the force of the 1870s. At the end of 1883, when he asked for a substantial increase in the force, Superintendent Doyle proposed implementing a graded system of pay based on seniority and modeled after similar systems in New York and London. He proposed that men who had been on the force longer than a year receive $1,000 a year in pay, those who had been hired in 1883 to receive $900 per year, and the new hires in 1884 to receive $62.50 a month for their first eight months with the force. This was a significant step toward giving officers incentives to stay with the police, since they would earn raises based on seniority. According to Doyle, the "quality most necessary to success in a police officer is ambition, tempered with sound discretion." As the force grew, however, there would be proportionately fewer superior positions to which capable men could be promoted. As a result, the leadership of the Department needed other incentives to recruit professional men and get them to stay on the police force. "I should like to see only such men apply for admission to the force as have made up their minds to make police business the avocation of their lives," Superintendent Doyle wrote. When they were poorly paid and given no raises, they had little reason to do so.[48]

Carter Harrison's new personnel policies might seem like a small step, but in fact, they constituted a serious civil service reform. They insulated the police from political changes in the city's leadership, ensured a greater degree of continuity in the force, and gave officers a greater incentive to follow orders and keep their jobs, even in good economic times when other employment opportunities were available. This push toward continuity was facilitated by Carter Harrison's long term in office. By the end of 1883, he had already been mayor for four and a half years, and it appeared likely that he would win the election in 1885, as well. The leadership of the police was already filled with men solidly committed to the institution. Before Harrison, the rank and file had experienced much greater turnover, especially during the 1870s, when the force was reduced from year to year and policemen were paid in city scrip. The stabilization of personnel meant that ordinary police officers would view their job as part of their identity, rather than a stopgap measure to "keep the wolf from the door."[49]

In 1885, the superintendent began keeping a merit roll of police officers who had "performed any distinguished act of bravery in the protection of life or property." A similar merit roll was established for the fire department. Mayor Harrison and Judge Lambert Tree, a Democrat millionaire with investments in various Chicago banks, the Chicago Dock Company, and the Chicago Gaslight and Coke Company, provided funds for a series of gold medals to be given to the men listed on the merit roll.[50] The exploits of the winners of the Tree Medal and the Harrison Medal were publicized, and the men received their awards in a ceremony by the trustees of the funds.[51]

Like the establishment of pay grades based on seniority, the merit roll and the gold medals gave police officers an incentive to identify with the force and try to get their names listed on the merit roll. They also helped to give the force positive publicity. By shifting the public's focus from police scandals, the toleration of gambling, underage drinking, and prostitution to the bravery of heroic police officers, these awards were intended to further rehabilitate the image of the police department. This rehabilitation, in turn, helped other officers feel pride in their connection with the institution.

Mayor Harrison also knew that it was crucial that the increasingly professional police department gain legitimacy among Chicago's workers. To this end, he had them refrain from breaking strikes. In 1882, for instance, a strike broke out at the North Side brickyards. The strikers threw stones at the strikebreakers and drove them away from the yards. Once the police arrived on the scene, the strikers stopped their assault, but they had already succeeded in driving off the strikebreakers. The police did not arrest a single striker. The patrolmen at the scene reported that they did not even know why they were sent to the yards and said that they had neither seen nor heard anything. Mayor Harrison even denied having sent any policemen.[52] This was a radical departure from the previous standard police procedure of arresting picketing strikers and escorting strikebreakers through picket lines, and both the police and the mayor made it clear to all involved that they were not going to implement the old policy. Another strike in 1882 at the Union Iron and Steel Company was more serious. The company provoked this strike when it tried to increase the hours of work for its 1,600 employees from eight hours a day to twelve hours. When the men went on strike in response, the company brought in Pinkerton guards and requested help from the mayor and the superintendent of police. A number of police officers were detailed to the plant, but they did not attack the crowd of strikers that kept strikebreakers from working. As a result, the strikers were successful in shutting down plant operations. The representative of the company claimed that the police would not attack the strikers because they lived in the neighborhood and were sympathetic to them. It was "not at all natural that a brother would be inclined to arrest a brother," the company representative said, "or a cousin a cousin." So he suggested that police be brought in from the North Side who were less likely to have personal connections with the strikers. But the department refused.[53] Although in the early 1880s the police department had hired men from the neighborhood to patrol the area around the mill who undoubtedly were sympathetic with the strikers, this was not the only reason that the police refused to arrest the strikers for attacking the strikebreakers: Carter Harrison had made an electoral alliance with the city's unions, and consistently refused to deploy the police against strikers.[54]

This policy allowed striking workers to defeat some of the city's most powerful employers, most dramatically at a strike at the McCormick Reaper

Works in the spring of 1885. In that strike, workers walked out to demand a raise and the dismissal of a hated foreman, and gathered in a crowd at the factory gates to prevent strikebreakers from entering. Cyrus McCormick Jr., the young heir to the agricultural machine company started by his father, met with Mayor Carter Harrison to request that the police keep the street in front of the Reaper Works clear of strikers and provide protection for his strikebreakers, but Mayor Harrison informed McCormick that he could not guarantee the help of the police, since the policemen were "largely in sympathy with the strikers and he could not very well interfere." Harrison advised McCormick to settle. Instead, McCormick hired Pinkertons, but workers defeated the Pinkerton guards in a series of running battles, took their weapons, and burned their vehicle. The police then arrested eight Pinkerton men for shooting at the strikers. The police offered to help McCormick bring supplies in and out of the plant, but they refused to disperse the picketing strikers. Philip Armour, founder of one of Chicago's original meatpacking companies and member of the Citizens' Association's Committee on Police, visited Cyrus McCormick and urged him to settle the strike. "He thought it would be better for us [the McCormicks] to end the matter even if we had to pay the men what they demanded," McCormick reported to his mother, "rather than to let matters go on as they were, for they were developing into open war." Following Armour's advice, the young McCormick agreed to a 10 percent pay raise for laborers and a 15 percent raise for molders, and he promised not to fire anyone for strike activity, although he refused the strikers' demand to fire the foreman. McCormick blamed his loss, among other things, on the lack of police protection. "If we had had 50 policemen on the ground on Tuesday morning," he wrote, "we could have overcome the whole matter."[55] He was probably right.

The Pinkertons provided employers a potential alternative to the police, though they were expensive and not very effective, as the 1885 McCormick strike showed. In addition to the Pinkerton guards defeated by the strikers in front of the plant, McCormick hired Pinkerton spies to report what his workers were thinking and doing. One of these Pinkerton spies submitted a report explaining that the company had lost the 1885 strike and the Pinkertons had proven unable to protect the strikebreakers or beat back the strikers because the leaders of the unions and the police were Irish immigrants who were hostile to the Pinkertons because of their role in the repression of the Molly Maguires in Pennsylvania. According to this spy, J. C. Harris, Captain O'Donnell and many of the police were members of the Ancient Order of Hibernians.[56] This was an old complaint, but it fails to account for

Harrison's shift in police policy. The police did not refrain from breaking the strike simply because many were Irish—rather, Harrison hired Irish police and refrained from breaking strikes in order to gain legitimacy for the police among Irish and other workers.

As outdated as its rhetoric was by 1885, Agent Harris's attack on the Irish police highlights an important point. Carter Harrison had made an effort to hire people from local ethnic groups into the police force for six years. The prominence of police officers from various ethnic backgrounds led Chicago's immigrants to differentiate between the legitimate police department and the illegitimate Pinkertons. This differentiation helped make the police a potentially effective strikebreaking force, while the Pinkertons were not.

J. C. Harris also pointed to a more threatening set of figures in the Chicago labor scene. "They [the workers] are also instigated by agents of the International Working Men's Association, known as socialists," Harris reported. "Parsons of this Anarchist Society, has been among McCormick's employees, advocating his ideas, how to make dynamite . . . and Parsons advises them to be all ready for such an emergency, and to keep their powder dry."[57] Harris here referred to Albert Parsons, the most prominent native-born leader of the radical Chicago labor movement. Harris and many Republican Chicagoans blamed Carter Harrison for allowing the anarchists to organize openly, but in fact, as with his policy toward immigrants, Carter Harrison's police policy was aimed at winning Chicago's workers to his brand of class collaborationist politics and away from the anarchists, who had gained greatly in appeal after the repression of 1877. Harrison's decision to not use the police against the McCormick strikers surely convinced many workers that they had a lot to gain by keeping him in office, and discredited the anarchists' claims that the police were simply tools of the business class.[58]

Obviously, J. C. Harris wanted to convince McCormick that the Pinkertons could be useful, even though they had failed to break the 1885 strike, but unlike the police, the Pinkertons lacked the force to effectively control large groups of men. The Pinkertons had proven themselves adept at spying on labor organizations and working with police in cases like the Molly Maguires, when a Pinkerton spy exposed the Irish militants to local authorities, who arrested and hung them. This kind of labor spying, though, was not the same as breaking a picket line. The police had two crucial advantages over the Pinkerton Agency: first, the Pinkertons did not command the same respect from the population and, second, they were not able to assemble as many men as the police force could. As long as the police remained neutral, McCormick could not defeat a crowd of a few hundred strikers with eight or a dozen armed Pinkertons.

The police also refrained from enforcing laws restricting drinking and gambling. According to the *Tribune*, Harrison protected the largest gambling operator in the city, Mike McDonald, in return for his political support.[59] Between 1879 and 1886, the police refrained from raiding gambling dens and overlooked the law requiring taverns to close at midnight. Tavern keepers did have to pay large licensing fees, but the city government was responsive to their needs. On April 18, 1885, for instance, the German Verein der Wirthe von Chicago (Saloonkeepers' Association of Chicago) petitioned the city government to consolidate the categories of liquor licenses. Up to that point, the city had sold licenses for selling malt beverages at a reduced price, but the Verein der Wirthe charged that many purveyors of liquor sold the full range of alcoholic beverages with only a malt license, which they considered unfair competition. The association also asked the city government to allow them to pay their license fees in installments. In response, the city council passed, and Mayor Harrison signed into law, an ordinance providing exactly what they wanted. The city council set the liquor license fee at $500 for the coming year, which was a large sum of money at the time and which made up a considerable part of the city's income.[60] This large fee helped "place the saloon business on a higher level" by protecting the "respectable tavernkeepers against the competition of the riff-raff."[61] More importantly, this cooperation among Harrison, the German saloonkeepers, and the police meant that the stable, property-owning elements within the German population dealt with the department in particular and the city government in general as an ally, rather than as an enemy. This helped to dispel some of the hostility toward the force that lingered from the Washburn-Medill period and cemented the acceptance of saloons by the Chicago Police Department that would continue for many decades.

Taken together, these reforms complicate the traditional distinction drawn by historians and contemporary observers between urban reformers and machine politicians. Historian Robert Fogelson, for instance, argues that by the mid-nineteenth century, police in New York, Philadelphia, Chicago, Kansas City, San Francisco, and other cities were largely controlled by political machines, tied in some cases to the Democrats, in other cases to the Republicans. These political machines were decentralized ward organizations that got out the vote on Election Day, gave contracts to local businesses, found jobs for immigrants, and demanded a great deal of say in the operations of the police department and other municipal departments.[62] They attracted the ire of elite urban reformers throughout the country, with Tammany Hall in New York the subject of particular denigration. Carter Harrison was in many ways the prototypical machine politician. He tolerated vice and curried favor among different groups within the city in order to build a broad electoral alliance that alienated some elements of the Protestant elite. At the same time, he implemented many civil-service reforms that weakened the strength of patronage politics and reinforced professional police officials. His police policy cannot be explained by reference to machine politics, however much he might have tried to build a machine. Instead, he used police policy in a concerted and politically conscious attempt to reconcile the increasingly hostile and clearly defined social classes born from the development of a wage labor economy.

Of course, the main activity of the police remained the apprehension and arrest of Chicagoans for disorderly conduct. Between 1878 and 1886, about half of all arrests were for that offense.[63] In 1878, 12,605 people were charged with disorderly conduct, or 46 percent of all arrests. By 1886, that figure had grown to 26,067, or 59 percent of the total. The next most common charges were prostitution, vagrancy, larceny, and violation of the dog ordinance, though each of these accounted for less than 5 percent of all arrests. Of those arrested, the vast majority were still poor and working class. Almost half of those arrested in 1883, a typical year, reported that they had no occupation. Of those whose occupations were recorded, almost a third were laborers and the next most common occupation was prostitution.[64] The increase in arrests paralleled the increase in the size of the police force. Superintendent Doyle also pointed to the growth of the city's population and the extension of the police telegraph service to account for the increase. But the character of those arrests changed very little. As before, the bulk of the patrolmen's work had little to do with crime. Rather, the police still focused on arresting people for disorderly behavior.[65]

Nevertheless, individuals who were arrested and held in the city bridewell for violating city ordinances could often secure release by the mayor's order, a longstanding Chicago tradition, especially when the Democratic Party was in power. Each week, Mayor Harrison released a form to the bridewell naming all the prisoners he had decided to release and enumerating the cause of their release. In most cases, prisoners were released because an important person or relative requested it. Some of these recommendations came from aldermen or the heads of city departments, though the largest number came from family members. This practice did not extend to convicted criminals held in the state or federal prisons, or for serious offenses like murder, but mostly applied to people who were sent to the bridewell because they could not pay their fines. So, for all of the professionalism of the police department, the ultimate enforcement of the city's laws was still largely personal. Carter Harrison and the city council retained the power to suspend the law's penalties whenever they chose.[66]

Harrison's reforms, then, did not change the basic activity of the police or the way that the city meted out justice. Despite the increased reporting of social service activities, patrolmen's daily activity remained fundamentally the same. Elected officials retained the ability to free their friends and allies from imprisonment. Harrison made the police force stronger and more legitimate in the eyes of the population, but he did not change its contradictory relationship with that population.

Despite their increased strength and the new emphasis on their social-service role, the police remained ill-equipped to deal with many of the human problems they faced every day. Other than the brief aid they could render, such as escorting people home, giving them a ride to the hospital, or saving them from drowning, force remained the primary tool available to the police, even under the reign of Carter Harrison, and this limited their ability to solve the social problems they were confronted with.

At the same time, the growth of the Chicago Police Department made possible massive new interventions, particularly in women's lives. This made potentially public what had previously been private. In the long run, this made possible a new reform impulse, which sought to use the power of the state to force people to change their behavior, in realms that had previously been family responsibilities. Yet even as the police of the 1880s increasingly intervened in women's private lives, they were still limited by the fact that force was their primary tool.

At about 12:30 P.M. on September 14, 1885, twenty-two-year-old Stanislaus Judas delivered a child in the bathroom of her employer, a junk dealer at 54 West Indiana Street. Judas was a Polish immigrant who had been in the country for just two months and had no friends in the city. She felt incapable of raising the child, so she thrust it down into the bathroom sink and drowned it. This caused the water to overflow the sink, and led her employer to discover her state and the child's body. He immediately notified the police. Officer Michael O'Donnell went to the scene and called a wagon to take the small body to the station and wait for the coroner. The officer then called in Dr. C. W. Leigh to look over the mother. Dr. Leigh reported that Judas was in no condition to be taken to the station, so Captain Bonfield gave her permission to remain at the house of her employer and to be treated there by Dr. Leigh. Bonfield also ordered Officer O'Donnell to check in on the girl, and to consider her his prisoner. After about a week, she was taken to the County Hospital, sent before the grand jury, and eventually taken to the county jail.[67]

The police officers in this case acted with compassion and according to the rules of discipline. They did not treat Judas brutally or drag her off to prison when she was still suffering from childbirth. Yet the police did not have a solution to the problems of a poor Polish immigrant woman who was caught in a hopeless situation. Ultimately, they sent her to jail. Clearly, Judas had committed the crime of infanticide, yet even the officers involved appear to have been aware that seeing Judas's case only in that light did not adequately sum up the situation. That Judas had no family in the city to help her either raise the child or conceal the crime certainly hurt her situation. But the increasingly bureaucratic procedures of the police also meant that, once the police were notified of the affair, it could end only with her imprisonment.[68]

The police also occasionally arrested practitioners of abortion, though until the 1880s nearly all of these arrests occurred after a woman died during the procedure. As early as July 1857, the *Tribune* reported that a woman named Regnat Larson was brought to Chicago against her will and forced to receive an abortion, which killed her. The police subsequently arrested both her seducer and the physician.[69] This type of arrest or at least investigation was relatively common for the next twenty-five years. On July 8, 1875, for instance, the *Inter Ocean* reported that a woman named Mattie Ross died at the hands of an abortionist. The police immediately arrested a Dr. Ingraham on the testimony of her landlord.[70] There were a few cases where the criminal justice system acted without death, but these seem to all have been prompted by a woman's complaint. For instance, in July 1878, a Miss Williams complained to the Grand Jury that she had been seduced by the heir of a banker named Floyd Reynolds in Lafayette, Indiana, when she was thirteen years old. When he tired of her charms, he sought to get rid of the girl, but she was apparently pregnant. She said that Mr. Reynolds brought her to a Dr. O'Farrell, also in Lafayette, who gave her some pills that he said would cause a miscarriage, and then sent her to Chicago. After this testimony, the grand jury issued an indictment against both Mr. Reynolds and Dr. O'Farrell. Williams eventually withdrew her complaint against the doctor, and the jury withdrew the indictment against him.[71] These types of prosecutions were relatively common, but before the 1880s, doctors who did not kill their patients or perform abortions against their patients' will seem to have been relatively safe from police interference with abortion.

As historians James Mohr and Leslie Reagan have shown, the medical and legal position of abortion changed dramatically over the late nineteenth century. Abortion had been legal earlier in the century, and the first laws to regulate it banned abortifacient drugs as poisons, rather than banning the medical procedure of terminating pregnancy.[72] But, starting in the 1850s, the American Medical Association launched a campaign to outlaw the process, which culminated in Illinois with the passage of a bill criminalizing abortion in 1867.[73] Reagan argues that this law was largely unenforced until an 1888 exposé in the *Chicago Times* equated abortion with infanticide and portrayed abortionists as profit-hungry exploiters. From the 1890s on, the Chicago police undertook an increasingly effective campaign laden with gender and class disdain to arrest illegal abortionists and support the AMA's campaign to medicalize the entire process of pregnancy and birth.[74]

However, in order for this campaign to take place, the police force required sufficient strength and legitimacy to carry it out. In fact, the newly strengthened department of the 1880s began to adopt a more vigorous policy of prosecuting all abortion providers even before the *Times* exposé. This new policy still did not result in a large number of arrests. Between 1882 and 1888, the police arrested only six people for this crime.[75] Most of these arrests continued to come after a woman died at the hands of an abortionist.[76] Yet the arrests of the early 1880s prefigure the antiabortion campaign of the Gilded Age and the Progressive Era and demonstrated that policing of abortionists was both possible and desirable, from the perspective of those seeking to prod the state to increase its control over women's bodies.

Starting in the early 1880s, the police increasingly arrested competent abortionists along with the incompetents that killed their patients. The case of Madame Vannornum illustrates this problem. On Saturday, December 23, 1882, the police raided an apparent abortion and birth clinic at 155 Centre Avenue and arrested Madame Vannornum and Dr. George Kellogg. The police had been gathering information on this clinic from a woman they sent there to pose as a patient. In contrast to the bloody work committed by most abortionists arrested by the police, Madame Vannornum's place appears to have been run as compassionately and competently as possible. It had an attending doctor, a comfortable bed in each room, and it offered women with unwanted pregnancies the choice of aborting or of staying there until they delivered naturally. The police suspected that Madame Vannornum left some of the unwanted babies on West Side doorsteps, where they had a chance of being cared for. Other women apparently went to the clinic to give birth to children they would keep. Apparently the most heinous crime in police eyes was that Madame Vannornum supposedly blackmailed the fathers of the aborted children to pay for the abortions. For instance, she was accused of extorting $2,500 from one wealthy man. He had fathered a child with a poor woman, then abandoned her to her fate and returned to his wife and other children. When she threatened to tell his family, he came up with the money. Madame Vannornum gave $2,000 to the mother, and kept $500 for herself. Most of her clients appear to have been wealthy women, though she would occasionally accept domestic services from poorer women in lieu of monetary payment. At the time of the raid, eleven women waited in the house to deliver or abort. According to witnesses, Dr. Kellogg performed about twelve abortions a week.[77]

After the raid, the police took two young women who had been at the house to the Desplaines Street Station. Their names were not publicly disclosed, and they were evidently working for Madame Vannornum as domestics to pay off their services. So that their former associates could not influence the women, the police intended to hold them at the station until the trial, when they would be brought as witnesses against Vannornum and Kellogg. The two women were apparently held against their will. While at the station, they were seen joking and "spooning" with various officers in the corners of the station house. After nearly four months, they escaped from the station and disappeared, effectively destroying any case the state had against the alleged abortionists.[78]

The strengthened police department, then, stands as one necessary part of the story of the criminalization of abortion in late-nineteenth-century America. The medical profession and legal system could only assert their control over pregnancy if they could deploy the police to enforce the laws. In this, as in other areas, the strengthened police department laid the groundwork for the increasingly intrusive regulation of women's lives at the end of the nineteenth century, with painful consequences for Chicago's women.

This also marked a more general shift in the willingness of the state to intervene in private matters. Before the late nineteenth century, regardless of whatever laws were on the books, no U.S. municipal government would have taken action to control a process as intimate and private as pregnancy and childbirth. This was outside the state's sphere. By the 1880s, however, the increasingly self-confident police force, charged with an increasingly broad mandate to maintain order throughout the city, was willing to extend its authority not just over women's traditional redoubt of the family hearth, but over women's reproductive organs.

The strengthened police force also had the capacity to address prostitution more forcefully. According to Superintendent Ebersold, the growth in street-walkers in 1885 was "the most vexing problem the police had to deal with."[79] Ebersold claimed that streetwalkers were responsible for a large share of the city's petty crime. They were even worse than prostitutes who worked out of bawdy houses, because at least the keepers of the bawdy houses had some stake in the safety of their prostitutes and customers. Ebersold was aware that dire economic straights caused most prostitution, though he also claimed that "bad women" from Chicago enticed many women from Michigan to come to the city. The police had no ready solution to the problem. Ebersold complained that "sympathy for these unfortunate women" often caused police officers to treat them lightly. And, according to Captain Bonfield, because the police only made them move along rather than fining or arresting them, the streetwalkers of his West Side District would simply change their venue and continue in the same profession.[80]

The problem had reached such proportions that, in the fall of 1885, the police department held a conference to discuss a solution. Superintendent Ebersold advocated imposing large fines on the streetwalkers. These fines might force them into the bridewell and discourage them from continuing in their profession. This policy might also dissuade other desperate women from joining the ranks of the streetwalkers. But in order for this policy to work, the police leadership needed to convince the rank and file that imposing harsh fines on desperate young women was somehow in those women's own interests.[81]

Prostitution, like unwanted pregnancy, illustrates the limitations of police methods. There was a sharp contradiction between the responsibility of professional police to try to solve the social problems of the city and the inability of police methods to point toward any real solutions to those problems other than the use of force. This contradiction derived directly from the fact that the police developed to keep order, not to solve social problems, yet they were nonetheless charged with policing those problems. This helps explain Superintendent Ebersold's policy. He knew that the police could not end prostitution. The best they could hope for was to push it off the streets. After Harrison's reforms, the police had the strength and discipline to undertake a concerted policy of fining streetwalkers and imprisoning those who could not afford to pay their fines. This policy was aimed at forcing prostitutes to seek employment in brothels. The police department's greater strength made a much more consistent policy possible. But the result was to reinforce the power of pimps and brothel owners over the whole industry. Chicago was well-known as a "wide-open" city, with a large red-light district known as the levee near downtown. The police did not eliminate prostitution. They simply made it more orderly.

One additional example further highlights how Chicagoans who sought to control the sex life of the city increasingly turned to the newly strengthened police department. In the 1880s, roller skating was enormously popular. New types of skates, fastenings, and styles of skating came out every year. Skating rinks were especially popular among young people who had the money to pay for the skates and the entrance fees to the rinks. Many skating rinks hired bands and organized races and demonstrations of technique to attract customers.[82] Skating had reached such a level of popularity by 1884 that saloonkeepers and theater managers complained of the loss of business, and investment in these rinks was growing. In Chicago alone in 1885 there were three new rinks, each of which cost over $150,000 to build.[83]

This new fad caught the attention of some churches, which launched a campaign against skating. The churches charged that skating rinks served as places where young people could meet in an unrestrained fashion, plan elopements, and "prepare the way for long lives of wretchedness." In New York City, men had even been reported dressing up like women at the roller rinks.[84] The Roman Catholic Archdiocese of Chicago issued proclamations against skating, and some small cities charged roller rink operators higher licensing fees than saloonkeepers.[85]

In response to all of this anti-roller-skating agitation, the rink operators established a Chicago Roller-Skating Association. This association was committed to upholding the reputation of the rinks by instituting rules of behavior. Among other things, its members pledged to keep young men from approaching young women not in their company unless they obviously needed assistance. They also pledged not to serve alcohol, and to enforce speed limits in their rinks. The goal of the association was to keep the rinks profitable by making them seem respectable to the pulpit, the newspapers, and the politicians.[86] Unlike New York City, Chicago had not yet experienced the "roller-rink evil" of men "disguising" themselves as women at the rinks.[87] Still, the sensational reports of sin at the roller-skating rink were enough to provoke a flurry of political activity.

By November 1885, this anti-roller-skating campaign had made its way into the city council. Alderman Lawles submitted a proposal backed by "citizens throughout the city" that the law department should prepare an ordinance to regulate the skating rinks. According to Lawles, "a great amount of disorderly conduct is indulged in where said rinks are located," despite the counterassertions of the Chicago Roller-Skating Rink Association. The invocation of disorderly conduct in this context linked the roller-skating rink with the general disorder that appeared to be increasing in the city in the last months of 1885. The final line of Alderman Lawles's proposal called for placing roller-skating rinks under proper police regulation.[88]

Ultimately, the city council placed Lawles's proposal on file and never acted on it. Still, it illustrates how the growth of the police department under Carter Harrison enlarged the potential for social control, even when that social control was presented as the protection of middle-class young people. It is unlikely that a proposal to use the police force to regulate roller-skating rinks would have been made in 1878, when the city was on the verge of financial ruin, the police were woefully undermanned, and the memory of 1877 stood much more strongly in the minds of the defenders of law and order than the fear of sin at the roller rink. The city council's grasp had exceeded its reach in the 1870s, but then they had wanted police to regulate more obvious disorderly behavior, such as skinny-dipping, or real health threats to the population, such as feral dogs. The idea that the police could be deployed to regulate the activity of middle- and upper-class young men and women was new, and it required a general sense of ease with the professionalism of the members of the force among the "respectable" elements of Chicago's population. Certainly, the regulation of skating rinks was a much less vexing problem than prostitution or the plight of young women like Stanislaus Judas, but it nonetheless reveals the burgeoning impulse to use the newly strengthened police force to regulate and reform all manner of behavior, especially sexual.

Taken together, these examples suggest that the progressivism that would flower in subsequent decades was made possible by the increased power of the police to regulate daily life. This was the crucial difference between antebellum reform and that of the Progressive Era. Instead of convincing people to drink less, it might be possible to ban drinking and use the police to enforce that ban. Instead of a church group proselytizing the poor into following Christian morality, it might be possible to enforce that morality with the police. The state might be used not just to ensure order on the most basic level, but to address the myriad social problems of the new industrial world. The rise of powerful police departments throughout the country was a necessary precondition for these attempts to use the state to regulate and reform daily life, even if the strengthened police still ultimately proved incapable of enforcing most of these reforms.

Harrison's police also showed that, despite their contradictions and limitations, only a public institution like the police could ensure order throughout the city. The Pinkertons who encountered such hostility at the McCormick Reaper Works were not constrained by such contradictions because they were not expected to deal with the city's social problems. During the early 1880s, the Pinkertons became especially well-known for uncovering a number of forgery rings, catching bank robbers, and arresting employees who were stealing from their employers.[89] On February 25, 1882, for instance, they drew public attention by catching two men suspected of stealing a hundred thousand dollars' worth of hogs from the stockyards over the previous two years.[90] Catching forgers and corporate thieves, however, did not legitimize the Pinkertons in the eyes of the population in the way that taking people to the hospital or saving them from drowning legitimized the police.

Faced with the growing power and reputation of the city police in the 1880s, Allan Pinkerton's expensive company began to suffer from competition. When, on April 2, 1883, the police took credit for arresting a man who had robbed a Pinkerton guard, Allan Pinkerton himself wrote a response that was published in the newspaper. The guard had been robbed by a former employee on a drunken spree, Pinkerton insisted, and the Pinkertons had at once suspected and arrested him. "The city police," according to Pinkerton, "had nothing whatever to do with it."[91]

Despite their limitations, the Pinkertons acquired a reputation as strike-breakers, but unlike the police, the strikers often defeated them as they had in the 1885 McCormick strike. On May 19, 1882, for instance, a squad of Pinkertons set upon some strikers in Muskegon, Michigan, then a major port for lumber, and beat up a number of them. In response, a crowd of workers assembled and threatened to attack the Pinkerton offices in that town.[92] In the fall of 1883, they helped break a strike of coal miners in Pennsylvania.[93] Pinkertons and strikers fought a series of pitched battles during another strike in the Hocking Valley of Ohio in 1884. The most violent conflict during this strike took place between Pinkertons, the company police force, and strikers in Murray City, Ohio. A group of strikers opened fire on the company police an hour after the Pinkertons went off duty. They were only defeated when the Pinkertons returned and protected the company's property. Later, local authorities arrested the entire Pinkerton force in New Straitsville, Ohio, both for rioting against the strikers and for impersonating constables.[94] Despite these arrests, the strike was eventually broken by the employers.[95] Then, in early 1885, when Jay Gould used the Pinkertons to try to break the Great Southwest Strike in Texas, the Knights of Labor defeated Gould and the Pinkertons, leading to a massive influx into the Knights by workers in Chicago and around the country.[96]

As Carter Harrison pulled back from deploying the police against strikers, the city's employers increasingly turned to the Pinkertons. In 1884, the Cribben and Sexton Company in Chicago hired Pinkerton detectives after iron molders struck at the plant. It also issued revolvers to its strikebreakers, since the police refused to protect them. On August 13, after a five-month strike, the union men fought the Pinkertons and nonunion men in a pitched battle in which one man died. Throughout the fight, no police arrived on the scene.[97] The police were willing to let Pinkertons and strikers fight it out, and because of the Pinkertons' limited resources, strikers actually had a chance of defeating them.

Taken together, these examples demonstrate why the tasks undertaken by the police could not be performed by a private agency like the Pinkertons. Strikers were more than willing to engage them in battle, and had at least a chance of winning. Private forces like the Pinkertons did not maintain order on a daily basis in working class neighborhoods, could not intervene in domestic affairs like unwanted pregnancy, had limited forces at their disposal, and were in fact hired guns, lacking completely in legitimacy among workers.

For this reason, while Harrison's policy of maintaining police neutrality in strikes helped build up the legitimacy of the force among workers, it did not succeed in tamping down class conflict. By 1885, the McCormick workers who fought the Pinkertons and were left alone by the police had every reason to expect such behavior from the two armed forces confronting them. The Pinkertons were known as enemies to everyone involved in Chicago's labor movement, while the police were at least under the control of a mayor who many workers considered their friend. As long as the police remained neutral, labor leaders had good reason to hope for continued success. Workers' perception that they could count on the neutrality of the police helped encourage the growth of the Knights of Labor and the eight-hour-day movement because workers had a reasonable chance of establishing effective pickets and blocking strikebreakers from taking their jobs if they struck. The Knights of Labor and the other unions had proven themselves capable of defeating the Pinkertons, even if they had lost almost every fight where the police were deployed against them. Employers, meanwhile, were increasingly dissatisfied with Harrison's police policy, and they clamored for the police department to contain the growing workers' movement.

By the middle of 1885, Harrison's cross-class alliance was falling apart. Harrison barely won reelection when even Democratic employers like McCormick turned against him. The Knights of Labor had grown into a mass organization, strikes were increasing in industries around the city, the eight-hour-day agitation was attracting growing numbers of workers, and the anarchists around Albert Parsons and August Spies were growing in strength and influence. A panic ensued among the business leaders of the city and among many city officials and politicians, including some within the leadership of the police department. These leaders knew that no private force like the Pinkertons could stem the tide of the growing workers' movement, and they clamored for a change in police policy.[98]

The turning point came at the beginning of July 1885, when the workers of the Chicago West Division Railway Company went on strike to protest the firing of their union leaders during a wage dispute. This strike attracted massive support. When the company first tried to run its horse cars on Madison Street with nonunion drivers, thousands of workers and their friends crowded onto the streets in front of the cars and blocked them from moving. The Cook County sheriff, Seth Hanchett, sent some deputies to the scene, but they were too few in number to force a path through the crowd.[99] Only the Chicago Police Department had the resources to break this strike.

At first, Mayor Harrison and the police tried to remain neutral. Police arrested some demonstrators, but Harrison released them the next day. Harrison called for arbitration, but the superintendent of the streetcar company refused, even after meat-packing magnate Philip Armour and some of his associates asked the superintendent to compromise. After the first day of the confrontation on June 30, Harrison made his usual prostrike pronouncement, calling on the company to avoid violence by keeping its cars from running as long as the strike continued. The strikers also assumed that Harrison would leave them alone. "Why," one striker told a *Chicago Times* reporter, "he told our committee . . . so help him God, that he wouldn't interfere with us."[100]

As the strike wore on, however, Harrison came under increasing pressure from the city's employers. On July 1, Levi Leiter, Marshall Field's wealthy Democratic partner, who owned stock in the streetcar company and was the founding president of the Chicago Commercial Club, requested that Harrison protect the cars. That night, the mayor assured the company it would get police protection, and he met privately with Police Superintendent Doyle. Two days later, the company sent out its streetcars, protected by Captain John Bonfield and a few hundred police, and followed by the mayor himself.[101]

These police officers beat their way through a throng of strikers and their supporters. They clubbed and then arrested anyone congregating near the tracks as well as anyone shouting the words "scab" or "rat." The police inflicted many serious injuries as they moved at a slow pace in front of the streetcars. No one in the vicinity of the tracks was safe from their onslaught. They even attacked workers digging a ditch on the street. After this violent confrontation, the strike was broken.[102]

The suppression of this strike marked a drastic shift in Carter Harrison's police policy that would soon extend to other strikes. As an indication of this change of direction, Harrison promoted Captain Bonfield to the position of inspector soon after he broke the strike. A few months later, Austin Doyle resigned and was replaced as superintendent by Frederick Ebersold.

However, the key element of this shift was not simply Bonfield's promotion or his willingness to use brutality. Mayor Harrison himself had ordered the suppression of the strike, and he had authorized the police to deploy nearly half the force to carry it out.[103] Harrison publicly defended the action of the police, arguing that it was their responsibility to enforce law and order. He lauded Bonfield for using clubs, instead of firing into the crowd, as some observers had urged. Superintendent Doyle also defended the repression of the strike. He insisted that any innocent person in the way of the police had been given ample opportunity to move on and that the police were entitled to arrest crowds because there was a city ordinance prohibiting loitering.[104] Despite his efforts to make the police more popular, there is no reason to believe that Doyle resigned because he was unwilling to carry out the new policies. In fact, upon his resignation, Doyle took a job as superintendent of the new Chicago Passenger Railway Company.[105] Journalist John Flinn attributed the hands-off approach of the police in the first days of the strike to the officers' natural sympathy for their fellows, which may have been real, but the initial policy of police neutrality was consistent with the standing police policy toward strikes.[106] And this sympathy was evidently not strong enough to overcome the discipline and esprit de corps that Harrison and Doyle had instilled in the force, once the determined Bonfield was put in charge of the squad protecting the strikebreakers.

The Chicago labor movement was split in its reaction to the clubbing. While the anarchists criticized the entire police force and Mayor Harrison, a section of the unions led by the Trades and Labor Assembly was unwilling to break with Harrison and instead laid the entire blame for the incident on Bonfield. They organized a petition drive and gathered statements from witnesses who detailed Bonfield's brutality. They submitted this petition to the city council's Committee on Police with over a thousand signatures from residents of the West Side and statements from five witnesses requesting that the city council and Harrison fire Bonfield from the force. One of the statements came from C. K. Billings, vice president of the Peoples Gas Light and Coke Company. He complained that Bonfield had assaulted and beaten some of his employees who were digging a ditch to lay pipe alongside the tracks.[107] Harrison had publicly upbraided Billings on July 3 for complaining about the police behavior when Billings owned stock in the Chicago West Division Railroad Company and thus personally benefited from the defeat of the strike.[108] A grocer named Robert Ellis claimed to have been struck by Captain Bonfield from behind as he was getting some vegetables from outside his shop. The Trades and Labor Assembly, then, tried to play down the class nature of the dispute, and gathered statements from reputable businessmen who objected to Bonfield's brutality although they did not question the role of the police in general.[109] This tactic yielded no results. Six months later, the Trades and Labor Assembly was still writing the city council asking what it had decided to do about Bonfield. Despite these union leaders' best efforts to avoid splitting with the mayor over this strike, the dispute eventually led to the collapse of labor's alliance with Mayor Carter Harrison.[110]

Meanwhile, on July 25, a number of the most important businessmen in the city, including Philip Armour, submitted a polite and respectful petition to Mayor Harrison requesting that Bonfield be kept on. "No good citizen having the credit and welfare of this city at heart," they wrote, "or having a proper respect for law and order could or would encourage or countenance mob rule and wanton destruction of property." According to the petitioners, "the surest, safest, and most sensible way to prevent bloodshed and loss of life and property in such an emergency is by prompt, vigorous and unfaltering action" by those like Bonfield. They insisted that it would set a "most dangerous precedent" if a man like Bonfield was fired for doing his duty. The city council received another letter thanking Bonfield that was signed by, among others, representatives of the Excelsior Iron Works, the Crescent Steel Works, and the Verona Tool Works.[111] The city's employers took heart from Harrison's change in policy and urged him to continue in this new direction. They recognized Bonfield as a man they could count on, and they were determined to defend him.

At the end of January 1886, while the unions continued to excoriate him, Captain Bonfield felt obliged to write a defense of his actions. He argued that the lives of members of the Trades and Labor Assembly were actually saved by his vigorous efforts, because otherwise further blood would have been spilled. According to Bonfield, Superintendent Doyle had called a meeting of all the police captains on the night of July 2 to discuss the situation. Doyle told them all to assemble with their men the next morning, warning them that the "reputation of the police and safety of the city" depended on them. The captains had performed their duties "faithfully and tearlessly," and ensured that those under them did so, as well. Bonfield said that, if they had failed, the militia would have been called, "with ball cartridge and bayonets instead of clubs," and that hundreds of people would have been killed. He referred to the actions of the militia in putting down the riots of 1877 in Pittsburgh, Cincinnati, and other cities when the clubs of the police proved insufficient and many people were killed. Bonfield also pointed out that he was in command of the force that confronted the strikers because the strike was taking place in his district and, as captain, it was his responsibility to lead the assault.[112]

Bonfield's insistence that he was carrying out orders makes more sense than the Trades and Labor Assembly's assertion that he alone was responsible for the brutality of the previous July 3. As the events of the ensuing months would make clear, Carter Harrison had by this time changed the policy of the police toward strikers. Before the streetcar strike, he had attempted to win over a segment of the unions and the working class from the socialists by allowing them to strike and showing that he had more to offer than men like anarchist leader Albert Parsons. But by mid-1885, under the almost unanimous pressure of the city's businessmen, he decided to change course. Bonfield may have acted more brutally than Harrison would have preferred, but in breaking the strike, he was, in all likelihood, merely following orders.

This is shown most clearly by the fact that after this strike, Harrison promoted Bonfield and disciplined police officers who refused to put down strikes. During a strike at the Maxwell Box factory in the winter of 1885–1886, Harrison removed Lieutenant Archibald Darrow from command of the Hinman Street Station after he refused to deploy the police against strikers who attacked strikebreakers. Local businesspeople urged the police to remove him, so the police apparently sent a spy to see what Darrow was doing. Darrow suspected the spy and told strikers that he was a scab, after which they attacked him. Superintendent Ebersold then had Darrow and two men under him removed because he refused to arrest the attackers when he knew who they were. Darrow was precisely the kind of officer who could move up during the early period of Carter Harrison's rule, since he was popular with the local population. But his unwillingness to toe the line once police policy changed cost him his job.[113] The strength of the personal aspersions cast on John Bonfield resonate so strongly through the years that even Richard Schneirov, whose *Labor and Urban Politics* is an excellent monograph on Carter Harrison's mayorship, attributes Darrow's removal to Captain Bonfield, rather than Superintendent Ebersold and, ultimately, Mayor Carter Harrison. After Darrow's removal, individual officers knew that they were now expected to move against strikers when ordered to do so, or face the consequences.

A few months later, another labor disturbance broke out at the McCormick Reaper Works and illustrated to all concerned that Harrison's police policy had changed definitively. On February 12, 1886, McCormick locked out his workers to preempt their call for a strike because he refused to meet their list of demands. He then prepared to reopen the works on March 1 with strikebreakers. The day before this attempt, Frederick Ebersold, the new superintendent of police, called the attention of every captain to the revised statutes and the Criminal Code of Illinois concerning large assemblies. This code ordered that wherever assemblies of twelve or more armed men or thirty or more unarmed men appeared dangerous or unruly, it was the responsibility of the authorities to go among them and order them to disperse in the name of the state, and to arrest all those who refused and fine them $500 or imprison them for a year. In preparation for the enforcement of this statute, Ebersold ordered 350 uniformed men to assemble on Blue Island Avenue from every precinct except the Irish neighborhood of Bridgeport, where many strikers lived. He also sent out many additional policemen in civilian clothes to mingle with the crowd.[114]

By 7 A.M. on March 1, about two hundred police, under the command of the same Captain O'Donnell who had refused to break the strike one year earlier, faced about three hundred locked-out men and their supporters on Blue Island Avenue. The police pushed the crowd about two blocks from the factory entrance onto open prairie. Shortly thereafter, a small stream of strikebreakers entered the factory. By 10 A.M., the *Tribune* estimated that two hundred men were in the plant, compared to the fourteen hundred who normally worked there. While the reaper works resumed a limited level of production, Captain John Bonfield and a squad of police attacked the Union House saloon near the plant, where strikers had gathered and were shouting "rats!" at the strikebreakers passing by outside. Bonfield and his men brutally beat scores of strikers.[115] At 11 A.M., McCormick offered a free meal to all two hundred police who were still guarding the entrance to his factory. They entered a dozen at a time, while their compatriots continued to guard the strikers. More strikebreakers came to work during the middle of the day so that, by late afternoon, when Superintendent Averill gave newspaper reporters a tour of the factory, between 300 and 400 men were at work.[116] Since the factory was able to continue its operations with these scabs after March 1, the strike was effectively broken. By March 5, about eight hundred men were at work, although the Knights of Labor still insisted that McCormick would be unable to ship out his completed machines because union switchmen would refuse to move cars carrying them. The lockout would continue for months, but the factory was able to operate continuously from that point on.[117]

The vigorous intervention of the police in this lockout had made all the difference. On March 5, 1886, Cyrus McCormick said that he "thought that, [but] for them, he would not be running his works at present."[118] The locked-out workers shared McCormick's appraisal. On March 2, the day after the plant reopened, anarchists organized a mass meeting of strikers to "protest against the armed force which had been enlisted against them." The anarchists wrote in their advertisement for the meeting that "these armed men, employed by the state, [the policemen] came forth at the behest of capital, struck down the peaceable citizen, clubbed and searched them, and cast them into the patrol wagons and hustled them off to prison."[119] All sides agreed that the change in police policy between April 1885 and March 1886 had been the difference between a victory for the strikers and a victory for the company.

This change in police policy broke Carter Harrison's ability to hold his electoral alliance together. The antipolice writings and speeches of Parsons and the anarchists made more sense to workers when the police openly attacked them. Ordering the police to break this series of strikes helped re-create the class divisions over the police that had been so apparent when Harrison first took office in 1879.

But the police of 1886 were not the police of 1879. They were more than twice as numerous, more disciplined, instilled with a greater esprit de corps, and more tied to the population where they worked. Many observers, including the Trades and Labor Council, viewed Mayor Carter Harrison as a friend of the working class. He certainly did curtail the repression of the period immediately following 1877. He allowed the unions to grow and kept the police from repressing strikes or immigrant leisure activities such as drinking. The foregoing story, however, suggests that Carter Harrison's administration had a very different long-term effect on Chicago, its working class, and their unions. It was in part through his electoral alliance with the unions that Harrison was able to build the police into a legitimate, powerful force that had roots in the population in every neighborhood. Whatever his intentions in building this force during the early 1880s, when his cross-class alliance became untenable in the middle of 1885, Harrison sided openly and vigorously with the employers. And he used the force he had helped create to repress his former allies. The long-term significance of his mayoralty lay much more in the strengthening of the police force than in any temporary gains made by the workers of Chicago.

CHAPTER 7

Chicago's Anarchists Shape the Police Department

The Chicago Police Department was transformed by its struggle with the city's anarchist and socialist movement in the 1870s and 1880s.[1] This struggle was distinct from the department's interaction with the wider labor movement and the working class generally. As previous chapters have shown, the relationship between the police and the city's working class was complex, often contradictory, and varied greatly from one period to the next. The relationship between the police and the militant workers' organizations, on the other hand, varied solely in degree. The police and the anarchists consistently faced each other with unalloyed hostility.

From their emergence on the city's political scene in the mid-1870s, Chicago's anarchists served as a constant potential threat to the order the police defended. As we have seen, the radical workers' movement initially tried to take control of the city government by mounting an electoral challenge to the People's Party in the 1870s. When that failed, they organized a series of demonstrations on behalf of the unemployed aimed at the Relief and Aid Society and the city government. These demonstrations sometimes confronted the police. But while they challenged the policies of first the People's Party and then the Republicans, the anarchists themselves were not a serious threat to order for most of the 1870s. The first real mass confrontation between the anarchists and the police took place during the 1877 upheaval, when the police broke up their meetings with violence. But in the 1880s, the anarchist organizations grew rapidly in size and increasingly set themselves against the police.

The conflict between the police and the anarchists played a crucial role in the development of the police department for two reasons. First, it gave the police a clear enemy. The crises of the 1870s and Carter Harrison's reforms showed that the police had to be legitimate in the eyes of the population to maintain order effectively. In order to ensure that legitimacy, the police could not be openly at odds with either the immigrant majority or the reformist part of the city's labor movement. But they could be consistently at odds with the anarchists. Second, the threat of mass strikes, riot, and revolution pushed the city's elite to seek a strong force that could be relied on to respond to the workers' movement. The disturbances of 1877 had helped consolidate elite support for the police, but the pressure of the anarchists served as a constant goad to strengthen the department at all costs. The workers' militias and the anarchists' open talk of dynamite and street fighting helped overcome elite reticence about taxes. Many wealthy Chicagoans had been willing to see the city government grind to a halt because they refused to pay taxes during the 1870s depression while the People's Party was in power. As we have seen, once they were convinced of the real threat of revolution, the city's elite was willing to raise funds for arms to give the police. They also made sure that the police department never again lacked for funds, no matter who occupied the mayor's office. And many police officers themselves kept the anarchist threat in the public mind in order to justify greater funding for the department, though they tended to deny that the anarchists had a large following. As Carl Smith has pointed out, the police, the eventual prosecution after Haymarket (see chapter 8), and much of the press portrayed the anarchists as both few in number and seriously threatening because of the effectiveness of dynamite.[2]

In fact, the anarchists were a real threat to the established order, and not just because of dynamite. Workers and the unemployed had already demonstrated in 1877 that they were capable of exploding in anger en masse. After the assault on the 1885 streetcar strike, Carter Harrison's policies were increasingly discredited and his attempts to diffuse class tension failed. The anarchists became a serious force, with a following in the thousands, and a hearing among wide swaths of the city's population. As many as a hundred thousand workers in the city would prove themselves willing to strike for the eight-hour day, which, though not in itself a revolutionary demand, was one the city's employers were absolutely determined not to yield on. The anarchists were the only group that advocated taking whatever steps were necessary to win that fight, and had things progressed differently, they might have gained the leadership of that massive movement. After observing the Paris Commune, Marx had written that "the working class cannot simply lay hold of the ready-made state machinery, and wield it for its own purposes."[3] Rather, the working class had to eliminate that machinery, and build its own anew. Chicago's anarchists had taken that lesson very much to heart. Chicago never reached a revolutionary situation, where the anarchists might have actually led the city's workers to put this into practice. In the spring of 1886, however, it was not at all clear that they would fail to do so.

The anarchists never gained the lead of the majority of Chicago's workers, in part because the working class remained deeply divided by ethnicity throughout this period. As Eric Hirsch argues, Irish Chicagoans developed their own organizations based on their concentration in low-wage industries, the density of Irish neighborhoods, the Irish reaction to nativism, and the Roman Catholic Church. This ethnic and religious identity led many Irish workers to take a much more conservative political stance than their German compatriots, and the Knights of Labor in Chicago likewise took a less radical position in order to attract Irish members. Irish laborers joined in all the mass strikes and demonstrations of the age, but Irish political activists generally worked either in nationalist organizations that endeavored to free Ireland, or within the city's political machine. As we've seen with the case of Francis O'Neill, many ambitious Irish Chicagoans were blocked from advancement in any realm other than through patronage jobs, and increasingly through employment with the police department.[4] As much as Anglo reformers might bemoan the Irish influence on Chicago's politics, this influence ultimately led many of Chicago's poorest workers away from the influence of the anarchists and toward a reformist version of labor politics that included employment on the police department.[5]

The changing Irish relationship with the police department helped both limit Irish involvement in anarchism and deeply shaped the department. During the 1880s, the share of Irish police officers began going up dramatically, and this trend continued well into the twentieth century, despite the declining Irish share of the city's population as other immigrant groups arrived. The police department did not record the ethnicity of its officers or patrolmen, but the discussions of the police from throughout this period and the lists of officer's names in Flinn's history of the department make the trend clear.[6] At the same time, the share of people of Irish nationality among those arrested declined. In 1865, the Irish accounted for more than 49 percent of those arrested, while by 1886 the Irish share was down to a little over 10 percent.[7] A large part of this is probably explained by the police recording the children of Irish immigrants as "Americans" rather than "Irish" and by the decline of the Irish share of the city's population, as the Irish would continue to figure prominently on both sides of the law for decades to come. Nonetheless, the prevalence of Irish policemen and the declining sense that the police department was primarily targeting them, which would have been largely true through the end of the Civil War, undoubtedly reduced the appeal of anarchism among Chicago's Irish.

Native-born Anglo workers were also much less attracted to radical politics than the Germans. Anglo workers did join unions, go on strike, and organize politically against their employers, as seen by their leadership of the 1867 movement for the eight-hour day, their involvement in the reformist Trades and Labor Assembly, and their successful creation of a large set of skilled trade unions. Yet many also undoubtedly accepted the nativist ideology so prevalent throughout the period as well as the idea that it was possible to move up with hard work, determination, sobriety, and education. Native-born workers also had middle- and upper-class counterparts who shared many of their traditions and assumptions, including Protestantism. Like the Irish, these Anglo workers were also involved in the city's political machine and formed a large bloc of Carter Harrison's voters. Some Anglos did join the radical movement, most famously Albert Parsons, but they were a small minority.[8]

. The anarchist movement, then, was largely German, but the German population was not largely anarchist: it was instead deeply divided by class and politics. There were prominent German businessmen and many Germans, like Michael Schaack, joined the police department and eventually played important roles in suppressing the anarchist movement. Nonetheless, the anarchists attracted a considerable following among Chicago's German population. The *Arbeiter Zeitung* and other German language anarchist newspapers each had circulations of over twenty thousand by the mid-1880s, far outstripping the English-language *Alarm*. Six of the eight men convicted after Haymarket were German, most of the anarchist unions were German, and a large majority of anarchist meetings were held in German and took place in German neighborhoods.[9] Yet it would be a grave error to view Chicago's labor problem or the question of order through an essentially ethnic lens. While German involvement in radical politics certainly contributed to nativism before and after Haymarket, and while that nativism in turn encouraged German workers to form a distinct brand of radical politics, it was their politics, not their ethnicity, that set the anarchists against the police.

Even before the Chicago anarchists had coalesced as a cohesive organization, the police and a segment of the press blamed them for the city's labor upheavals. During the strike of 1877, future anarchist leader Albert Parsons gave a speech advocating that workers join the Workingmen's Party and use their ballots "for the purpose of obtaining State control of all means of production, transportation, communication and exchange." The following day, he found himself fired and blacklisted from his job at the *Chicago Times*. Soon after, two armed men brought Parsons to the office of Superintendent of Police Hickey, along with another activist of the Workingmen's Party, Philip Van Patten. In a room filled with a crowd of scowling officers along with the mayor and the corporation counsel James Bonfield (John Bonfield's brother), Superintendent Hickey asked Parsons if he didn't "know better than to come up here from Texas and incite the working people to insurrections." At the end of the interview, several officers urged that Parsons be lynched. Bonfield warned that Parsons and Van Patten would be held "responsible in the eyes of the law for any destruction of property or loss of life" ensuing from the strike. Finally, the superintendent said that his men had been shadowing Parsons and urged him to leave the city for his own safety, since "those Board of Trade men would as leave hang you to a lamp post as not." The two men were released to witness the next day's defeat of the strikers at the battle of the Halsted viaduct and the subsequent raiding of Turner's Hall.[10]

This interview reveals an early strand of police thinking that blamed all labor troubles on the influence of the socialists and anarchists. According to this line of reasoning, Parsons and Van Patten were responsible for bringing the strikes of 1877 to Chicago by making speeches and distributing handbills. If that were true, then the most efficient way of dealing with labor troubles would be to eliminate the influence of the leftists. The leaders of the police demonstrated by their actions that they were not so naive, but they nonetheless reinforced this view of strikes. In his book on the strike wave of 1877, *Strikers, Communists, Tramps and Detectives*, Allan Pinkerton blamed Chicago's "communists" for all of the labor trouble that shook the city. Although not a policeman, Pinkerton most clearly expressed the police view of leftist influence in the working class. According to Pinkerton, Chicago contained "as pestilential a crew of communists as any city in the world." "It was this class and no other, that precipitated the riot in Chicago." According to those like Pinkerton who saw labor troubles this way, there would never have been any strikes, and there certainly would not have been violence, but for the baleful influence of the communists. "In every instance the men quietly quit work, and remained peaceably about their different resorts," Pinkerton wrote of the railroad strikers, "while it is only a simple matter of justice to state that, in all the subsequent riot and trouble, the striking trainmen were guilty of no single act of violence." Rather, all the violence was caused by the communists. And, Pinkerton continued, "it is a notable fact in connection with these communists, that their viciousness and desperation were largely caused by the rantings of a young American communist named Parsons."[11]

This set of ideas remained a central strand of the police viewpoint on labor troubles before Haymarket, but it was tempered by the marked growth of nonrevolutionary unions such as those allied with Harrison. The rise of these nonrevolutionary unions led even hostile observers to recognize some union activity as legitimate and to admit that workers had real grievances. Detective Michael Schaack gave this more nuanced view its clearest rendition by a police officer in his book *Anarchy and Anarchists*. Schaack wrote that workers had legitimate problems, even concluding that those problems gave the anarchists the opportunity to organize. But he still insisted that the open class warfare of the period was caused by the anarchists. In his description of the McCormick lockout of 1886, for instance, Schaack argued that "the real state of affairs in that trouble was greatly exaggerated," and that the anarchists instigated "violent resistance to the installation of new men, or 'scabs.'" For Schaack, workers' legitimate grievances could have been peacefully resolved but for the meddling of the anarchists.[12] Schaack also criticized the anarchists for spreading class consciousness among workers. To him, America was the land of individual opportunity. If workers would only concentrate on upward mobility instead of fighting their bosses, there would be no labor trouble. If the anarchists were stopped from spreading their doctrines, workers would embrace the American dream and concentrate on moving up in the world.[13] From 1877 to 1886, then, a segment of the police and their Pinkerton allies viewed the anarchists as the primary cause of the labor troubles that constituted the most threatening expression of disorder in the city. Simply stated, in the opinion of the police and the Pinkertons, the anarchists were the most dangerous force in Chicago, and if they were removed, class conflict would cease.

While Chicago's business community and the Republican Party had a long tradition of associating anarchism, labor troubles, and immigration, under Carter Harrison, the city government in general downplayed this connection. This succeeded for a time in winning many Germans and the more conservative unions to join Harrison's coalition. Historian Carl Smith points out that after the bombing at Haymarket, much of the press labeled the anarchists as foreign, and attacked them as such, but this was not the police department's line of reasoning.[14] Neither Schaack nor the rest of the police stigmatized the anarchists for being foreigners, although most of them were. Because most of the city's population and a large portion of the police department were also foreign born, Schaack instead attacked the foreign origin of the anarchists' ideas, which was a crucial difference. In addition, the prominence of Albert Parsons, and the anarchists' own emphasis on the international nature of the workers' movement, undercut the potential nativist critique of the anarchist movement, at least within Chicago. This meant that, for all concerned, the

central questions were political, not ethnic, even if the majority of the anarchists were Germans.

Albert Parsons was the single person most representative of the anarchist
threat in Chicago. Parsons's role as the most hated symbol of revolution for
the city's "powers that be" began during the upheaval of 1877. Between 1877
and 1886, he became the most prominent English-speaking revolutionary in
the city. Born in Texas, Parsons had fought for the Confederacy and served
as Jefferson Davis's secretary during the Civil War. He then worked for the
Reconstruction governments in Texas in various capacities, including secretary of the Texas State Senate and chief deputy collector for the Internal
Revenue Service. He married Lucy Gonzalez in 1872, a woman he described
as a "charming young Spanish-Indian maiden," but who police insisted was
black. Regardless of her race, Lucy Parsons remained a prominent anarchist
organizer long after Albert's death. In 1873, he left Texas for Chicago and
got a job as a typographer with the *Chicago Times*, where he joined the Typographical Union Number 16 and became interested in the "Labor Question." Parsons would come to represent the native-born American strand of a
movement that would claim 2,800 members in Chicago by May 1886.[15] Other
than Parsons, the movement was dominated by German immigrants imbued
with the ideas of Marx and reformist socialist Ferdinand Lasalle. In October
1884, the members of the International Working People's Association (or the
International) elected him editor of the *Alarm*, the new English-language
newspaper for Chicago. In its pages, Parsons attacked the city's capitalists,
the state apparatus at all levels, and Carter Harrison's cross-class alliance.[16]

Chicago's anarchist movement mounted the first sustained intellectual
criticism of Chicago's need for a police department since the city had created
the force in 1855. This criticism regularly filled the pages of the *Arbeiter-
Zeitung*, the anarchists' German language paper, and the *Alarm*. The anarchists attacked the police on two fronts: as an institution, and as individuals
who took advantage of their power. Their main line of attack charged that
the police were part of a broader set of institutions that defended capitalist
exploitation of the working class. Parsons and the other writers attacked all
of these institutions in the pages of the *Alarm*, including the army, the state
militia, "statute law," the prison system, and the Pinkertons, in addition to
the police force. But they also attacked individual officers, and those attacks
raised the immediate ire of the police more directly than the International's
ideological criticism of the capitalist state.

The basic line of the anarchists' reasoning was evident in an early *Alarm*
article on Lieutenant General Philip Sheridan, commanding general of the

army. The *Alarm* quoted at length Sheridan's summary of the main threats facing the country in the mid-1880s. There was little threat of a foreign invasion, he concluded, but the danger of a military conflict between labor and capital was very real. Sheridan pointed out that commercial buildings might be blown up by "an infuriated people with means carried with perfect safety to themselves *in the pockets* of their clothing," a reference to dynamite.[17] The *Alarm* used this quotation to attack the institution of the military, but not Sheridan's personal character. "The army, navy and police," commented the *Alarm*, "are instruments of tyrants to enslave their fellow men." The newspaper conceded that General Sheridan was "a brave man and a skilled general," but his position rendered him the enemy of the working class. The *Alarm* went on to celebrate the dynamite which Sheridan feared as the great equalizer between the propertyless people and the armed defenders of property. The article closed by declaring, "hail to the social revolution! Hail to the deliverer—*Dynamite!*"[18]

This invocation of dynamite was intended to assure readers of the *Alarm* that it was possible for workers to defeat the militia or army, rather than as an immediate call to action. During this period, the International was still trying to build anarchist workers' morale after their defeat in 1877. Still, articles like this antagonized all who stood for order. The paeans to dynamite reinforced elite support for the police, and undoubtedly alienated many workers as well.

This raises the question of whether or not the anarchists actually organized a conspiracy to bomb the police on May 4, 1886.[19] Certainly, the anarchists were determined revolutionaries who carried out concerted propaganda against the state and called for the use of violence against it, and historian Timothy Messer-Kruse presents considerable, convincing evidence that the anarchists were making bombs and preparing for armed confrontation, something they admitted freely.[20] Yet to assert that the trial fit the evidentiary standards of the day serves more to illustrate the anarchists' point that the justice system was patently unfair than to indict them in the eyes of history.[21] The prosecution's case actually linking the defendants to the bombing was sketchy at best, and the assistant prosecutor admitted that the state prosecuted the leading anarchists in order to decapitate the movement, not because they were at the meeting where the bombing was supposed to have been planned.[22] The anarchists did not receive a fair trial.

Messer-Kruse's argument that the Haymarket bombing was part of a transnational conspiracy fails to accurately capture the nuances and divisions within Chicago's anarchist and socialist movement because he does not locate Chicago anarchism within the context of the city's working-class political economy.[23] Messer-Kruse defines anarchists as those who reject legal reforms and voting, advocate collective and individual violence, and believe in the imminence of mass insurrection. This formalistic definition misses the point of the anarchists' critique of the policies of Carter Harrison and the unions allied with him. He attributes the anarchists' isolation from the mainstream of Chicago's labor movement entirely to the drift in anarchist politics over the mid-1880s and fails to account for their reaction to Carter Harrison's policies and the role Harrison played in shifting the political landscape of the city. Instead of antiunion advocates of "propaganda of the deed" versus prounion, proreform socialists, the split was between trade-union-based reformers allied with the Democrats and anarchist and socialist revolutionaries, a division that would continue into the twentieth century.[24]

Bombing as a precursor to a more general uprising fits with the anarchists' basic ideas, but the general uprising never occurred, and the anarchists generally advocated overthrowing capitalism by means of mass strikes and worker uprisings, like that of 1877, rather than advocating individual terror bombings. They were dedicated to winning workers to their ideas and organizing them to confront the capitalists and the state. In this light, it seems much more likely that an individual or group of people linked to the anarchists and influenced by their ideas threw the bomb that day, and unlikely that Spies, Parsons, and other leaders of the movement had abandoned the politics of mass mobilization and resorted to disorganized individual terrorism.

The anarchists certainly were, however, opposed to the institution of the police, and they resisted it in many ways, not just through the use of violence. For instance, to further the aim of showing workers that they could run a society without the capitalist state, the members of the International organized activities that would prove working people did not need the police to protect them. The main justification the authorities gave for expanding the police department was that, if left to their own devices, ordinary people would descend into drunken riots and orgies, destroy property, and hurt or kill each other. They maintained that police were needed to ensure that everyone respected basic morality. In order to undercut this idea, the International hosted regular dances, marches, and picnics, at which they refused entrance to the police.[25] For example, two thousand people reportedly attended the anarchists' picnic at Ogden's Grove on July 26, 1885.[26] At this picnic, they refused police protection and reported no untoward incidents.[27] The *Alarm* made the case that this peaceable event proved that people were perfectly capable of taking care of themselves without the help of the police even when they drank large quantities of beer and wine.

Many anarchists, including Albert Parsons, had personal reasons to hate and fear the department, but this personal animosity ran in both directions because, in addition to their ideological critiques, the anarchists also assailed acts of brutality by individual police officers. On December 13, 1884, the *Alarm* featured a headline that read "OUTRAGED. A Working Girl Imprisoned And Then Brutally Ravished By A Police Officer." The article went on to describe the case of Martha Seidle, a seventeen-year-old German maid accused by her employer of taking a silver ring. Seidle reported that the arresting police officers took her to the Chicago Avenue Station, where Desk Sergeant William Patton raped her repeatedly until she passed out. She was held in the station for four days before seeing a police magistrate, who assigned her $600 in bail. She could not pay this sum and so was held in jail, where she fell ill. Her story was discovered because the doctor who was eventually called to tend to her in jail reported that she had been raped.[28]

A week after the incident, August Spies, editor of the *Abieter Zeitung* and Parsons's close collaborator in the International Working People's Association, heard her story and brought the case to the attention of a judge, who issued a warrant for Patton's arrest. The *Alarm* doubted that justice would ever be done, especially since the police and the city's other newspapers immediately began to cast aspersions on Seidle's character and to charge that her extreme illness predated her arrest and had caused her to hallucinate. With Patton likely to avoid punishment, the *Alarm* invoked "Judge Lynch." Thus, not only had a leading socialist directly involved himself in indicting a police officer for rape, but the anarchists' English-language organ recommended the lynching of that officer if justice should miscarry.[29] Even in this period, while Mayor Harrison's police reform was in full swing, the anarchists remained willing to antagonize the department and its members with actions as well as words.

The *Alarm* was correct in its prediction of how the case would proceed. A string of police witnesses swore that Patton could not have committed the crime, attacking Seidle's character. The defense attorney searched for any small inconsistency in her testimony and accused her of being hysterical before her arrest.[30] Patton was acquitted, and just a few months later, Seidle was charged with larceny for stealing $50 worth of money, clothing, and jewelry from her employer.[31] As the anarchists had predicted, the police department had rallied around one of their own at the expense of a vulnerable young immigrant woman.

This dispute formed one part of a long running anarchist critique of the general way the police treated women. The members of the International consistently defended women's right to participate in politics and the labor movement, including the right of suffrage. But the police, as we have seen, were sworn to defend elite notions of order. Women's proper behavior formed an integral part of that order. The most basic conflict between the police and the anarchists stemmed from the fact that the two groups denied each other's organizational right to exist. But the police and the anarchists also fundamentally disagreed over the proper role of women in society, and fought over the most effective way to deal with the problems facing the thousands of impoverished and desperate women in Chicago.

Many women played important roles in the revolutionary movement. According to historian Bruce Nelson, women formed a small portion of the actual membership in anarchist organizations in Chicago, but a few of them occupied prominent roles. Lizzie Swank was one important example. She was assistant editor of the *Alarm* and a frequent contributor to the paper before the Haymarket bombing, eventually becoming associate editor. Lucy Parsons was another prominent anarchist militant, and she would become even more famous after her husband's execution. Both of these women gave speeches to mixed gender crowds. Other women taught in the anarchist Sunday schools and participated in theater groups. The very choice of the name "International Working People's Association" instead of "Working-men's" marked the anarchists' attempts to include women as equals.[32]

Captain Michael Schaack's 1889 book on the anarchists, *Anarchy and Anarchists, A History of the Red Terror and the Socialist Revolution in America and Europe*, devoted a section to these "female anarchists," deploying images of "unwomanly" women in order to attack the movement. According to Schaack, the many "squaws" active in the movement "proved the most bloodthirsty."[33] He recounted an episode in which a Pinkerton agent was discovered among the anarchists. Schaack wrote that the women at the meeting wanted to kill the agent, but the men were more restrained and allowed him to escape with his life. Schaack also criticized the personal appearance of the revolutionary women. "At one meeting, held on North Halsted Street," he reported, "there were thirteen of these creatures in petticoats present, the most hideous-looking females that could possibly be found." He particularly criticized their "unwomanly" behavior and appearance, noting that they held snuff-boxes, that one was six feet tall, and that another wore her husband's boots.[34] These descriptions dehumanized the anarchists and so helped justify their later repression, while they also reinforced the gender norms of the day, which the police sustained. For Schaack and his readers, the idea of six-foot-tall women speaking in front of crowds, snorting snuff, and wearing their husbands' boots was almost as threatening to order as the socialist call to expropriate capitalist property, and it presented a more visceral threat than general calls for collective ownership of the means of production.

The anarchists, meanwhile, accused the police of keeping thousands of Chicago women in misery. In November 1885, the anarchists organized a mass meeting to discuss the problem of prostitution, soon after the police held their conference on the same subject (discussed in the previous chapter). Both the anarchists and the police agreed that poverty was the basic cause of prostitution, but the anarchists contended that the men of the "better classes," among whom there was "ten times as much prostitution" as among the poor, caused prostitution by denying women an alternative way of earning a living. Locking these women up would not help them; removing the social system that created these problems would. The hypocrisy of "bourgeois morality" to the anarchists lay precisely in expecting women to conform to a standard of behavior that the rule of the bourgeoisie rendered inaccessible, and then in sending the police against those unable to meet the standard.[35] Thus, the anarchists and the police had opposite views of the problems facing women, their causes, and their potential solutions, and these views contributed to these groups' hostility toward each other.

In addition to their overall critique of the state and their discussions of police brutality, especially toward women, the anarchists condemned the other parts of the forces of order. They made a series of criticisms of the prisons and jails that contained both specific attacks on the capitalists who profited from prison labor and general critiques of the role of prisons in a capitalist society. This line of reasoning set the police within a broader system of justice weighted against the poor.

As we saw in the previous chapter, the police deployed punishment and force as their only tool, and many of their leaders thought that this was the best way to help prostitutes in particular learn the error of their ways. The anarchists attacked this logic directly. "It is a lie to say that a person is punished for his own good," the *Alarm* wrote in an article comparing prisoners to Jesus and Socrates. "He is punished for the sole purpose of sustaining the position of those who punish him."[36] A few months later the anarchists pointed out that, of the 7,860 people committed to the bridewell in 1884 for petty crimes and charged a small fine, only two hundred were able to pay those fines. The remainder languished in prison, forced to work to pay off their fines, "in every instance . . . the victims of poverty."[37] Thus, the police and the prison system oppressed those who lacked the cash to buy their release, and funneled the poor into a labor system exploited by a few well-connected industrialists. A few months later, the *Alarm* reported that residents in the bridewell were often flogged or starved to death, and that all were "driven as galley slaves in the service of the Amazonian Hosiery Corporation, an institution whose stock and goods are handled by the millionaire merchant prince, Marshall Field." This article went on to point out that Field was a member of the Humane Society for the prevention of cruelty to animals, but that "the inmates of the bridewell are not animals but human beings, and therefore do not come within the protecting care of this Christian philanthropist."[38] These were just a few in a series of articles critiquing the bridewell, the politically connected beneficiaries of prison labor, and the use of the police, prisons, and courts to control the problems caused by poverty.

The *Alarm* here highlighted one of the most glaring contradictions in the late-nineteenth-century ideology of free labor. Throughout the industrializing north, increasing numbers of mostly poor young men were subjected to conditions of prison labor based on physical and mental torture for the profit of contractors. The most famous prison of the era was Sing Sing, in New York State. Its inmates, like those in the Chicago bridewell, worked for private contractors and their lives were organized according to the demands of those contractors. Historian Timothy Gilfoyle writes that in the 1880s, "New York penitentiaries were little more than large factories where profit determined most things, with convict bodies sold to the highest bidder."[39] By pointing out that the prison system in Illinois worked the same way, the *Alarm* argued that the private enterprise system was deeply implicated in the growing state apparatus aimed at controlling the poor and working class through compulsion and physical violence. The anarchists thus set the state, embodied by the prison system as well as the police, as their enemy, as much as the wealthy the state served.

The *Alarm* also contained a series of rejoinders aimed at the Pinkertons, and encouraged workers to prepare to confront them. The paper recounted with glee every armed battle in which the Pinkertons were defeated by strikers, such as the fighting between Pinkertons and miners in the Hocking Valley of Ohio in the fall of 1884.[40] It also repeatedly warned its readers of the danger of infiltration by the Pinkertons. In the October 17, 1885, issue, the *Alarm* published a summary of a Pinkerton flyer advertising the services of the Pinkerton Preventive Patrol to businesses anticipating labor trouble. The flyer suggested that strikes were caused by a small ring of individuals interested in stirring up trouble, and that companies could hire Pinkertons to find out who these men were. By "discovering the ring leaders and dealing promptly with them," trouble could be avoided.[41] The *Alarm* published this article to warn labor organizers among its readers to beware of Pinkertons.

The *Alarm* also excoriated the moral character of the men who worked for the Pinkerton agency. In order to be a Pinkerton, the paper argued, a person must possess "ever readiness to lie. . . . Must, if ordered, shoot down defenseless workingmen, women and children . . . [and] must renounce all claims to manhood and become a willing, pliant, miserable tool in the hands of whomsoever pays his masters, the Pinkerton Brothers, $6.00 for services per day, of which he gets about $10.00 per week." In the *Alarm*'s view, these were the "cardinal characteristics of a good detective." The Pinkertons had stolen letters out of the mail, promoted marital disputes, blackmailed and drugged people. Because they were not as effective as the police, the Pinkertons were falling out of favor with many employers, and so the agency was now using the "bug-bear of our aristocrats, Socialism, to blackmail trembling millionaires and exploiters of labor."[42] In other words, the Pinkertons scared employers with the threat of socialism to drum up business. For the *Alarm* and its readers, the Pinkertons, even more than the police, were the ultimate symbol of armed force at the beck and call of capitalists.

The anarchists also suggested that the Pinkertons were unabashed *agents provocateurs*. In an article titled "Infernal Machines and Detectives," a taunting reference to the series of books by Allan Pinkerton with similar titles, the *Alarm* suggested that the Pinkertons had planted two bombs in order to drum up business. The anarchists recounted that one of the bombs was discovered on the porch of a mansion by a servant and the other was addressed to a "wage slave" of the Chicago, Burlington and Quincy Railroad. Since the owner of the mansion was known to be in Europe, the *Alarm* argued that no socialist or anarchist would have sent the bombs since they could only have hurt fellow wage slaves. "What can have been the motive of the attempts?" the *Alarm* asked. "Money," it answered, "the lifeblood of modern Christianity, the ideal of our civilization, and the greatest motive power in the land." The anarchists went on to report that the Pinkertons had been hired to investigate the case, and thus, they were the only organization that stood to gain from the attempted bombings.[43] This foreshadowed the anarchists' later interpretation of the Haymarket bombing as the work of a similar *agent provocateur* willing to kill police officers in order to provide an excuse to repress the anarchists.

Thus, Chicago's anarchists set themselves against every institution meant to protect order or serve the city's businessmen. They saw the capitalists' order as the greatest impediment to working-class democracy, and portrayed the army, the police, the courts, the jails, and the Pinkertons as weapons deployed by the capitalists to maintain their control. These anarchists were not in favor of using the state against business. Instead, they viewed the state as a tool of the businessmen and believed that one would have to be removed to get at the other. And their ideas received a hearing among a significant segment of Chicago's workers. This threat both to the police and to order itself contributed in pushing the city's elite to rally to the police.

In addition to their ideological confrontations, the anarchists and the forces of order also began to face off in a series of incidents before the eight-hour-day strikes began. While these confrontations did not lead to bloodshed, they exacerbated tensions on both sides and confirmed both the police appraisal that the anarchists were a threat to order and the anarchists' perception of the police as tools of the business class. On April 28, 1885, the anarchists organized a demonstration of a thousand people to protest the dedication of a new building for the board of trade, which was then the tallest building in the city and the first commercial building to have electric lighting. In response to a request from the board of trade for protection, Superintendent Doyle assembled two hundred officers, with two hundred in reserve and another two hundred available to be assembled within twenty minutes using the Police Alarm Telegraph System, and placed them under the command of Captain Ebersold. These two hundred men were assembled into five units and placed at every intersection leading to the new building. The marching anarchists, led by a full band and singing "The Marseillaise," confronted Colonel Welter and a force of about twenty-five police at the corner of Adams and LaSalle Streets. Albert Parsons, at the head of the procession, asked Colonel Welter to permit them to pass, but Welter reportedly told him that the street was too crowded with pedestrians and carriages and that they should march elsewhere. After some shouting, the procession marched away, without serious incident other than a brick thrown through the window of the carriage of one board of trade member.[44]

The lack of bloodshed or open repression of the anarchists in clashes like this one during the first five years of Harrison's mayoralty led businessmen, police officials, and Republican Party politicians to complain later that Carter Harrison's policies allowed the militant organizations to grow, but this was certainly not his intention. Harrison's policy toward the anarchists corresponded with his general approach toward the growing militancy of the working class. He intended to undercut them by building a broad coalition that would gain the support of Chicago's Trades Assembly and win the city's workers away from revolutionary influence. He allowed the anarchists and socialists to speak, hoping they would function as a safety valve, letting the more angry elements of the city's population blow off steam without provoking the kind of confrontation that had occurred in 1877. This policy had helped undercut the socialist electoral threat to the Democratic Party. But as the city's business leaders, its press, and the Republican Party insisted later, it had also allowed the anarchists to grow into a large and threatening body by the spring of 1886, and gave them the space to help organize the strikes for the eight-hour workday. Harrison's policies were not primarily responsible for this growth. Rather, the anarchists grew because of the resonance of anarchist ideas among a wide swath of Chicago's working class. Also, as stated above, Harrison's policies ultimately allowed the city to strengthen the police force in such a way that it could contain the anarchists when called upon to do so. Still, the anarchists did take advantage of the space afforded them during Harrison's administration, regularly parading, drilling, and picnicking throughout the city. As with his efforts to tamp down class conflict more generally, Harrison's attempts to undercut the anarchists ultimately failed. As the anarchists themselves predicted, they would be defeated by armed force, not by political persuasion.

After the bombing at Haymarket, Harrison clarified and defended his treatment of the socialist and anarchist movement, making his goals clear. "When the Socialists made their first appearance in the city," he explained on May 8, 1886, "they were a species much more refined in their expressions, and I gave them permission to hold their meetings." Furthermore, "owing to the avowed purpose of this sect, they were antagonized by some of the citizens, and their gatherings were frequently broken up by riotous proceedings." In response to a request for aid and in order to avoid these disturbances, Harrison claimed to have told the anarchist leaders that if they would inform him in advance of the times and locations of their meetings, he would furnish them police protection. In other words, Harrison tried to demonstrate that the police could act neutrally, and in this way prove the anarchist arguments' false. But he denied having actually protected them, and said that if anyone had tried to break up their organizations, he would have approved, especially since more "nihilistic" elements had taken the lead in the period leading up to the eight-hour strikes.[45] This contradictory assessment reveals the limitations of Carter Harrison's policies. He hoped to defuse the situation and win workers to accept the political compromise he offered, instead of rallying to the anarchists. He did not want to repress the anarchists, but as they grew in strength and roundly critiqued the limitations of his policies, he hoped that someone else would crush them.

From the moment of his inauguration, Carter Harrison put forth the view that the anarchists were not such a serious threat that they needed to be contained by repression. He granted that some citizens (implicitly the Republican

Party and the Citizens' Association) feared "an organized resistance to authority," but he did not think such an organized resistance existed, although
if it did, the police and the citizenry would not tolerate it. This marked a
significant shift away from Mayor Heath's policy and the demands of the
Citizens' Association, but it fit with Harrison's insistence in 1877 that the
police could control the mobs. It was also an implicit critique of the police
attacks on peaceful socialist gatherings during that disturbance. The mayor's
affirmation of their rights contrasted with the treatment the socialists and
anarchists had come to expect from the forces of law and order.[46] And Harrison even attended some socialist events like the fifteenth anniversary of the
moderate Vorwarts society. At that meeting he again affirmed his support
for the freedom of speech and said he was "confident that this overpowering
idea of a new freedom shall have its birth in our city."[47] This policy was intended to win support from those who otherwise might be drawn to socialist
electoral politics, and in this it succeeded. But one unintended consequence
was that it gave the anarchists the upper hand within the socialist movement
as moderates left to support Harrison.

When Harrison first ran for mayor in 1879, the Socialist Labor Party candidate, Ernst Schmidt, received 20 percent of the vote. He had run on a
temperate program. At the time, the main socialist group in the city favored
electoral methods and looked to the reformist ideas of Lasalle rather than the
revolutionary ideas of Marx. But soon after the election, the Socialist Labor
Party split and went into decline, and the anarchist International Working
People's Association grew to become the largest radical group in the city. The
IWPA looked more to Marx than Bakunin. It advocated organizing workers
to directly oppose their employers and the state, instead of running in elections.[48] This move to the left put the radicals in more direct conflict with the
police than ever before.

In fact, their consistent opposition to Carter Harrison and his policy of
class collaboration was the single issue that most clearly distinguished the
anarchists from the rest of Chicago's labor movement. From the time it began
publication in 1884, the *Alarm* criticized workers who supported either of
the two mainstream parties. It editorialized that the votes of workers who
had cast their ballots for either the Democrats or Republicans "have brought
them nothing worth the having. Themselves and their families are as destitute,
yes, more poverty stricken since than before the election."[49] This opposition
to Harrison's brand of politics reached its zenith with the streetcar strike of
1885. On July 5, 1885, the anarchists held a mass meeting on the streetcar
strike, at which Spies, Samuel Fielden, and others spoke. They argued that

the strike was lost because the trade unionists relied on their alliance with Harrison. "As long as they looked upon Carter Harrison and the police force as their friends," one of the speakers argued, "they ought to be clubbed." The *Alarm* also reported that "one Rodgers," a representative of Carter Harrison's administration, told a meeting of the striking streetcar workers that "he sympathized with them and so did Carter H. Harrison," and that the police would not intervene.[50] The *Alarm* made much of this after the police smashed the strike. After Harrison began deploying the police against strikes in mid-1885, their consistent opposition to Harrison also won the anarchists considerable support among the city's working class. This was not just because, as newspapers and politicians claimed afterward, Harrison's lenient policies had given the anarchists room to grow. Rather, by gaining time, support, and resources for the police department, Harrison's policies ultimately led to the successful repression of the anarchists after Haymarket. The anarchists grew because they were the only group in the city who saw clearly that Harrison would eventually turn against the working class, and this insight rather than Harrison's policies themselves gained the anarchists support once their prediction proved correct.

For all of their criticisms of Harrison's policies and striking rejoinders to the police and the Pinkertons, however, Chicago's anarchists misunderstood the nature of state repression that was about to descend upon them. The *Alarm* was filled with articles describing how masses of workers could defeat an army. They also advertised the activities of the anarchist militia, the Lehr und Wehr Verein, and protested the practices of the state militia. For instance, the anarchists held a mass meeting on December 9, 1885, to protest the "street riot drill" of the First Regiment on Thanksgiving Day.[51] This kind of drill, they believed, was intended to overawe any potential rioters and to prepare the militia for a confrontation with the increasingly numerous anarchists. Apparently, the anarchists expected the type of repression that they had faced in 1877—a shoot-out between strikers and military-style units—that seemed likely to break out around the eight-hour-day strikes scheduled to begin on May 1, 1886. They also saw the major actions of the police to break the streetcar strike in 1885 and the McCormick strike in 1886 this way. If the workers would only fight back, they could defeat the strong-arm tactics of the police.[52] But this was not the kind of repression that the movement would actually encounter.

Although the police force and the Pinkertons were not political organizations that advertised their feelings about Chicago's anarchists, many individual officers must have felt threatened by the anarchists. Until May

1886, the police force remained disciplined and carried out Mayor Harrison's orders to refrain from openly repressing the anarchists. It came out later that the Pinkertons had infiltrated the IWPA, but no violence took place between the Pinkertons and the anarchists. A deep fault line was emerging within the police department between those, led by Michael Schaack and John Bonfield, who wished to persecute the anarchists more forcefully with the aid of the Pinkertons, and those who were more loyal to Harrison's policy, like Superintendent Ebersold. But both of these groups within the police as well as the Pinkertons agreed that anarchists were to blame for most of the labor trouble facing the city.[53] In this view, they were in line with most of the city's press and employers. By the beginning of 1886, the police department's hostility to the anarchists was like a coiled spring, held down by discipline, but ready for release when the time came.

For six years before the massive 1886 strikes for the eight-hour workday, Chicago's anarchists and police confronted each other with increasing hostility. The city's anarchist movement was becoming dominated by people who saw the police as a tool of the capitalists. They had a well-developed and very public condemnation of both the department and the behavior of its members, particularly their treatment of women. This hostile attitude increasingly antagonized the police themselves. At the same time, the threat that the anarchists posed to order pushed the city's elite to harden its support for the police. Finally, the growth of the anarchists contributed to elite concern over Harrison's policy of tolerance and cooptation. These six years set the stage for the consolidation of Harrison's reforms and the police force as a whole following the fateful confrontation of May 1886.

The Eight-Hour Strikes, the Haymarket Bombing, and the Consolidation of the Chicago Police Department

The Haymarket bombing forever changed what it meant to be a member of the Chicago Police Department. It gave the police their own set of martyrs and made being a patrolman meaningful in a way that gradual pay raises and merit awards could not. It made clear what the forces of law and order were defending civilization against. Most importantly, Haymarket and its aftermath consolidated a positive image of the Chicago Police Department in the eyes of the respectable citizens of the city. The image of the gallant blue line between anarchy and civilization, of men ready to risk their lives to defend the sanctity of life, liberty, and property replaced the old image of the police as drunken or corrupt men cavorting with prostitutes and taking bribes from gamblers. This shift facilitated some institutional changes that favored police officers, like the funding of a pension. The city also invested considerable resources to fund improvements in police buildings, and pay for a dramatic increase in the size of the force. But most of all, from that point forward, only citizens willing to risk being identified with the anarchists would criticize the institution itself, though of course police corruption, brutality, and inefficiency would remain issues to this day. Still, the police department proved its ability to protect the constituted order from the most serious crisis yet born out of the development of a wage labor economy, and in doing so, it cemented its place in the pantheon of state institutions.

The police department was not dramatically reshaped in this process. The changes that did take place were a continuation of reforms along the lines of those already implemented by Carter Harrison's administration. Nevertheless, the police emerged from the 1880s a much stronger institution than they had been before Haymarket. By the end of that decade, the Chicago Police

Department had established its institutional form, self-image, strength, and respectability, and defined its role in ways that would never be reversed.

The Haymarket affair was part of a national labor upheaval that was centered in Chicago and reached its high point with the massive strikes for the eight-hour workday that began on May 1, 1886. This episode has been thoroughly covered elsewhere, but some essential points relate directly to the story of police development. First, calls for violence began with the general strike for the eight-hour workday, rather than the bombing and subsequent police riot at Haymarket. An aura of fear and anticipation pervaded the city in the days leading up to May Day.[1] The strike had been planned for months, and workers joined the Knights of Labor and the anarchist organizations in anticipation. Many workers, police, and business leaders expected the eight-hour strikes to lead to violence, and some anarchists and businessmen argued that it would be better if these strikes did involve physical fighting.[2] In January 1886, the *Tribune* twice editorialized about the need for a regular army garrison in Chicago.[3] In anticipation of the conflict, the Commercial Club, led by Philip Armour, subscribed $2,000 to furnish the First Infantry Regiment with a machine gun.[4] While the police and the anarchists had not violently confronted each other openly since 1877, the police had confronted striking workers with violence on a number of important occasions, most dramatically in the 1885 streetcar strike and the McCormick strike of 1886. All of this contributed to the tension in the city before the strikes even began. But despite the anarchists' invocation of dynamite, both sides expected the violence coming out of the May 1 strikes to resemble the clashes of 1877: a mass confrontation between possibly armed strikers and a collection of state forces, including militia units, the police, Pinkertons, and possibly the army.

By the time the eight-hour strikes began, the anarchists formed just one faction in a large and diverse workers' movement in the city. Many native-born craft workers were organized in the Trades and Labor Assembly. This assembly supported Carter Harrison, was generally hostile to the anarchists, and was a precursor to the American Federation of Labor's "pure and simple" unionism that would come to dominate the labor movement after the Haymarket bombing. The anarchists had organized a Central Labor Union that included predominantly central European workers. The Central Labor Union was a "dual union," organizing revolutionary workers outside of the Trades and Labor Assembly, skilled and unskilled alike. Finally, many Chicago workers, especially the Irish, were organized in two district assemblies of the Knights of Labor. Unlike the Trades and Labor Assembly, the Knights included many unskilled workers. By the time of Haymarket, the Knights of Labor had 27,000 members in Chicago, more than either trade union federation. The anarchists had an ambivalent relationship with the Knights. Many had been members, including Albert Parsons, Chicago's first Knight, but they fought with the leadership of the Knights over program, strategy, and politics and broke with them before the eight-hour strikes began. All three of these labor federations participated in the eight-hour strikes, and the anarchists by no means dominated them, even if they were important, active participants who tried to push the strikes as far as they could go.[5]

The city's employers knew that the eight-hour strikes were coming and began preparing well in advance. A year before, in May 1885, the Commercial Club held a meeting to decide whether or not to "make the necessary efforts to secure the location of the new artillery school and military station near Chicago."[6] In March 1886, the Commercial Club resolved that "the public importance of a military post near Chicago is manifest," and began soliciting subscriptions from the wealthiest Chicagoans to purchase land for the proposed base. They also resolved to purchase and outfit an armory in the city.[7] The Commercial Club quickly raised $300,000 in donations from all the biggest names in Chicago business: merchants Marshall Field and Levi Leiter, hotelier and real-estate investor Potter Palmer, industrialist Cyrus H. McCormick, meatpacking magnates Gustavus Swift and Philip Armour, bankers Franklin MacVeagh and Lyman Gage and many others.[8] Then on April 13, 1886, the Commercial Club met to discuss "The eight-hour movement—its advantages, disadvantages, and probable results."[9] The city's employers knew the strike was coming and they were organized to oppose it.

The police did not plan to crush the strikes or repress the anarchists from the outset. On April 30, Superintendent Ebersold reported that he expected no trouble. "All this talk about reserves, police preparation, and special orders is pure nonsense," Ebersold told the *Tribune*. "I have had no call for police protection," he continued, "and I have received no intimation from any of my subordinates that they anticipated any serious difficulty tomorrow."[10] Ebersold's expectations proved correct, when on May 1, the strikes began peacefully. Between 30,000 and 110,000 Chicagoans went on strike the first day in a range of industries, and 80,000 people marched down Michigan Avenue in a parade led by the anarchist International Working People's Association. The marchers and strikers did not confront the police.[11] Private security forces hired by some employers did see action in the first few days of eight-hour strikes, but they were overwhelmed by the sheer number of strikers. For instance, on May 3, at the Cary, Ogden and Parker paint factory on Eighteenth Street, a crowd of about 500 strikers from the lumber district pulled out the remaining workers at the plant and chased away four watch-men. One of the guards fired his pistol at the strikers as he ran away, but no one was hurt.[12] The strikers faced resolute economic opposition, especially from the railroads who were determined not to give in on the main demand for the eight-hour day. But the strikers responded to this in the first few days by organizing a number of large demonstrations, pickets, and open air meetings. There was little violence until the confrontation in front of McCormick Reaper Works on May 3.

On that day, the armed truce was broken when striking lumber workers organized a rally on the Southwest Side near the McCormick Reaper Works. By that time, there were about 80,000 to 100,000 Chicagoans on strike for the eight-hour workday, but the determination of the employers was as strong as ever, especially after word came that afternoon that Jay Gould had defeated a big strike by the Knights of Labor on his southwestern railroads. But the spirit of Chicago's strikers also remained strong. In addition to as many as 10,000 striking lumber workers, this meeting attracted August Spies and perhaps 200 men who had been locked out of McCormick's months earlier. The eight-hour strikes had restarted the strike at McCormicks, and about 800 workers had come out on April 30, leaving only the 600 or 700 strikebreakers McCormick had brought in earlier.[13] While Spies was talking to the crowd, the shift-change bell rang at the Reaper Works, and strikebreaking workers began streaming out of the plant. The McCormick strikers present at the meeting turned and attacked the men who had replaced them. These men were guarded by just a few police, so they quickly called for reinforcements using the Police Alarm Telegraph System. As four or five patrol wagons and approximately 200 police officers pulled up, they opened fire on the strikers and then fell upon them with their clubs. In the ensuing melee, between two and six McCormick strikers were killed, and many more were wounded. The rest of the strikers fled before the columns of police, and the lumber workers followed suit.[14]

The first blood had been spilled and, as predicted, it had taken place in a massed police assault on strikers. Spies later concluded that this killing was carried out on purpose to break the eight-hour strikes.[15] The battle served to harden the two sides in opposition to each other.

The police concluded from this confrontation that they were perfectly prepared to deal with violence during the strike wave. They saw it as a proof of the efficacy of the Police Alarm Telegraph System and of their own discipline. "I believe we are strong enough to suppress any uprising," Inspector Bonfield reported in the aftermath of this clash, and "I do not believe it will be necessary to call out the militia." He predicted that there might be some more rioting and even bloodletting, but said that he did not anticipate a repeat of 1877 because the police were so much stronger and better able to control the city.[16] Schaack later insisted that the attack on the McCormick strikebreakers had been planned by the anarchists in order to spark an insurrection and take over the city. "Their plans had been carefully concocted," he later wrote, "and their network of conspiracy extended in every direction." He wrote that in the meeting in front of McCormick's, "the first opportunity was presented for a general upheaval." But there is no evidence to confirm Schaack's appraisal, and no police sources at the time seemed to fear such an insurrection.[17]

In response to the killing of strikers in front of McCormick's, Spies drafted his famous "Revenge" circular that would play such a prominent role in his prosecution a few months later. Spies wrote it in English and German, with a headline that read "Revenge! Workingmen to Arms!!! Your masters sent out their bloodhounds—the police." Spies continued, "they killed six of your brothers at McCormick's this afternoon. They killed them to show you 'Free American Citizens,' that you must be satisfied and contented with whatever your bosses condescend to allow you, or you will be killed!" The circular ended with a rousing cry to action. "If you are men, if you are the sons of your grand sires, who have shed their blood to free you, then you will rise in your might, Hercules, and destroy the hideous monster that seeks to destroy you. To arms, we call you, to arms!"[18] In the context of the rest of the anarchists' speeches and writings, Spies's "hideous monster" probably referred to capitalism, but in the aftermath of Haymarket, State's Attorney Grinell portrayed this circular as a call to literally destroy the police. The anarchists distributed this circular throughout the city and called for a demonstration the next day at the Haymarket to protest the killing of strikers by police in front of the Reaper Works.

This flyer was not the only thing galvanizing working-class hostility to the police. The killings and the general temper of the city in the middle of the strike meant that a large portion of the city's population was extremely hostile to the police by the evening of May 3. When the police finally tried to escort the strikebreakers trapped in the Reaper Works to their homes later that night, women attacked them with sticks and stones and cursed them. In response, the police charged these women with clubs drawn and drove them off the streets.[19] In another incident, some strikers attacked an officer escorting a wounded man home and, according to the officer and Michael Schaack, threatened to lynch him.[20]

Thus, by May 4, the city was increasingly divided between employers who expected the police to protect them and strikers who saw the police as the "bloodhounds" of their enemies. A large group in the middle led by Mayor Carter Harrison that included some antisocialist trade unionists like Andrew Cameron still tried to maintain the mayor's cross-class alliance.[21] In the excitement of the great strike, though, the ground was quickly disappearing beneath Harrison's feet. The class divisions that had been so evident in 1877 had reappeared. Harrison's policy of reform and class collaboration had maintained peace in the city for seven years, but the strike had pushed the city's business leaders to call for more vigorous repression.

While the strike continued to spread to include laundry girls, high school students, and garment workers, in addition to the lumber workers, freight handlers, and factory workers already out, the opposition of the employers remained strong.[22] George Pullman refused the demands of a committee of his workers. The Furniture Makers' Association resolved that they would not grant shorter hours or negotiate with unions at all. The railroad managers made sure no road gave in, and the Metal Manufacturers' Association forced machine shops that had already agreed to the eight-hour demands to rescind their agreements.[23] The employers sought to starve out the strikers, but they also counted on the police to maintain order.

Later on, both sides would accuse each other of planning for bloodshed in advance, but there is little evidence of this. In the trial of the anarchists, much would be made of a meeting held on the night of May 3. According to Schaack and some anarchists who turned state's evidence in return for cash and safe passage out of the country, the anarchists made plans at that meeting to attack the police. William Seliger later testified that he, Louis Lingg, and a few other anarchist comrades made between thirty and forty bombs to defend themselves when the police "came to protect the capitalists."[24] It appears, however, that the anarchists planned to fight only if the police attacked. This meeting, then, did not mark a significant departure from the normal plans of the workers' militias.[25] At the same time, some employers called on Governor Oglesby to bring the state militia into Chicago to break the strike. This certainly would have increased tension and might have led to a battle reminiscent of 1877. But, fearful that the militia's presence would incite further violence, Oglesby refused, instead ordering the militia to disband until further orders.[26] Thus, despite the tension, and despite both sides' readiness for conflict, neither group appears to have organized plans for the bloody conflict that was to ensue.

On the evening of May 4, perhaps three thousand people met at the Haymarket Square to protest the previous day's killings and to rally workers for the eight-hour movement. No one appears to have suspected violence; Parsons even brought his wife and two children. Spies, Parsons, and Samuel Fielden, another leading revolutionary, spoke in general terms while the crowd began to shrink because of the cold and the lateness of the hour. Mayor Harrison and a large group of police officers attended the rally. By 10 P.M. Harrison told Inspector Bonfield that the speakers were tame and he expected no violence. Bonfield reportedly agreed. Nevertheless, at about 10:20, a column of police moved toward the remaining crowd of about five hundred, led by Bonfield and Captain William Ward, who ordered the crowd to disperse. Fielden, who was on the speakers wagon, objected at first, but then agreed to leave and began to climb down. At that moment, a bomb exploded in the midst of the police.

From that point forward, accounts of the night differ widely. The police (almost unanimously) reported that the moment the bomb went off, people in the crowd began firing. But every other account, whether from socialists, nonpolitical workers, or even some businessmen, alleges that only the police fired revolvers. In any case, it is clear that the police did not run, but drew their weapons and fired into the crowd and, in their panic, probably into each other. People in the crowd ran as fast they could, but many were felled by the bullets of the scared and enraged police. No one knows precisely how many members of the crowd were killed, but at least five were confirmed dead by official accounts and more than forty-five were wounded. The first police fatality was Patrolman Mathias Degan, who died instantly in the blast, and six more officers died in the ensuing days. Sixty policemen were wounded and brought into the Desplaines Street Station in a scene that reminded Superintendent Ebersold of the aftermath of a Civil War battle.[27]

The subsequent trial would turn on the prosecution's idea that the anarchists had planned this attack as part of an attempted coup d'état, and the jury would accept this reasoning. The focus was less on who threw the bomb, though the police believed it was thrown by an anarchist named Schnaubelt, than on whether or not the bombing was part of a concerted and planned attack on law and order. While it is impossible to determine who threw the bomb, it seems highly unlikely that the leaders of the anarchist movement knew about the plan. Although Schaack and other officers claimed that the anarchist leaders planned the bombing as the beginning of an armed uprising, no evidence supports this: no other action was carried out in concert with the attack, and the crowd at the meeting seemed as shocked as the police at the explosion. Also, such a plot would have run counter to the anarchists' own ideas about mass action, especially when they were in the middle of a widespread, enormous strike that still seemed to have a chance of reaching its goal. Nonetheless, the police did present considerable material and eyewitness evidence indicating that the leading anarchists did make bombs.[28] At the same time, given the genuine esprit de corps of the police department, it seems equally unlikely that the bomb was thrown by a police officer acting as an agent provocateur, as some on the left would later charge. It is possible that an agent working for a private citizen or one of the detective agencies threw the bomb, but there is no evidence of this. Historian Paul Avrich suggests that the bomb was probably thrown by George Meng, an anarchist acting independently, while Timothy Messer-Kruse thinks the police had solid evidence pointing to Schnaubelt and a wider conspiracy.[29] But whoever threw the bomb, its detonation could hardly have benefited the Chicago Police Department as an institution more. At the same time, the bomb had dire consequences for the city's anarchists.

After the bombing, the police turned on the anarchists with a fury. Captain Michael Schaack of the Chicago Avenue Station, nearest to the North Side strongholds of the anarchists, led the charge, accompanied by Officers Michael Marks and Horace Elliot, as well as a number of Pinkertons hired to assist in the investigation. In addition to making arrests, breaking up labor meetings, and seizing property, these men infiltrated the anarchists. "At each Anarchist meeting," Schaack later bragged, "I had at least one man present to note the proceedings."[30] This is surely an exaggeration, but the police certainly posted men at places the anarchists were known to congregate. On May 30, 1886, for instance, Officer Michael Marks was detailed to "special duty," which consisted of going to the saloons at 58 Clyborn Avenue and at Archer Avenue and Dearborn, where "anarchists congregate."[31]

The police were particularly vigorous in shutting down the revolutionary press. The day after the explosion, May 5, Inspector Bonfield led a raid on the offices of the *Arbeiter-Zeitung* and arrested August Spies, his brother Chris, Michael Schwaab, Adolph Fischer, and fifteen or sixteen compositors. The police also shut down the *Alarm* and confiscated the files of both papers, which Schaack would later use to write his book, *Anarchy and Anarchists*. These papers would also be presented as evidence in the trial that eventually convicted Spies, Parsons, Schwaab, Fischer, and four other anarchists of murder in connection with the bombing.[32] The repression of the revolutionary press, however, did not end with shutting down the two main newspapers. On May 28, for instance, Officer Patrick Costelle reported that he was detailed to raid 41 Kendall Street, where there was reported to be a press in the basement of a grocery store.[33] On May 30, Horace Elliot and Officer Crowe searched 236 Dayton Street and "captured large amounts of copies of the London and

New York *Freiheit*," another anarchist newspaper.[34] For the next eight weeks or so, the police prevented the anarchists from publicly airing their side of events. This gave the police and their allies a monopoly over public perception of the repression.

The repression was highly effective, even though the mass street battle the *Alarm* had been predicting never occurred. The police arrested about two hundred people in all. Between the destruction of the anarchist press, the arrests, and the fear the police spread within the movement, they effectively crippled the anarchists' operations. These measures prevented the anarchists from assuming leadership of the strike movement and assured its defeat. A few skilled trades won the eight-hour workday, but after losing the massive strike, the labor movement as a whole in the city was pushed back for a whole period. This defeat marked the end for the Knights of Labor as well. It left the city's labor movement in the hands of the same craft unionists who had allied with Harrison, and who had thus facilitated the construction of the police force that smashed the strike.[35]

The leadership of the police force did not direct the repression of the anarchists, though they certainly did not stop it. Schaack later claimed that Superintendent Ebersold stood in his way at every step. Carter Harrison never publicly approved of the repression, though he did take credit for the success of the police force that he had built. When the city council passed a resolution to hire a hundred additional police on May 24, 1886, with money in the city's contingent fund, Carter Harrison vetoed the resolution. He claimed that paying for the additional police out of the contingent fund was entirely illegal, since the contingent fund was set up to pay for legal claims made against the city. More importantly, Harrison argued that such an increase was unnecessary. "The late riots and the bold suppression thereof by the police," he wrote in his veto, "instead of showing a necessity for such an increase, rather prove the present satisfactory efficiency of the force." He further argued that the Police Alarm Telegraph System had made the police as effective against riots as a force double its size. He compared the victory of the police force over the anarchists to the city's rebirth from the fire. The efficient persecution of the anarchists allowed Chicago to boast that "she can put down lawlessness and bloody anarchy without an appeal for the aid of the soldier."[36] Thus, while he maintained his basically moderate stance throughout, Harrison clearly approved of the repression.

Captain Schaack vigorously countered Harrison's attempts to take credit for the performance of the police force. Schaack claimed to have led the destruction of the anarchists himself, despite the interference of Ebersold and

Harrison. He also claimed that he acted with the support of a private group of citizens. When he later recounted hiring Pinkerton agents already familiar with the anarchists from their work for private companies, Schaack reported that "the funds for this purpose were supplied to me by public spirited citizens who wished the law vindicated and order preserved in Chicago."[37] Editor of the *Chicago Daily News* Melville E. Stone reported that immediately after the bombing he hired William Pinkerton to shadow the leading anarchists, and it is likely that these were the Pinkerton agents who worked with Schaack.[38] These agents and funds gave Schaack the latitude to carry out the repression of the anarchists without the explicit approval of Ebersold and Harrison. Schaack and his men became a force within the force, in effect the first red squad in American history.[39]

The Haymarket incident launched a whole new period of police development. First of all, the local and national press transformed the Chicago police into heroes. This began immediately after the bombing and had important long-term consequences for the relationship between the police, the press, and the city government. As a result of the strikes, the activity of the anarchists, the Haymarket bombing, and the subsequent trial, Bonfield and Schaack emerged into the national spotlight as major players in the most captivating news drama of the day. But they were only the most prominent figures in a department basking in acclaim. When Officers John Barrett and George Mueller died on May 6 from wounds sustained in the bombing, the *Tribune* referred to them as "Two More Dead Heroes," which constituted the first time the paper had called police officers "heroes."[40] On May 29, which was then called Decoration Day, the precursor to Memorial Day, the city organized a parade of 650 officers down LaSalle Street to accompany the memorial march of the Grand Army of the Republic. Chief Ebersold, Inspector Bonfield, Captain Schaack, and five others led the procession on horseback. A marching band played martial music and an exceptionally large crowd of onlookers cheered them as living heroes, equating them with the honored dead from the Civil War.[41]

The police also received large amounts of money from private citizens to disburse to members of the force. By August 15 they had received $70,361.43. This was an impressive amount of money when the total police expenditures for 1886 totaled slightly more than one million dollars and a first-class patrolman earned just a thousand dollars a year.[42] The board of trade was the largest single contributor. It gave two donations, one of $6,000 and another of $7,700. The Lumberman's Exchange donated $7,500, the second largest single contribution. Large donations also came from Cyrus McCormick, the Peoples Gas Light and Coke Company, the railroads, real-estate magnate Potter Palmer, the Western Union Telegraph Company, and even some police officers, including Austin Doyle and John Bonfield.[43] Some of the money went to the immediate aid of those officers wounded at Haymarket or to the families of those killed. Most of the rest was earmarked for the Policemen's Benevolent Association, and it was enough for the captains in charge of the fund to propose starting a pension for the police.[44] The *Tribune* also initiated a drive to erect a statue commemorating the fallen officers at the Haymarket, for which they eventually received thousands of dollars more in subscriptions from wealthy Chicagoans. The bronze monument of an officer holding out his hand was erected on Memorial Day 1889.[45]

The Commercial Club also brought together the city's leading businessmen to draw practical conclusions from the strike and bombing. The day after the Haymarket bombing, the Commercial Club held a meeting titled "The late Civil Disorder—its causes and lessons."[46] It also acted to strengthen the military and militia presence around the city. On May 15, less than two weeks after the bombing, the Commercial Club used some of the funds it had raised to buy land for a military post to purchase the property of the Washington Boulevard Skating Company. The Commercial Club paid $18,000 for this building and then donated it to the Second Regiment of the state militia as an armory.[47] Every subscriber to the initial fund consented to this purchase. J. H. McVickers of the McVickers Theater wrote on his consent form that "there are more savages and unruly people to be found here than our frontiers now contain," so the armed might of the nation should be directed against the "rabble," rather than against the Indians.[48]

The Commercial Club spent the rest of the money purchasing 632 acres just north of the city for an army post.[49] The army occupied this post a year later and in 1888 named it Fort Sheridan, to recognize General Sheridan's role in pacifying the city after the fire of 1871. Fittingly, the garrison posted at Fort Sheridan would occupy the city in 1894 during the Pullman strike. Chicago's businessmen drew the same basic conclusion from the eight-hour strikes and the Haymarket bombing that they had drawn from the events of 1877: it was worth spending considerable funds to ensure that the forces of order could meet any threat posed by the city's workingmen and radicals.

The establishment of a pension fund for men who retired from the force was the most important professional transformation to come out of Haymarket. The state legislature took up the proposal in the session following the bombing. The initial bill proposed to pay officers half of their pay upon retirement after twenty years of service or after a shorter period of service

if they were wounded in the line of duty. It included a provision to pay a
fallen policeman's family the full pension. The state proposed to pay for
these pensions out of saloon license fees, dog taxes, fines levied against
members of the department, some other tax revenue, and $1 a month from
the officers themselves.[50] The proposed bill would amply fund a generous
pension. Police Controller Schwabb actually complained that the bill's initial provisions would give the police fund an annual income of $50,000,
much more than they could use. Chief Ebersold came out strongly in favor
of the bill, arguing that the provision of a pension would increase the loyalty
of the force.[51] The sponsors of the bill asked that every member of the police
department vote on the pension proposal. They threatened that if even one
fourth of the men on the force voted against it, they would withdraw the
pension bill. But fewer than 60 of the 900 men voted no. Those few who
were against the bill objected to the proposed $1 a month deduction from
their pay and resented the provision of higher pensions for higher-ranking
officers.[52] John A. Roche, soon to be mayor of Chicago, helped push the
bill through the state legislature, and it passed easily during the summer
session of 1887.[53]

The passage of the pension bill marked a dramatic turnaround from the
fiscal situation facing the force just ten years before. In 1877, wealthy Chicagoans could barely be persuaded to pay their taxes, and the police department
had to cut its personnel on the eve of that year's riots. Even during Carter
Harrison's years, when the city rapidly increased police expenditures, no one
proposed a pension. But after Haymarket, the police were assured of a decent
retirement, and the wealthy citizens and institutions of Chicago competed
with each other to see who could donate more money to the pension fund, as
well as to the department as a whole, to the state militia, and to the military.

The police also demanded that citizens address them more respectfully
after the Haymarket bombing. On January 20, 1887, salesman S. L. Black went
before Justice C. J. White on the charge of speaking to a police officer without
permission. Black apparently asked Patrolman Thomas Sullivan for directions
while Sullivan was on his beat. Sullivan at first ignored him, but when Black
asked again, Sullivan arrested him. A police justice eventually released the
salesman. But the police complained to the press that this release showed
that the justices were not cooperating with the police against the criminal
element. "A policeman on his beat," the *Tribune* reminded its readers, "is
like a Judge on the bench, and 'May it please your Honor' is the only safe
way to begin a conversation with either of them."[54] Certainly, police officers
would have liked to be treated with respect before Haymarket. But the fact
that a man could be arrested for failing to show the proper deference when

asking a patrolman for directions shows how this expectation among both the police themselves and the public as a whole reached an entirely new level after Haymarket, even if the case was dismissed.

Haymarket had a national impact on the reputation of the police. *Harpers* magazine, which until that time had only mentioned the Chicago Police Department to tease it for putting rubber tires on patrol wagons, praised the "heroic fidelity and bravery of the police of Chicago in the late street battle with brutal ruffians." *Harpers* contrasted the vigorous action of the police with the "extraordinary incompetency of the other municipal and State authorities," and argued that the "most complete and summary methods of repression are the plainest duty." This article insisted that the actions of the police demonstrated "what brave and noble stuff the police force of this country is composed." Suggesting that the police who died that day should be considered martyrs, the journal concluded that "those who were murdered in Chicago fell in the discharge of the most patriotic and humane duty."[55] These words cast the Chicago police in an entirely new light, and like soldiers in a war, put them on a plane beyond reproach. Police throughout the country could bask in the reflected glory and demand increased respect.

A few years after the event, this image of the Chicago police as brave men standing firm against the forces of disorder had been cemented in the popular imagination. In a June 1888 article in the magazine *Century* titled "The Philosophy of Courage," Horace Porter, former brigadier general and secretary to President Grant and current vice president of the Pullman Palace Car Company, invoked the Chicago police response to Haymarket as the best image of what courage could do. "Before that event," he wrote, "the police had been strictly on the defense; their small squads huddled together for protection had been boldly attacked, and they had been ordered from pillar to post to rescue their comrades from the fierce onslaughts that were being made upon them by a foe whose reckless acts and exaggerated numbers had almost paralyzed the community." After the suppression of the Haymarket riot, Porter wrote, "the police went forth wearing the laurels of success, they swaggered like the returned heroes of Austerlitz; each man seemed to feel two feet higher in stature and competent to cope single-handed with an army of anarchists." He went on to insist that "one of these policemen undertook to guard a railway station where a dozen were required the day before; they searched single-handed for anarchists like ferrets for rats; the city was safe from that hour."[56] All of this was untrue, of course. The police had never been attacked by the anarchists before Haymarket. They did not have to rescue their comrades. And they generally guarded railway stations and made arrests single-handedly as a matter of course. Nevertheless, articles such as this reinforced the image of these officers as soldiers bravely protecting civilization despite the danger to themselves.

The repression carried out by Bonfield, Schaack, and their men proved devastatingly effective at destroying the organizations built by the anarchists, but it also kept public attention on the anarchists and the role of the police in destroying them. The activity of the police officers culminated in preparations for the trial. This included gathering evidence for the prosecution and even re-creating and detonating bombs like the one used to kill the seven dead patrolmen. Many of the police conclusions were exaggerated. One of the Pinkertons on Schaack's staff later wrote that "the false reports written about anarchists as told me by the writers themselves would make a decent man's blood boil."[57] In 1889, Ebersold issued a public statement that the anarchist plots had been greatly exaggerated and even that Schaack wanted the police to organize anarchist societies that they could then repress, in order to keep himself in the public eye.[58] But however exaggerated, these activities and reports helped keep the "anarchist threat" in the public mind, and the police who repressed them in the spotlight until Spies, Parsons, Fischer, and Engel were executed on November 11, 1887.[59]

Of course, not everyone viewed the police as the heroes of Haymarket. Just as the police killed at the square were transformed into martyrs for the advocates of law and order, so the eight sentenced anarchists became martyrs for the world's socialist and anarchist movements. Soon after the repression following Haymarket, the *Alarm* reappeared under the editorship of Dyer D. Lum and Lizzie Swank.[60] The *Alarm* took up mocking the new image of the forces of law and order. On November 19, 1887, for instance, Lizzie Swank wrote an article subtitled "Glorious Victory Won by the State Over Two Women and Two Small Children." This article excoriated John Bonfield for arresting Lucy Parsons and her children during the execution of Albert Parsons. "On Friday, Nov. 11, mention is made of a certain Capt. Bonfield, who 'came into the jail flushed from the arrest of Mrs. Parsons and her children and friends,'" Swank wrote. "Like a warrior flushed with the excitement of a great victory, like a noble knight fresh from conquering a brave adversary, the doughty captain stood before his brother braves and recounted the great, courageous act he had performed," Swank continued, mocking the tone of the mainstream press. "The power of a mighty state had put forth its strong arm, in him personified, and behold: two grief-stricken women and two weeping children lay in dungeons gloomy and dark, completely vanquished!"[61] Despite the impact of articles such as this, the *Alarm* was forced to close a few months after it resumed publication due to a lack of funds.

By early 1891, the anarchists were able to attract two thousand people to a meeting at Turner's Hall. But their rebuilt organization lacked the verve and immediacy of its predecessor. Instead of the spirited celebrations of the armed strength of the proletariat so common in the 1880s, the anarchists were now confined to discussing European politics and promising the eventual organization of a political club.[62] Their meetings were also openly attended by the police. At one commemoration of the Haymarket martyrs in 1891, the police even forced the anarchists to fly the U.S. flag among their red flags.[63]

Some anarchists invoked the repression after Haymarket as a call to arms, and they rededicated themselves to the movement. Lucy Parsons was the most notable of these. She became a lifelong activist, who traveled the world speaking on behalf of anarchist ideas. But within the city, the police portrayed Parsons as crazed, vindictive, and unwomanly. On June 20, 1888, for instance, the police arrested her for distributing handbills. As they arrested her, Parsons called the police "blue coated murderers" and protested her arrest because she had children to care for at home. But Captain Bonfield dismissed Parsons's claims of motherly responsibilities by saying, "You should have thought of that before."[64] By 1888, the police could dismiss Lucy Parsons as an impotent threat to order. A large part of the difference between the treatment of Lucy Parsons and that of her husband can be explained by the fact that she was a woman involved in politics, but there was still a major change in the police reaction to anarchist women as a result of Haymarket. Bonfield's self-satisfied rejection of Parsons's right to the claims of motherhood is very different from the shrill warnings about unwomanly anarchists issued by the press and the police just a few years before. The biggest difference is that, before Haymarket, the anarchists had a large and imposing set of organizations with armed militias. They could defend themselves from the police, and it was not so obvious who would win in an armed confrontation. But the execution of the leading anarchists, the arrests of many more, the open repression of the anarchists' fighting organizations, and the destruction of the anarchist press had effectively disarmed the movement. By 1888, Lucy Parsons was working with a small and marginal group that the police no longer feared.

As May Day spread as an international workers' holiday dedicated to the fight for the eight-hour workday and the memory of the Haymarket martyrs, the Chicago police earned a reputation for brutality and summary justice among leftists around the world. But within the city, people with even reform-ist socialist politics were politically marginalized after Haymarket and the police had achieved new status as the successful defenders of order against anarchy. The anarchists had already made their major impact on the Chicago police, and while they would eventually reemerge, for the next decade their influence would continue more as a negative referent than a real threat.

Haymarket also pushed the rhetoric of Chicago's politics far to the right and gave the promoters of law and order increased political power against those who advocated a continuation of Harrison's class collaborationist style. In retrospect, the police reaction to Haymarket vindicates Carter Harrison's policies, at least from the businessman's perspective. When the big confrontation finally occurred, the police department was more than capable of protecting order. And despite the massive growth of the anarchists and the labor movement between 1877 and 1886, despite the strike wave that surpassed anything the city had ever seen, the police were able to keep the situation entirely under control. From the perspective of the city's elite, Harrison's police force had proven itself capable of at least containing the problem of order that had wracked Chicago for fifteen years. But Harrison's policies had run their course, and he was no longer the man for the job.

Harrison's political isolation first revealed itself in the fight over increasing the police force immediately after the Haymarket bombing. As discussed above, Harrison vetoed a proposed increase of the force and insisted that the police had proven themselves capable of handling the situation. But because of the widespread feeling of panic, the city council passed an increase in the force over Harrison's veto on June 7, 1886.[65] To pay for it, the council proposed a November referendum for the voters to approve hiring more police by transferring $100,000 from funds otherwise earmarked.[66] That was not all. That same day, the city council formally expanded the powers of the police under the municipal code, though this expansion only covered the things they were already doing in their pursuit of the anarchists.[67] They also authorized the purchase of grenade-style fire extinguishers for use in police stations, public libraries, and city hall.[68] The press, the city's elite, and many of its politicians blamed Harrison for coddling the anarchists. Their insistence on increasing the size of the force, its legal powers, and its tools amounted to a rejection of Harrison's policies.

Under the pressure of mounting criticism, Harrison first declined the Democratic nomination to run for reelection in 1887. He then reversed himself and accepted, but he faced such denunciations from the Democratic press that he later dropped out. After this turmoil, there was no Democratic candidate for mayor in the April 1887 municipal election. This turned the election into a contest between the Republican candidate, John A. Roche, and Labor candidate, Robert S. Nelson. The bulk of the Democratic politicians of the city and their voters went for Roche, who won by a vote of 51,268 to 23,410.[69] As had happened in Medill's election after the 1871 fire, the "law-

and-order" ticket had been able to assemble a large electoral majority in the aftermath of a major crisis. But given the universal ire heaped on Nelson and labor in general by the press, his ability to garner almost one-third of the vote was remarkable evidence of the continued strength and resiliency of the city's labor movement despite the destruction of the anarchist organizations and the defeat of the eight-hour-workday strikes. Nonetheless, the outright victory of the "law-and-order" candidate, just like after the fire or the strikes of 1877, is another instance of a dramatic political shift to the right after a major crisis.

Roche stood for an end to Harrison's collaboration with labor and "coddling" of the anarchists, but he did not propose a radical departure in policy. Harrison's policy had run its course because his tolerance toward strikes and toward the anarchist organizations had, in the eyes of the city's elite, led directly to the strikes and bombing of May 1886. But Harrison had also succeeded in building up a powerful police department that was able to defeat the workers' movement. Upon his election, Roche promised to undertake a "thorough examination of the working of every department, and the personnel of its members," but upon examination, he found that most departments worked relatively well.[70] At first he even supported the police department leadership put in place by Harrison. Despite his antianarchist rhetoric, Roche also tried to avoid alienating the city's workers. He said that they created the wealth of the city, and that they had a right to demand just treatment, but that they did not have the right to do so by force. He insisted that "the mistaken men who, while enjoying the benefits of a free government, are seeking to undermine and overthrow it under the guise of Socialism and Anarchy, must learn that this is not the soil for the growth of their un-American doctrines."[71] This marked his attempt to split the bulk of Chicago's workers from the anarchists, and win them to more moderate ideas. At the same time, he wanted to consolidate what had proven to be an effective police force. The only way to accomplish these two goals was to maintain many elements of Harrison's police policy along with the personnel that had implemented them.[72]

Roche retained Ebersold as superintendent of the force and Bonfield as inspector. Most of his early communications with the superintendent regarded the same types of day-to-day matters that had occupied the force for decades. His first official communication to Ebersold urged the superintendent to vigorously enforce "the 'dog' ordinance, especially the provision relating to unmuzzled dogs," hardly a major issue.[73] Throughout the year, most of his letters to Ebersold dealt with similarly mundane matters. He asked the police to take a census of saloon owners and double-check their licenses, and he urged them to enforce the ban on fireworks sales before the Fourth of

July. He also tried to ensure that the police restricted auctions taking place at unauthorized locations. In sum, despite the rhetoric accompanying his election, Roche did nothing major to change the force he had inherited from Harrison.[74]

Roche also refused to continue the level of repression against strikers carried out by the police immediately after Haymarket. In fact, by October 1888, Roche was coming under pressure for not repressing a streetcar strike as vigorously as the streetcar company's owners wished. In that month, Charles Yerkes, president of the Chicago Streetcar Company, complained to the press that he was not receiving sufficient police protection to run streetcars during a strike. And Yerkes wasn't the only one who complained about the insufficient vigor displayed by the police against this strike. The new editor of the *Illinois Staats-Zeitung*, Hermann Raster, called for the federal government to declare that the horse-drawn streetcars in the big cities were postal routes. This would justify sending the army against the strikers, a foreshadowing of the Pullman strike six years later.[75] In rhetoric reminiscent of Carter Harrison, Roche claimed that the police had stationed enough men to protect all the cars that the Chicago Streetcar Company could run. "If you are unable to run cars for want of conductors," Roche wrote to Yerkes, "it is not the fault of the city or the Police Department."[76] Nevertheless, Roche deployed considerable numbers of police against this strike on the West and North Side lines. Police guarded company property, fought crowds of strikers, and charged mobs to help move cars, much as they had in the 1885 streetcar strike.[77] At the same time, Mayor Roche tried repeatedly to get Yerkes and the union leaders to compromise and end the strike, an effort that eventually succeeded.[78] His policy in the strike as a whole, in both deploying the police and attempting to arbitrate, was almost identical to Carter Harrison's policy during the streetcar strike of 1885, though there was no mass clubbing in 1888. The only difference was that this strike represented a continuation of ongoing police policy, rather than a major change.

The 1888 streetcar strike also demonstrates the continued perception among a section of the city's businessmen that labor trouble was invariably due to anarchist agitation. North Side streetcar workers had struck because they were paid less than West Side men, and the West Side men had struck in sympathy. The *Tribune*, however, reported that the West Side workers had voted to strike because of the influence of labor "demagogues" and "centurions" George Schilling and Luke Coyne. The West Side workers' vote to join the North Side strikers was a "survival of the days of Communism and Anarchy." A member of the South Side Street Car-Men's Union, who had attended the meeting as a disinterested observer, objected strenuously to this accusation. He argued that the West Side men had struck because "they knew too well that if their brethren across the river were defeated the tocsin of defeat or reduced pay would soon be heralded by Mr. Yerkes' luminaries on the West Side."[79] As this unionist argued, and as time would demonstrate, Chicago's labor conflicts were not simply the creation of communists, anarchists, or outside agitators of any sort, even though leftist organizations and ideas played an important role. This notion, however, continued to give police in Chicago and throughout the nation a negative referent to justify their interventions against strikes for decades to come.

The streetcar strike of 1888 also illustrates how new respect for the police reduced the role of private detective agencies. During this strike, Yerkes hired "specials" from a private company, Mooney and Boland, because he did not think the police were repressing the strikers vigorously enough. These Mooney and Boland men would give Yerkes an extra measure of force beholden only to him. Mayor Roche saw the matter differently. To him the employment of Mooney and Boland men was an "incitement to disorder," and he asked Yerkes to fire them. Because he feared losing the substantial support the city police were already providing, Yerkes complied with the mayor's wishes.[80] Thus, the success of the police worked to the detriment of private strikebreakers. Roche felt confident that the police could protect Yerkes' property and did not want to encourage the use of "specials." Mayor Roche was also able to stand above the conflict between Yerkes and the strikers. However much the strikers might view the police as their enemies when they helped move cars and clubbed people out of the way, the police did not present themselves as hired guns for the company. As a result, they retained much more legitimacy both among the "public" represented by the newspapers and among the strikers. The strengthening of the police, their success in controlling strikes, and their new status as heroes after Haymarket limited the possible role of strikebreaking companies like the Pinkertons and Mooney and Boland, though they continue to play an important role in antiunion efforts to this day.

By late 1888, the courts also set about restoring some of the free-speech rights that had been suspended arbitrarily after Haymarket. In addition to the republication of the *Alarm* and the *Arbeiter Zeitung*, a group of German workers who had been active with the anarchists sought to found a new organization, called the Arbeiter Bund. This organization planned and advertised a founding meeting at Plasterer's Hall on December 23, 1888. The police, led by Inspector Bonfield but under orders from the superintendent, arrived in force and kept members of the Arbeiter Bund from entering the hall, saying that they had no right to meet. The Arbeiter Bund sued the police for this right, and on January 15, 1889, the court found in their favor. Judge Tuley ruled that the police could not bar any group from meeting solely on the basis of "information and belief." The police argued that they had the responsibility to prevent crime, and thus the authority to break up a meeting that they thought would lead to crime. Judge Tuley declared that giving the police such broad powers would amount to a suspension of *habeas corpus*. Under the department's interpretation, "a policeman could, without warrant, invade the citizen's home, tear down his house, arrest the citizen, and detain him for an indefinite time in prison cells." The department's approach would also give the police the power to "prescribe the hour at which a person must close his store or put out his lights." In sum, if the police were permitted to do whatever they thought necessary to prevent crime, they would subsume the Legislative, Judicial and Executive powers at once, and this was clearly unacceptable. Judge Tuley insisted on the rights of free speech and free assembly and wrote that the police only had the right to arrest people for crimes they had committed, not because of organizations to which they belonged. In fact, Judge Tuley's decision rendered formal what had previously seemed to depend on the discretion of the mayor and the leadership of the police. His decision fit with Carter Harrison's earlier arguments about the anarchists' free-speech rights and established a precedent that later groups of socialists and anarchists would refer to, though he certainly was not ruling for their benefit. Nevertheless, in some ways, the expanded deployment of police authority in the aftermath of Haymarket forced the courts to establish definitive boundaries for the policing of political activities.[81]

The improved reputation of the police among the political and economic elite meant that the city government was more willing to allocate funds for hiring more officers, purchasing equipment, and creating a pension fund. By the end of 1888, the new superintendent, George Hubbard, could boast that "an unusually large amount of material improvement has been completed or undertaken in the Department during the past year, exceeding in value and importance the improvements made in any previous year in its history."[82] This was hyperbole, since the creation of the police alarm system was undoubtedly more important than the improvements made in 1888. But the department did add a sixth precinct on the South Side. It also built new stations in five of the twenty-one districts. In addition, the department added over 100 men, to end the year with 1,255 police compared to 1,145 in 1887, 1,036 in 1886, and 926 in 1885. In the aftermath of Haymarket, the police added more than 300 men in three years, or an increase of about one-third.

While the previous force had been sufficient to suppress the anarchists and break the eight-hour-workday strikes, this increase allowed the police to patrol the city more effectively on a daily basis. This effectiveness should not be exaggerated, since police patrols still largely could not enforce municipal policy in most areas, and workers would continue to pose serious challenges to the constituted order that the police force could not contain. Nonetheless, these improvements further consolidated police power in the city.[83]

In the years immediately after Haymarket, Chicago's police department divided between those who promoted more vigorous prosecution of any who threatened order and those who advocated a continuation of Harrison's policies. If the internal rivalries of the 1870s were nearly a tragedy for the department, those of the late 1880s were more of a farce. Superintendent Ebersold became a target for ridicule within the force, in part because he continued to support Carter Harrison's policies. Mayor Roche asked for Ebersold's resignation on February 13, 1888, apparently because he was unable to deter officers from speaking ill of him, which undercut the discipline of the force. Roche had been contemplating this move for some time but had held back because "prominent businessmen" asked him to keep Ebersold on after his effective handling of the anarchists.[84] Ebersold thus fell because he was seen as too linked to Harrison.

The main leaders of the attack on the anarchists fared little better, however. Shortly after Ebersold's removal, the *Chicago Times* and the *Arbeiter Zeitung* both accused Captain Schaack and Inspector Bonfield of taking money from saloonkeepers and prostitutes and selling stolen property, including some that belonged to Louis Lingg, one of the Haymarket martyrs.[85] Schaack and Bonfield blamed the accusations on an anarchist revenge conspiracy and promptly arrested the editors of both the *Times* and the *Arbeiter Zeitung*, charging them with libel.[86] But this did not suffice to squelch the scandal, as Bonfield came under increasing accusations of betraying his superiors and using officers under his command for personal gain. On April 13, 1889, Bonfield was eating with friends at Billy Boyle's restaurant when J. J. West, editor of the *Times* and a defendant in his libel suit, entered with a group of friends. Bonfield accosted him, brandishing a pistol and calling him a "blackmailer, a coward, a dog, and a dog-faced villain!"[87] This was the last straw, and Bonfield was forced out of the department. He eventually moved to Salt Lake City and worked for the Mormons before returning to Chicago to provide private security services for the Columbian Exposition in 1893.

Captain Schaack, meanwhile, kept quiet only until he published his book, *Anarchy and Anarchists*. This book was a broadside directed at former superintendent Ebersold, who was brought back on the force as inspector after

Bonfield resigned. Ebersold responded by attacking Schaack as a liar, charging that the entire book was a fabrication that must have been written by someone else since, according to the former superintendent, Schaack could not even write a police report. Ebersold also accused him of manufacturing a lot of plots and excitement after Haymarket. "My object was to quiet the excitement," Ebersold said, "while he was trying to keep everything in a turmoil so as to make capital out of it." Ebersold went on to accuse Schaack of trying to get his hands on police funds and of trying to make arrests just to keep the pot boiling. Police Lieutenant Shea also attacked Schaack: "There's a lot of these 'coppers' who are crazy on anarchy and lived off it since the Haymarket riot," Shea said. "When the Supreme Court sustained the verdict [against the Haymarket martyrs]," Shea continued, "Schaack took a revolver in each hand, went down into the basement of the station and emptied both of them—had a regular celebration all by himself."[88] On the other hand, ignoring public criticisms of the book, the Pinkerton Company distributed Schaack's book to potential clients as evidence of their effectiveness against labor activists.[89]

In an ironic twist, Schaack was appointed to replace Ebersold as inspector in 1891 when Ebersold resigned. Schaack would remain in that post until his death in 1898.[90] He was a highly controversial figure for the remainder of his career, but he also played a prominent role in numerous important cases. Despite the lack of respect for the chain of command that Schaack demonstrated by attacking his superiors in his book, he earned a reputation among his subordinates as a disciplinarian. He even tried to order officers under him to wear their uniforms even when they were off duty.[91] More than anything else, Michael Schaack was the prototype of the police officer whose whole identity was subsumed by his job and who was completely committed to law and order. Well before his death, the jealousies engendered by Haymarket had cooled, while Schaack's role in repressing the anarchists still came up enough in the press to ensure his legacy.

Despite these internal divisions, continued corruption, and ongoing scandals, the police department had established itself as a powerful, permanent institution. Each of these men had played a major role in building and reinforcing that department, but the department was much stronger than any of them and survived these scandals no worse for wear. This was the mark of how far the police department had come. Unlike the 1860s, when Mayor Wentworth could threaten the very shape of the department and fire its entire force, unlike the 1870s, when Mayor Medill and the Committee of Seventy almost broke the department with their impossible demands, by the end of the 1880s, the Chicago Police Department could survive the shenanigans of any individual officer without threats to its institutional structure. In years to come, reformers and machine-style politicians would continuously wrangle over what policies the department should carry out and who it should employ. Observers of many stripes would decry the corruption, inefficiency, and drunken habits of the police. Journalist William Stead, for instance, wrote in 1894 that "The policeman divides his time in unequal proportions between keeping a sharp eye upon every evil doer whom he must arrest and in winking both eyes hard when he comes across those other evil doers who have either in money or in 'pull' established their right to be invisible to the patrol."[92] Nonetheless, from this point forward, the basic shape of the department, its status as a crucial municipal institution, and its relatively high funding levels were secure.

By the end of the 1880s, the Chicago Police Department had proven that it was an essential institution for meeting the threat posed by the transition to an economy composed largely of wage workers. In the aftermath of the crisis facing the police during the 1870s, Carter Harrison's Democratic administration undertook the basic reforms that turned the police into the strong, stable (relatively), disciplined organization that faced the city's anarchist movement in 1886. The department's conflict with that movement, culminating in the repression following the Haymarket bombing, consolidated both this transformation and elite support for the department. The Chicago Police Department's successful performance as the defender of property and order from the threat of revolution had solidified its support and status among the wealthy and the politicians of the city. From this moment forward, Chicago's elite counted on the police to protect the city's basic social, economic, and political order. This support was ensured by the deaths of seven police officers in the explosion at Haymarket, and of four anarchists brought to the gallows by those fallen officers' comrades.

The Pullman Strike
and the Matrix of State Institutions

The upheaval of 1886 was not the last important labor struggle that accompanied the rise of a wage labor economy in the United States. In 1894, the Pullman strike erupted. It was the largest and most important strike of the nineteenth century, and its epicenter was in Chicago. It thrust the question of order back on the national stage. This strike revealed as a failure George Pullman's attempt to apply a modified earlier version of order, based on the pre-police idea that a paternalistic system of organization could embed wage workers within an ordered system controlled by their employer. This strike also revealed the limits of police power, since the Chicago Police Department did not have the will or the force to break it. By 1894, Chicago already possessed a strong, bureaucratically organized, disciplined police department. Yet the strike was primarily broken by the army, with the police department playing only a supporting role. This was in part because, despite its impressive growth and power, the Chicago Police Department was still quite limited when faced with a mass strike of this magnitude. William Novak argues that one of the central strengths of American state power is that it is so widely distributed among so many different institutions.[1] The Pullman Strike illustrates one aspect of this: municipal police departments were just one set of institutions within the broader matrix of state power, including the state militias and the military, that was built to maintain the businessmen's order in the nineteenth century. Nonetheless, while it was unable to break the strike, before the arrival of federal troops, the Chicago Police Department was able to maintain order in the city, and almost all of the violence accompanying the strike was carried out by soldiers, federal deputies, or strikers acting against those forces, not the police.[2]

As Carl Smith points out, Pullman's model town was one of three strategies that U.S. elites formulated to solve the crisis of order in the Gilded Age. The other two were progressive reform and the use of armed force.[3] The strategy of progressive reform evolved slowly and was both messy and complicated. It included Jane Addams's and others' efforts to reshape the social and cultural life of the poor, and Carter Harrison's and others' policies that sought to convince a plurality of the new polyglot working class that their interests could best be promoted by reformist politicians. The continued efforts of workers and their unions would eventually lead to what Richard Schneirov has called modern liberalism when a section of politicians and employers elaborated a new vision of politics that was much better at co-opting working class activism than the previous versions.[4] One of the most important implications of this study is that this strategy of accommodation and cooptation was facilitated by the existence of a powerful police force that could serve as the stick to supplement the liberal, progressive carrot.

The model town of Pullman was the most important U.S. example of a third strategy to escape the disorder that had so wracked Chicago and other cities after the Civil War. Pullman "hoped to show that industrialization need not lead to social disintegration" and that the disorder of industrial cities could be replaced by "the planned order of an industrial community."[5] George Pullman created his town for some of the same reasons that Chicago's businessmen pushed to create the police department. In many ways, the two attempted to serve similar functions, by regulating the everyday lives of wage workers. But Pullman took things quite a few steps further.

Pullman was a central figure among Chicago's elite. Like many of his peers, he came from New York, arriving in 1855, and first started a construction firm before launching the famous Pullman sleeping-car company that brought him fortune. In 1867, he married Harriet Sanger, daughter of a railroad contractor, and they built one of the largest mansions on the city's elite Prairie Avenue in 1873. He also owned three other residences: an islet in the Saint Lawrence River; a house in Albion, New York; and an estate in Long Branch, New Jersey.[6] Pullman was a founding member of the Commercial Club, and socially integrated into the city's business community. He was thus intimately familiar with the deep crisis of order that had accompanied Chicago's creation as a center of wage labor.

It was in the context of his class's search for order that Pullman built his new factory in 1880 in the Calumet region south of the city. By providing an orderly existence for his workers, including homes, a church, even a theater, he expected his town to ensure that no labor unrest would ever trouble his business. "The love of order is the keynote to a great system," a reporter commented about Pullman in 1892, and the town of Pullman was built as a highly organized system.[7] Pullman famously attempted to regulate his workers' lives in much the way that reformers had pushed the police to restrict working-class activities, but to greater effect. The town had no brothels, and the only saloon was in the elite hotel. Because they didn't go there, workers could only drink outside of town. This kept the disorder associated with immigrant leisure activities at arm's length and removed an otherwise commonplace opportunity for workers to build a social life with their coworkers. Pullman provided other activities for his workers, though again, under his control, including a reading room, a billiards hall, and outdoor sports.[8]

All these enterprises were profit making for the company, which limited the effectiveness of the model town for reducing worker discontent. For example, workers were barred from owning their own homes. This was part of Pullman's plan, since complete ownership of land gave Pullman control over the built environment, yet it also removed one of the key ties workers could develop to the community and to their jobs. "Nobody regards Pullman as a real home," one journalist reported in 1885, "and, in fact, it can scarcely be said that there are more than temporary residents in Pullman."[9] It also engendered resentment against Pullman as a landlord, in addition to resentment of Pullman as a boss. Estimates from local real-estate agents and the strike commission put rents in Pullman somewhere between 25 and 33 percent higher than in neighboring towns for comparable housing.[10] Pullman also charged considerably more for municipal services than did Chicago utilities. In 1893, for instance, Pullman sold gas to resident-workers for $2.25 per thousand cubic feet, compared to $1.25 in Chicago.[11]

While some observers gushed over the possibility that Pullman's model town might offer a solution to the labor crisis of the era, others saw it as a backward-looking attempt to resurrect the social order of a bygone age. Progressive reformer and economist Richard Ely, who was also a particular critic of socialism, wrote that the town of Pullman "is benevolent, well wishing feudalism."[12] Other observers made similar critiques, not least the anarchists, who hated George Pullman as much as they hated the police department.[13] Yet he did not seek to reestablish the precapitalist past of embedded social and economic relations; rather, he sought to combine the orderly aspects of preindustrial society with the capitalist profit motive.

Pullman's experiment failed during the depression of 1893, when his strive for order clashed with his drive for profits, and this failure was the immediate cause of the strike. While the Pullman Company continued to make significant profits from the leasing of its cars, new orders declined almost to nothing, and Pullman kept his construction company operating only by putting out bids at a loss. To offset the losses in the construction division, Pullman laid off workers, reduced hours drastically, and cut wages to the bone. Rents to live in his model town, however, remained high. The workers were driven into penury, some famously receiving as little as a dollar for two weeks' work after rent was deducted.[14] The Pullman strategy for achieving an industrial version of the preindustrial system of order had broken down in the face of the industrial business cycle and Pullman's own determination to make a profit from every one of his enterprises.

The strike that followed was like no other that had taken place in the nineteenth century. It was a national railroad strike like that of 1877, but it was infinitely better organized and touched, if possible, an even deeper nerve of worker discontent. The Pullman strike was centered in Chicago, which was the center of the nation's railroad network and the headquarters of the American Railway Union (ARU), but it was a national strike. The strike started in the town of Pullman in May 1894 and became national when the delegates to the national convention of the ARU agreed to refuse moving any trains with Pullman Palace cars if Pullman continued to refuse to negotiate with his workers by June 26, 1894. The union intended to cut off Pullman's revenue stream. Because the railroads' General Managers' Association refused to remove Pullman cars from the trains, this boycott of Pullman cars shut down the nation's entire rail system. The boycott was more effective than anyone in the leadership of the ARU expected, having touched a nerve of anger among railroad workers faced with wage cuts and deteriorating working conditions. As with the other major railroad strikes, it quickly garnered support from other workers and the unemployed in Chicago and across the country.[15]

Both the Chicago city government and the Illinois state government were in the hands of men elected by workers, who promised to support the rights of the strikers. Mayor John Hopkins had owned a store in Pullman but was evicted and personally held a grudge. He was also the first mayor elected after the assassination of Mayor Carter Harrison, and ran on a proworker platform. He even donated $1,500 to the Pullman relief fund, though he did so before the strike spread outside of that company.[16] Governor John Altgeld was elected with labor votes and famously pardoned the anarchists convicted after Haymarket. However, as they did with Mayor Carter Harrison, many historians and contemporary observers have overstated the importance of these liberal politicians. Despite the avowed sympathies of the mayor, the

Chicago police helped the companies break the Pullman strike under the direction of the mayor and police leadership. Mayor Hopkins ordered all 3,000 city policemen to maintain order during the strike, hired 500 additional men who had police experience to help, and even fired an inspector of police and suspended all the patrolmen of the First District when he thought they were unduly lax toward the strikers.[17] The police also acted under the mayor's orders to clear the tracks of strikers, and in fact performed most of this central task to getting the railroads moving again throughout the strike.[18]

For instance, at 4 A.M. on July 2, 1894, Lieutenant Keleher and a detail of twenty policemen broke the strikers' lines and began escorting trains into the stockyards. They met determined opposition from strikers, but "the officers put them to rout." By noon, the police had brought 467 cars into the stockyards.[19] The police then attempted to escort the cars out of the yards through the crowds of strikers. "Toward evening an effort was made to take a Swift and Company train of dressed beef intended for eastern markets out of the Michigan Central yards west of Halsted Street," according to then-chief clerk Francis O'Neill. "Coupling pins were repeatedly pulled and the engineer and trainmen were mercilessly jeered and stoned. The police were well nigh powerless in such a mob." Eventually, O'Neill arrived on the scene with reinforcements and "stationed policemen along both sides of the train and together we succeeded in clearing the tracks after driving the mob out into the plank road."[20] The police, then, did not refrain from attempting to break the Pullman strike. Rather, as Chief Clerk O'Neill put it, "the police were well nigh powerless" in the face of a well-organized strike that engaged a broad swath of Chicago's working class and that was national in scope. As in the early stages of the 1877 strike or the eight-hour workday strikes of 1886, the police did not have the force to overwhelm such a large group of mobilized workers. So the police guarded railroad property and ran a few trains of perishable merchandise through the strikers' picket lines, and very effectively maintained order in the city before the arrival of federal troops.

This point has broad implications because historians have consistently overestimated the importance of political rhetoric in determining state policy. Had Chicago had an openly probusiness mayor, the rhetoric undoubtedly would have been different. The mayor would not have donated to the strike fund. But short of arresting the leadership of the ARU, the police did not have the power to break the strike, no matter what the political rhetoric of the city's leadership.

The attitude of Governor John Altgeld probably made more of a difference. He refused to enforce a federal injunction against the strikers issued on July

1. He also complained vigorously about the intervention of federal troops from Fort Sheridan, and said that this amounted to "an unconstitutional centralization of power in the hands of a 'military government.'"[21] But these protests did not have any serious effect, and despite the fact that Governor Altgeld and President Grover Cleveland were both Democrats, his support of the strikers allowed Altgeld to maintain his position as a friend of labor, even while soldiers broke the strike with a great deal of violence.

The General Managers' Association had developed a plan to turn to the federal government before the boycott even began. While they immediately hired private detectives to identify strike leaders and fire them, they also tried to enflame public anger over the strike to justify federal intervention. During the hearings after the strike, ARU officials accused the General Managers' Association of deliberately attaching Pullman cars to mail trains, freight trains, and even local commuter trains.[22] On July 2, just a few days after the strike had begun, John Egan, leader of the General Managers' Association, testified that the strike had effectively shut down the railroad network and urged the intervention of troops from Fort Sheridan. "It is the government's duty to take this business in hand, restore law, suppress the riots, and restore to the public the service which is now being deprived by conspirators and lawless men."[23] Egan's appeal was successful. The federal government used every means at its disposal, including injunctions, the army, and the federal prison system, where Eugene Debs, the most prominent leader of the strike, was imprisoned. Egan and the General Managers' Association had learned the lessons of the preceding generation of labor upheaval. Since the first May Day strike for the eight-hour day in 1867, Chicago businessmen had turned to the armed force of the state to solve their labor problems. In 1894, as in 1877 and 1886, that force proved effective.

Historian Richard Schneirov persuasively argues that the Pullman strike was a key event in the evolution of modern liberalism. "Pullman played an important role in defining the crisis of the 1890s, shaping a changing legal environment, spurring the development of the regulatory state, and fostering a new politics of progressive reform."[24] Schneirov saw Governor Altgeld and Mayor Hopkins as advocating a middle road of conciliation between labor and capital as a solution to the crisis of the 1890s, and the strike helped push their type of policy to the fore in the coming decades. For Schneirov and John Jentz, this politics of compromise followed from the policies that Carter Harrison began to implement in Chicago during the 1880s after the 1877 upheaval, and it was reestablished after Pullman.[25] In the aftermath of the strike, Jane Addams articulated a new progressive vision of "mediated conflict through democratic process."[26] The Progressive Era succeeded the Gilded Age in part because of the labor movement and the crises it engendered. However, this interpretation explains only half the story.

The Pullman strike also clearly reveals that by the end of the nineteenth century the United States had developed a matrix of state institutions to curtail the labor movement.[27] The ARU represented the culmination of a generation of railroad-worker organizing and upheaval and was the most powerful union American workers had ever built up to that time. An industrial union of its strength, class consciousness, and organization would not be seen again until the mass production unions of the Congress of Industrial Organizations (CIO) were built in the 1930s.[28] Employers had also learned from a generation of labor disputes and formed their own organizations, including the General Managers' Association among the railroads, and the Citizens' Association and Commercial Club within Chicago. But the state itself had also expanded dramatically and had much more force at its disposal in 1894 than it had in 1877. The police departments of every major city were radically stronger, more disciplined, and more legitimate institutions by that time. State militias of local businessmen and their allies had new, castellated armories spread throughout the northern cities.[29] When these institutions failed, the army could still intervene as it had in 1877, cloaked in the legal authority given by courts increasingly willing to issue injunctions against the labor movement.[30] The courts were also perfectly capable of convicting and executing the most radical leaders of the workers movement, in the case of the anarchists after Haymarket, or imprisoning them, as in the case of Eugene Debs, the main leader of the ARU. This reinforced armed might of the state undergirded all subsequent attempts at reform. This matrix of institutions, police, state militia, army, courts, and prisons beat back labor's challenge to the business order of the Gilded Age. This was not the end of the struggle by any means, as the history of labor in the Progressive Era shows, but from this point forward, businessmen would have access to armed forces no one would have predicted the existence of fifty years earlier.

This matrix also allowed different state actors to carry out strategies of repression and accommodation at the same time, as the Pullman strike illustrates so well. Altgeld and Hopkins could gain credit among workers for nominally backing the strikers, even as the federal government was breaking the strike. Thus a strike broken by a Democratic president could reinforce support for the Democratic Party among strikers in Chicago. That employers had a smorgasbord of armed institutions they could turn to helped make liberal politics and progressive reform on the local level palatable to a segment of businessmen, since they always had other levels of force available. If the police and state militia would not or could not break the Pullman strike, the army could. This also helps explain the old bugbear of U.S. labor history. Part of the reason American workers never developed as strong a socialist movement as their European counterparts is because liberal politicians like Harrison, Altgeld, and Hopkins could seem to support workers demands and even their movements, without denying employers the use of state power against those same working class movements. This strategy was not foolproof, as the growth of the Socialist Party and the Industrial Workers of the World (IWW) soon after these events illustrates, but it certainly helped liberal politicians establish some support among the country's wage workers.

Violent labor disputes continued into the twentieth century. The Teamsters' strike of 1905 pitted a range of craft unions, organized together in a sympathy strike, against businessmen organized in an Employers' Association who raised considerable funds for strikebreakers and private guards. Strikers and their supporters fought the police and the strikebreakers in battles that cost the lives of twenty-one people and left over four hundred injured. The defeat of this strike both through accusations of union corruption and through a great deal of violence carried out largely by the police weakened Chicago's unions for decades to come.[31] Chicago's workers were not tamed by police violence, though, as the strike waves of 1919 and the 1930s illustrate. Workers would continue to resist their exploitation in the wage labor economy that had been firmly established by the dawn of the twentieth century, and they would continue to face the police and other armed branches of the state, which had also been firmly established by this time.

The Pullman strike reveals the place of the Chicago Police Department within an increasingly national state apparatus dedicated to defending the new order that had arisen with the development of a wage labor economy. The crises of the nineteenth century gave birth to the police. The crises of the twentieth century would increasingly engage the federal government and lead to a similar massive expansion of its powers.

The United States is the only country that remained a republic with a high degree of democratic participation throughout the traumatic experience of industrialization. The development of the Chicago Police Department suggests that this was largely possible because democratic participation did not mean democratic control of state institutions. During the period of this country's most rapid industrialization, control over the police was removed from the realm of popular elections and put in the hands of supposedly neutral experts. With the firm backing of the urban elite, these experts built a powerful armed apparatus that defended order as they understood it. The rapid transition from a nation of independent producers to one of wage workers, with its accompanying increase in the concentration of wealth and power, was only possible because crucial armed institutions like the police were dedicated to protecting an order that facilitated this transformation. This transition was concentrated in cities, and the power of armed state institutions developed most strikingly at the municipal rather than the national level.

But the police were not born in a day to meet the demands of the elite. The institution evolved over the course of thirty years before it was able to maintain order in the city. This development was driven by the series of crises that accompanied the urban economic development of the second half of the nineteenth century. In Chicago, these crises generally moved from earlier conflicts over immigrant leisure activities to increasingly strident class conflict that culminated in the massive strikes for the eight-hour workday and the Haymarket bombing in 1886. Each of these crises was more severe than the one that preceded it. At each turn, those who were threatening the constituted order grew more organized, more radical, and more intellectually clear in their opposition to the basic structure of society. At the same time, these crises increasingly unified the otherwise politically heterogeneous elite around the need to strengthen all the forces that could defend their power, especially the police force. The threat of strikes, riots, and anarchist militias pushed the elite to take more flexible political positions regarding drinking, municipal services, and the incorporation of immigrants into city institutions in order to draw as many urban residents as possible away from the radical threat. These crises also led the wealthy to consent to a certain level of taxation.

Focusing on the police highlights a crucial aspect of the state that historians often lose sight of: the state serves first of all to protect and promote a particular political and economic order. While business and the state have a long history of contestation over regulation, at a deeper level the state is crucial to the basic functioning of business because it protects a particular form of property relations.[32] This protection takes the form, first of all, of eliminating threats to the existing order. These threats took various forms in late-nineteenth-century Chicago, including drunken immigrants, vagrants, thieves, anarchists, and most threateningly, mass workers' struggles. Before it could play any other role in society, the state had to ward off those threats.

This might seem an obvious point, but without it the development of the police and of capitalism more broadly cannot be explained.

However, in order to be effective, the police had to play a contradictory role. In Chicago, the key period of transformation for the police department took place during the mayoralty of Carter Harrison, when the police department refrained from breaking strikes and emphasized its usefulness to the population. Before the 1880s, police legitimacy was tenuous and the physical resources of the department were barely sufficient to meet the challenge of disorder. The department's legitimacy was secured by becoming a useful city service, as much as it was secured by protecting capitalism from anarchy. Paradoxically, the police could only protect bourgeois order and property by tolerating a certain amount of disorder.

Yet the police also set real threats to capitalism and the deep interests of the capitalists outside the pale of acceptable behavior. The anarchists were not part of the polyglot urbanity tolerable to the police by the 1890s. Neither were the strident demands of workers for the eight-hour day. The craft unions that allied with Carter Harrison and eventually became an integral part of the city's economic scene were tolerable. Thus, police policy in the late nineteenth century helped shape the political economy of the workers' movement in ways that would resonate at least into the 1930s.

It is easy to lose sight of the contingent aspect of the state because the police are now so ubiquitous that it is hard to imagine a time before they existed. But in fact, as this book illustrates, the police evolved relatively late in U.S. history. This is not to suggest that the police might never have been created. The threats to the established order in the second half of the nineteenth century were dire enough that they could be solved only with the help of such an institution. It is inconceivable that the urban elite would have surrendered their political and economic hegemony to groups like the anarchists without trying first to build a state apparatus that could ensure their continued power. The elite had the power to build a police force because they controlled the economic and political means to do so—they could mold the state to meet their needs, and so they did. However, this was still a remarkably difficult task to accomplish because the elite's power was far from absolute. This power was limited by the department's need to retain legitimacy among at least a large section of the city's workers. The elite was also constrained by the divisions within its own ranks. And, most important, the active resistance of those it sought to control set severe limits on how far elite power could extend. In the end, the elite was able to build an institution that could defend its conception of order, even if this institution did not take precisely the shape that the elite would have preferred.

If this book illustrates one point, it is that the messiness and contradictory nature of state building and the occasional apparent autonomy of state institutions do not change the fact that at a deeper level those institutions are built by specific groups of people to meet their needs. In the case of the police force, the business class that dominated municipal politics throughout the nineteenth century built the police to protect themselves from threats to their power, real and perceived.

NOTES

Abbreviations

RCAC	Records of the Citizens' Association of Chicago, Chicago History Museum, Chicago
CHM	Chicago History Museum, Chicago
HADC-CHM	Haymarket Affair Digital Collection, Chicago History Museum, Chicago
HWL	Harold Washington Library Center, Chicago
IGDRJD	Illinois Government Document Depository at Richard J. Daley Library, University of Illinois at Chicago
PCCCC	Proceedings of the Common Council of the City of Chicago, Illinois Regional Archive Depository at Ronald Williams Library, Northeastern Illinois University
WPA-FLPS	Works Progress Administration Foreign Language Press Survey, Harold Washington Library Center, Chicago

Introduction

1. Bernard Bailyn, *The Ordeal of Thomas Hutchinson: Loyalism and the Destruction of the First British Empire* (Cambridge, Mass.: Harvard University Press, 1974), 35–36.

2. Mary Ryan, *Civic Wars: Democracy and Civic Life in the American City During the Nineteenth Century* (Berkeley: University of California Press, 1998); Michael Feldberg, *The Turbulent Era: Riot and Disorder in Jacksonian America* (New York: Oxford University Press, 1970).

3. David Grimstead, *American Mobbing, 1828–1861: Toward Civil War* (New York: Oxford University Press, 1998).

4. Susan Davis, "Making Night Hideous: Christmas Revelry and Public Order in Nineteenth-Century Philadelphia," *American Quarterly* 34, no. 2 (1982): 184–199.

5. Grimstead, *American Mobbing*; Feldberg, *Turbulent Era*; Daniel Walker Howe, *What Hath God Wrought: The Transformation of America, 1815–1848* (New York: Oxford University Press, 2007), 430–434.

6. Nigel Cliff, *The Shakespeare Riots: Revenge, Drama and Death in Nineteenth Century America* (New York: Random House, 2007), 213–230; Paul Weinbaum, *Mobs*

and Demagogues: The New York Response to Collective Violence in the Early Nineteenth Century (Ann Arbor: University of Michigan Press, 1979), 37–39.

7. Moses I. Finley, *The Ancient Economy* (Berkeley: University of California Press, 1973), 17–18.

8. http://www.hmcourts-service.gov.uk/aboutus/history/magistrates.htm (accessed January 28, 2011).

9. See Erik Monkkonen, *Police in Urban America, 1860–1920* (Cambridge: Cambridge University Press, 1980); Roger Lane, *Policing the City: Boston, 1822–1855* (Cambridge, Mass.: Harvard University Press, 1967); Allen Steinberg, *The Transformation of Criminal Justice: Philadelphia, 1800–1880* (Chapel Hill: University of North Carolina Press, 1989); Robert M. Fogelson, *Big City Police* (Cambridge, Mass.: Harvard University Press, 1977); Gerald Astor, *The New York Cops: An Informal History* (New York: Charles Scribners' Sons, 1971); Dennis Rousey, *Policing the Southern City: New Orleans, 1805–1889* (Baton Rouge: Louisiana State University Press, 1997), among others.

10. *Chicago Police Department Annual Report*, 2010, 54, https://portal.chicagopolice .org/portal/page/portal/ClearPath/News/Statistical%20Reports/Annual%20Reports/ 10AR.pdf (accessed March 28, 2013).

11. For the fullest discussion of this transformation, see John Jentz and Richard Schneirov, *Chicago in the Age of Capital: Class, Politics and Democracy during the Civil War and Reconstruction* (Urbana: University of Illinois Press, 2012).

12. Richard Bensel, *The Political Economy of American Industrialization, 1877–1900* (New York: Cambridge University Press, 2000).

13. William Forbath, *Law and the Shaping of the American Labor Movement* (Cambridge, Mass.: Harvard University Press, 1991).

14. Harold Platt, *Shock Cities: The Environmental Transformation and Reform in Manchester and Chicago* (Chicago: University of Chicago Press, 2005).

15. For other types of order, see especially Paul Boyer, *Urban Masses and Moral Order in America, 1820–1920* (Cambridge, Mass.: Harvard University Press, 1978); and Robert Wiebe, *The Search for Order, 1877–1920* (New York: Hill and Wang, 1966).

16. In 1976, Mark Haller pointed out that the police received no legal training as late as 1900. Mark Haller, "Historical Roots of Police Behavior, Chicago, 1890–1925," *Law and Society Review* 10, no. 2 (1976): 303.

17. William Stead, *If Christ Came to Chicago!: A Plea for the Union of All who Love in the Service of All Who Suffer* (Chicago: Laird and Lee Publishers, 1894), 102.

18. Frederick Cople Jaher, *The Urban Establishment: Upper Strata in Boston, New York, Charleston, Chicago, and Los Angeles* (Urbana: University of Illinois Press, 1982), 453–456.

19. Ibid., 456.

20. Edward Bubnys, "Nativity and the Distribution of Wealth: Chicago, 1870," *Explorations in Economic History* 19 (April 1982): 101–109.

21. Stead, *If Christ Came to Chicago*, 69–98.

22. Jaher, *Urban Establishment*, 472–517.

23. This development is explained most fully in John Jentz and Richard Schneirov, *Chicago in the Age of Capital: Class, Politics, and Democracy during the Civil War and Reconstruction* (Urbana: University of Illinois Press, 2012).

24. Congressional Globe, 30 Congress, 2 Session, Appendix, 103, quoted in Eric Foner, *"Free Soil, Free Labor, Free Men:" The Ideology of the Republican Party before the Civil War* (Oxford: Oxford University Press, 1995), 17.

25. See, for instance, Bruce Laurie, *Artisans into Workers: Labor in Nineteenth-Century America* (New York: Hill and Wang, 1989; repr. Urbana: University of Illinois Press, 1997); Sean Wilentz, *Chants Democratic: New York City and the Rise of the American Working Class, 1788–1850* (Oxford: Oxford University Press: 1984); David Montgomery, *The Fall of the House of Labor: The Workplace, the State, and American Labor Activism, 1865–1920* (New York: Cambridge University Press, 1987), and *Beyond Equality: Labor and the Radical Republicans, 1862–1872* (Urbana: University of Illinois Press, 1981); Alan Dawley, *Class and Community: The Industrial Revolution in Lynn* (Cambridge, Mass.: Harvard University Press, 1976); and Jentz and Schneirov, *Chicago in the Age of Capital*.

26. See among others, Boyer, *Urban Masses and Moral Order in America*; and Jentz and Schneirov, *Chicago in the Age of Capital*.

27. See Bruce Nelson, *Beyond the Martyrs: A Social History of Chicago's Anarchists, 1870–1900* (New Brunswick, N.J.: Rutgers University Press, 1988)

28. See especially Eric Hirsch, *Urban Revolt: Ethnic Politics in the Nineteenth-Century Chicago Labor Movement* (Berkeley: University of California Press, 1990); and Jentz and Schneirov, *Chicago in the Age of Capital*.

29. Jentz and Schneirov, *Chicago in the Age of Capital*.

30. Michael Funchion, "Irish Chicago: Church, Homeland, Politics, and Class—The Shaping of an Ethnic Group, 1870–1900," in *Ethnic Chicago: A Multicultural Portrait*, ed. Melvin Holli and Peter Jones (Grand Rapids, Mich.: Wm. B. Eerdmans, 1995), 57–92; for first arrest records, see PCCCC, January 14, 1856, doc. 1874A.

31. Hirsch, *Urban Revolt*.

32. Mimi Cowan, "Ducking for Cover: Chicago's Irish Nationalists in the Haymarket Era," *Labor: Studies in Working-Class History of the Americas* 9, no. 1 (2012): 53–76.

33. Erik Monkkonen, *Police in Urban America, 1860–1920* (Cambridge: Cambridge University Press, 1980).

34. This pessimistic view of human nature runs through the main police-produced works of the time, including the annual reports, Michael Schaack, *Anarchy and Anarchists: A History of Red Terror in America and Europe* (1889; repr. New York: Arno Press, 1977); Francis O'Neil, *Chief O'Neill's Sketchy Recollections of an Eventful Life in Chicago* (Evanston, Ill.: Northwestern University Press, 2008); and police reports in the newspapers, such as John Bonfield's defense of police actions against striking transit workers in the *Chicago Tribune*, January 31, 1886.

35. Bruce Nelson, *Beyond the Martyrs*; Eric Hirsch, *Urban Revolt*.

36. See *Report of the General Superintendent of Police of the City of Chicago to the City Council for the Fiscal Year ending December 31st, 1878–1894*, Municipal Reference Collection, HWL.

Chapter 1. Drunken Immigrants, Businessmen's Order,
and the Founding of the Chicago Police Department

1. Police report on arrests for month of April 1855, printed in *Chicago Tribune*, May 1, 1855.

2. John Flinn, *History of the Chicago Police* (1887; repr. New York: AMS Press, 1972), 70–74; Robin Einhorn, *Property Rules: Political Economy in Chicago, 1833–1872* (Chicago: University of Chicago Press, 1991), 156–162

3. For nonpolice elite reactions to this increased disorder, see Paul Boyer, *Urban Masses and Moral Order in America, 1820–1920* (Cambridge, Mass.: Harvard University Press, 1978).

4. PCCCC, March 12, 1855, doc. 2139A–2207A. These documents are the official oaths of all the watchmen, constables, and policemen of the city.

5. Flinn, *History of the Chicago Police*, 71–72.

6. PCCCC, April 30, 1855, doc. 294A.

7. Richard Schneirov, *Labor and Urban Politics: Class Conflict and the Origins of Modern Liberalism in Chicago, 1864–97* (Urbana: University of Illinois Press, 1998), 27 and 52; Einhorn, *Property Rules*, 156–162; Richard Wilson Renner, "In a Perfect Ferment: Chicago, the Know-Nothings, and the Riot for Lager Beer," *Chicago History* 5 (1976): 163–165; Flinn, *History of the Chicago Police*, 70–79.

8. *Chicago Tribune*, April 24, 1855.

9. For similar stories in other cities, see Roger Lane, *Policing the City: Boston, 1820–1885* (Cambridge, Mass.: Harvard University Press, 1967); Allen Steinberg, *The Transformation of Criminal Justice: Philadelphia, 1800–1880* (Chapel Hill: University of North Carolina Press, 1989); Sidney Harring, *Policing a Class Society: The Experience of American Cities, 1865–1915* (New Brunswick, N.J.: Rutgers University Press, 1983); Erik Monkkonen, *Police in Urban America, 1860–1920* (Cambridge: Cambridge University Press, 1980); Robert M. Fogelson, *Big City Police* (Cambridge, Mass.: Harvard University Press, 1977).

10. "Act of Incorporation for the City of Chicago, 1837," Electronic Encyclopedia of Chicago, http://www.encyclopedia.chicagohistory.org/pages/11480.html (accessed January 2008).

11. Flinn, *History of the Chicago Police*, 58.

12. Daniel Walker Howe makes a nearly identical observation about eastern cities in *What Hath God Wrought: The Transformation of America, 1815–1848* (New York: Oxford University Press, 2007), 432.

13. Andrew Todd Harris, *Policing the City: Crime and Legal Authority in London, 1780–1840* (Columbus: Ohio State University Press, 2004), chapter 1. See also Henry Fielding's classic account of a thief taker, *Jonathon Wild* (1743; repr. New York: Oxford University Press, 2008).

14. PCCCC, December 8, 1851, doc. 1290A.

15. See especially the inaugural speeches of Mayors Boone, (http://www.chipublib.org/cplbooksmovies/cplarchive/mayors/boone_inaug.php, accessed March 30, 2013) and Wentworth (http://www.chipublib.org/cplbooksmovies/cplarchive/mayors/wentworth_inaug_1860.php, accessed March 30, 2013).

16. PCCCC, December 8, 1851, doc. 1290A.

17. See especially David R. Johnson, *Policing the Urban Underworld: The Impact of Crime on the Development of the American Police, 1800–1877* (Philadelphia, Pa.: Temple University Press, 1979).

18. For police budget, see PCCCC, April 2, 1852, doc. 71A. For population, see Census Report, August 9, 1852, in *Early Chicago, 1833–1871: A Selection of City Council Proceedings Files from the Illinois State Archives* (Springfield: Illinois State Archives Publication Unit, 1986), doc. 23.

19. Einhorn, *Property Rules.*

20. James MacKay, *Allan Pinkerton: The First Private Eye* (Hoboken, N.J.: Wiley, 1996).

21. Frank Morn, *The Eye That Never Sleeps: A History of the Pinkerton National Detective Agency* (Bloomington: Indiana University Press, 1982).

22. Sally Hadden, *Slave Patrols: Law and Violence in Virginia and the Carolinas* (Cambridge, Mass.: Harvard University Press, 2001).

23. Dennis Rousey, *Policing the Southern City: New Orleans, 1805–1889* (Baton Rouge: Louisiana State University Press, 1997).

24. Wilbur Miller, *Cops and Bobbies: Police Authority in New York and London, 1830–1870* (Chicago: University of Chicago Press, 1977).

25. The British historiography of policing is greatly superior to the American. See especially David Taylor, *The New Police in Nineteenth-Century England: Crime, Conflict and Control* (Manchester, U.K.: Manchester University Press, 1997), 1–12.

26. PCCCC, May 12, 1853, doc. 409A.

27. Ibid.

28. Ibid.

29. PCCCC, May 2, 1853, doc. 280A.

30. PCCCC, August 8, 1853, doc. 800A; *Daily Chicago Journal*, August 8 and 9, 1853.

31. *Daily Chicago Journal*, August 10, 12, and 17, 1853; for the number of men, see PCCCC, March 15, 1854, doc. 1817A–1872A. These are the official oaths of all the constables, night and day watchmen in the employ of the city of Chicago as of that date.

32. *Chicago Tribune*, May 17, 1853.

33. http://www.measuringworth.com/uscompare (accessed August 2011).

34. PCCCC, March 12, 1855, doc. 1861A.

35. For more detailed descriptions of this booster system, see especially Jeffrey S. Adler, *Yankee Merchants and the Making of the Urban West: the Rise and Fall of Antebellum St. Louis* (Cambridge: Cambridge University Press, 1991); Einhorn, *Property Rules*, and Donald Miller, *City of the Century: The Epic of Chicago and the Making of America* (New York: Simon and Schuster, 1996).

36. PCCCC, April 30, 1855, doc. 294A; PCCCC, June 11, 1855, doc. 647A; PCCCC, July 10, 1855, doc. 768A; Schneirov, *Labor and Urban Politics*, 27, 52; Einhorn, *Property Rules*, 156–162; Flinn, *History of the Chicago Police*, 70–79.

37. PCCCC, April 30, 1855, doc. 294A.

38. Illinois Central Railroad Company, *Report and Accompanying Documents of the Illinois Central Railroad Company, made by order of the Stockholders at their Annual*

Meeting held at Chicago, March 19, 1856 (New York: George Scott Row, Printer and Stationer, 1856).

39. *Daily Chicago Journal,* August 17, 1853.

40. John W. Starr Jr., *Lincoln and the Railroads; a biographical study* (New York: Dodd, Mead & Company, 1927), 57–79.

41. William K. Ackerman, "History of the Illinois Central Railroad Company," in *History of the Illinois Central Railroad Company and Representative Employes* (Chicago: Railroad Historical Company, 1900); Bessie Pierce, *A History of Chicago, 1848–1871,* vol. 2, *1848–1871* (London: Alfred A. Knopf, 1940).

42. Carlton J. Corliss, *The Main Line of Mid-America: The Story of the Illinois Central* (New York: Creative Age Press, 1950), 59.

43. PCCCC, April 30, 1855, doc. 294A; Pierce, *History of Chicago,* 198.

44. Corliss, *Main Line of Mid-America,* 52.

45. Illinois Central Railroad Company Directors, *Report of the Directors to the Stockholders of the Illinois Central Railroad Company, March 15, 1854* (New York: Geo. Scott and Roe, Stationer and Printer, 1854.)

46. Ibid.

47. Peter Way, *Common Labor: Workers and the Digging of North American Canals, 1780–1860* (New York: Cambridge University Press, 2003), 200–205

48. Peter Thompson, *Rum Punch and Revolution: Taverngoing and Public Life in Eighteenth-Century Philadelphia* (Philadelphia: University of Pennsylvania Press, 1999), 101.

49. Bruce Laurie, *Artisans into Workers: Labor in Nineteenth-Century America* (New York: Hill and Wang, 1989; repr. Urbana: University of Illinois Press, 1997), 37.

50. See ibid.; Sean Wilentz, *Chants Democratic: New York City and the Rise of the American Working Class, 1788–1850* (Oxford: Oxford University Press: 1984); and David Montgomery, *The Fall of the House of Labor: The Workplace, the State, and American Labor Activism, 1865–1920* (New York: Cambridge University Press, 1987).

51. For the fullest development of this idea, see Roy Rosenzweig, *Eight Hours for What We Will: Workers and Leisure in an Industrial City, 1870–1920* (Cambridge: Cambridge University Press, 1983). For a rich description of saloon life, see Perry Duis, *The Saloon: Public Drinking in Chicago and Boston, 1880–1920* (Urbana: University of Illinois Press, 1983).

52. PCCCC, April 30, 1855, doc. 294A.

53. Ibid.

54. For New York and London police see Miller, *Cops and Bobbies;* Ignatieff, "Police and People"; for the Boston police, see Roger Lane, *Policing the City: Boston, 1822–1855* (Cambridge, Mass.: Harvard University Press, 1967).

55. Allen Steinberg, *The Transformation of Criminal Justice: Philadelphia, 1800–1880* (Chapel Hill: University of North Carolina Press, 1989), 119.

56. Ibid., 143–145.

57. Ibid., 149.

58. Laurie, *Artisans into Workers,* 74.

59. See, for instance, Alfred Young, *The Shoemaker and the Tea Party: Memory and the American Revolution* (Boston: Beacon Press, 1999), for a description of cross class crowds during the revolutionary period.

60. Schneirov, *Labor and Urban Politics*, 27, 52; Einhorn, *Property Rules*, 156–162; Renner, "In a Perfect Ferment," 163–165; Flinn, *History of the Chicago Police*, 70–79.

61. A. T. Andreas, *History of Chicago*, vol. 2 (1884; repr. New York: Arno Press, 1975), 86; Flinn *History of the Chicago Police*, 75–76; undated clipping, John D. Shea scrapbooks, CHM.

62. Flinn, *History of the Chicago Police*, 75–76; see also Ralph Marrow and Harriet Carter, *In Pursuit of Crime; the Police of Chicago: Chronicle of a Hundred Years, 1833–1933* (Sunbury, Ohio: The Flats Publishing Company, 1996), 16–20; for arrest statistics, see PCCCC, June 11, 1856, doc. 44A.

63. Lawrence McCaffrey, Ellen Skerret, Michael Funchion, and Charles Fanning, *The Irish in Chicago* (Urbana: University of Illinois Press, 1987), 3.

64. PCCCC, January 14, 1856, doc. 1874A.

65. Ibid.

66. Ibid.

67. Ibid.

68. Alfred Young, *The Shoemaker and the Tea Party: Memory and the American Revolution* (Boston: Beacon Press, 2000), 42–46.

69. See, for example, Pierce, *History of Chicago*, and Flinn, *History of the Chicago Police*.

70. Robin Einhorn, "Lager Beer Riot," in *The Encyclopedia of Chicago*, ed. James Grossman, Ann Durkin Keating, and Janice L. Reiff (Chicago: University of Chicago Press, 2004).

Chapter 2. Paternalism and the Birth of Professional Police Organization

1. *Chicago Tribune*, March 12, 1856.

2. Mark Haller makes this point most clearly in "Historical Roots of Police Behavior, Chicago, 1890–1925," *Law and Society Review* 10, no. 2 (1976): 303–323.

3. See Amy Bridges, *A City in the Republic: Antebellum Reform in New York and the Origins of Machine Politics* (Cambridge: Cambridge University Press, 1986.

4. Kenneth Finegold makes a similar argument about the role of experts in the clash between reformers and machine politicians in *Experts and Politicians: Reform Challenges to Machine Politics in New York, Cleveland, and Chicago* (Princeton, N.J.: Princeton University Press, 1995).

5. For statistics on arrests, see PCCCC, February 2, 1857, doc. 1710A.

6. See, for example, PCCCC: March 11, 1856, doc. 2169X; March 17, 1856, doc. 7A; October 27, 1856, doc. 1192A; December 8, 1856, doc. 1449A; January 26, 1857, doc. 1640A.

7. PCCCC, March 17, 1856, doc. 7.

8. PCCCC, January 26, 1857, doc. 1640A.

9. Don Fehrenbacher, *Chicago Giant: A Biography of "Long John" Wentworth* (Madison, Wisc.: American History Research Center, 1957).

10. *Chicago Tribune*, March 5 and 11, 1857; Ralph Marrow and Harriet Carter, *In Pursuit of Crime; the Police of Chicago: Chronicle of a Hundred Years, 1833–1933* (Sunbury, Ohio: Flats Publishing Company, 1996), 23–24; Fehrenbacher, *Chicago Giant*, 142–161.

11. John Wentworth's first inaugural speech, reproduced in the *Chicago Tribune*, March 11, 1857.

12. *Chicago Tribune*, March 11, 1857.

13. PCCCC, April 13, 1857, doc. 171A.

14. PCCCC, May 4, 1857, doc. 282A.

15. PCCCC: May 26, 1860, doc. 47A; May 25, 1860, doc. 46A.

16. PCCCC, June 4, 1860, doc. 63A.

17. PCCCC, June 4, 1860, doc. 60A.

18. John Flinn, *History of the Chicago Police* (1887; repr. New York: AMS Press, 1972), 88; Fehrenbacher, *Chicago Giant*, 142–162.

19. *Chicago Tribune*, March 21, 1857; Marrow and Carter, *In Pursuit of Crime*, 24; Fehrenbacher, *Chicago Giant*, 143; Donald Miller, *City of the Century: The Epic of Chicago and the Making of America* (New York: Simon and Schuster, 1996); Richard Lindberg, *To Serve and Collect: Chicago Politics and Police Corruption from the Lager Beer Riot to the Summerdale Scandal, 1855–1960* (Carbondale: Southern Illinois University Press, 1998), 8–9.

20. Donald Miller, *City of the Century: The Epic of Chicago and the Making of America* (New York: Simon and Schuster, 1996), 103–117.

21. *Chicago Tribune*, July 18, 1857; Lindberg, *To Serve and Collect*, 9; Flinn, *History of the Chicago Police*, 85–86.

22. *Chicago Tribune*, June 20, 1857; Fehrenbacher, *Chicago Giant*, 146.

23. *Chicago Tribune*, October 12, 1857.

24. Ibid.; Lindberg, *To Serve and Collect*, 10–11.

25. Fehrenbacher, *Chicago Giant*, 145; Marrow and Carter, *In Pursuit of Crime*, 23–26; Flinn, *History of the Chicago Police*, 82–88.

26. Flinn, *History of the Chicago Police*, 88–90. The total count of police and their approximate ethnicities were derived from the complete role of policemen at the end of Haines's second term, found in PCCCC, March 3, 1860, doc. 833A.

27. An example of a rejected petition under Haines can be found in PCCCC, April 5, 1858, doc. 87A.

28. Flinn, *History of the Chicago Police*, 92–93; Fehrenbacher, *Chicago Giant*, see esp. 142–176.

29. Reports made to the 22nd General Assembly of the State of Illinois, January 7, 1861, IGDRJD.

30. Warden's report to the 22nd General Assembly of the State of Illinois, December 1, 1860, IGDRJD.

31. Bessie Pierce, *A History of Chicago*, vol. 2, *1848–1871* (London: Alfred A. Knopf, 1940), 316.

32. Gerald Astor, *The New York Cops: An Informal History* (New York: Charles Scribner's Sons, 1971), 24–31.

33. Phillip Ethington, "Vigilantes and the Police: The Creation of a Professional Police Bureaucracy in San Francisco, 1847–1900," *Journal of Social History* 21, no. 2 (1987): 197–227.

34. See Richard Bensel, *Yankee Leviathan: The Origins of Central State Authority in America, 1859–1877* (New York: Cambridge University Press, 1991) for the fullest discussion of this development.

35. See, for instance, Tyler Anbinder, *Nativism and Slavery: The Northing Know-Nothings and the Politics of the 1850s* (New York: Oxford University Press, 1994).

36. *Public Laws of the State of Illinois, passed by the Twenty Second General Assembly* (Springfield: Bailhache and Baker, Printers, 1861), 151.

37. Ibid., 152.

38. PCCCC, November 17, 1862, doc. 203A; *Chicago Tribune*, March 22, 1861; Flinn, *History of the Chicago Police*, 95–96.

39. *Chicago Tribune*, April 9, 1861.

40. PCCCC, March 20, 1861, doc. 305A; Flinn, *History of the Chicago Police*, 98.

41. PCCCC, November 17, 1862, doc. 203A.

42. Ibid., for a description of the "creaker," see Flinn, *History of the Chicago Police*, 88.

43. These recollections come from an undated file of clippings at the CHM, so the exact date is unknown. Given the mention of Chief Kipley, they are probably from 1897, when Kipley was appointed by Mayor Carter Harrison II.

44. Undated clipping, John D. Shea scrapbooks, CHM.

45. Finegold, *Reformers and Politicians*.

46. PCCCC, November 17, 1862, doc. 203A.

47. Chicago *Tribune*, March 1, 1861.

48. *Chicago Tribune*, and April 3, 1861.

49. PCCCC, November 17, 1862, doc. 203A; Flinn, *History of the Chicago Police*, 98; A. T. Andreas, *History of Chicago*, vol. 2 (1884; repr. New York: Arno Press, 1975), 86.

50. PCCCC, November 17, 1862, doc. 203A; *Chicago Tribune*, June 18, 1862; Fehrenbacher, *Chicago Giant*, 194–195.

51. Bensel, *Yankee Leviathan*; Theda Skocpol, *Protecting Soldiers and Mothers: The Political Origins of Social Policy in the United States* (Cambridge, Mass.: Harvard University Press, 1995); Iver Bernstein, *The New York City Draft Riots: Their Significance for American Society and Politics in the Age of the Civil War* (New York: Oxford University Press, 1990).

Chapter 3. The Police and the First May Day Strike for the Eight-Hour Day

1. Bruce Laurie, *Artisans into Workers: Labor in Nineteenth-Century America* (New York: Hill and Wang, 1989; repr. Urbana: University of Illinois Press, 1997); David

Montgomery, *The Fall of the House of Labor: The Workplace, the State, and American Labor Activism, 1865–1925* (Cambridge: Cambridge University Press, 1987).

2. Richard Schneirov, *Labor and Urban Politics: Class Conflict and the Origins of Modern Liberalism in Chicago, 1864–97* (Urbana: University of Illinois Press, 1998), 19–25; John Jentz and Richard Schneirov, *Chicago in the Age of Capital: Class, Politics, and Democracy during the Civil War and Reconstruction* (Urbana: University of Illinois Press, 2012), 12–50.

3. Herbert Harris, *American Labor* (London: Oxford University Press, 1939), 69; Joseph Rayback, *A History of American Labor* (New York: Free Press, 1966), 114.

4. Montgomery, *Fall of the House of Labor*, 22.

5. Laurie, *Artisans into Workers*; Montgomery, *Fall of the House of Labor*.

6. Bessie Pierce, *A History of Chicago*, vol. 2, *1848–1871* (Chicago: University of Chicago Press, 1940), 160–168.

7. Schneirov, *Labor and Urban Politics*, 34–35.

8. Eric Hirsch, *Urban Revolt: Ethnic Politics in the Nineteenth-Century Chicago Labor Movement* (Berkeley: University of California Press, 1990), 6.

9. Schneirov, *Labor and Urban Politics*, 34–35.

10. David Montgomery, *Beyond Equality: Labor and the Radical Republicans, 1862–1872* (Urbana: University of Illinois Press, 1981), x.

11. John Flinn, *History of the Chicago Police* (1887; repr. New York: AMS Press, 1972), 98–109.

12. Robin Einhorn, *Property Rules: Political Economy in Chicago, 1833–1872* (Chicago: University of Chicago Press, 1991).

13. Schneirov, *Labor and Urban Politics*, 32.

14. Montgomery, *Beyond Equality*, 111, 113, 155, 177.

15. *Workingman's Advocate*, September 1 and 8, 1866.

16. PCCCC, April 10, 1867, doc. 1122A.

17. Ibid.

18. PCCCC, April 1, 1866, doc. 262A.

19. Montgomery, *Beyond Equality*, 296–302.

20. Ibid., 302.

21. Schneirov, *Labor and Urban Politics*, 33–34.

22. Eric Foner, *Free Soil, Free Labor, Free Men: The Ideology of the Republican Party before the Civil War* (New York: Oxford University Press, 1971); Montgomery, *Fall of the House of Labor* and *Beyond Equality*.

23. Brian Greenberg, *Worker and Community: Response to Industrialization in a Nineteenth-Century American City, Albany, New York, 1850–1894* (Albany: State University of New York Press, 1985), 26.

24. This set of ideas is described in Greenberg, *Worker and Community*, and Montgomery, *Beyond Equality*.

25. Montgomery, *Beyond Equality*, 306.

26. See, for example, *Chicago Republican*, April 30, 1867; *Chicago Tribune*, May 1, 1867; *Chicago Times*, April 30, 1867.

27. For a fuller discussion of this debate, see Jentz and Schneirov, *Chicago in the Age of Capital*, 93–100.

28. Jentz and Schneirov, *Chicago in the Age of Capital*, 50.

29. *Chicago Republican*, April 30, 1867.

30. Montgomery, *Beyond Equality*, 308.

31. *Chicago Republican*, April 30, 1867.

32. *Chicago Republican*, May 1 and 2, 1867; *Chicago Tribune*, May 2, 1867.

33. *Chicago Republican*, May 2, 1867; *Chicago Tribune*, May 2, 1867.

34. *Chicago Tribune*, May 2, 1867

35. *Chicago Tribune*, May 3, 1867; *Chicago Republican*, May 3, 1867; Schneirov, *Labor and Urban Politics*, 35.

36. *Chicago Republican*, May 3, 1867; *Chicago Tribune*, May 3, 1867.

37. *Chicago Republican*, May 3, 1867; *Chicago Tribune*, May 3, 1867.

38. Schneirov, *Labor and Urban Politics*, 35.

39. *Chicago Republican*, May 3, 1867.

40. *Chicago Tribune*, May 3, 1867.

41. *Chicago Times*, May 3, 1867.

42. Foner, *Free Soil, Free Labor, Free Men*.

43. *Chicago Tribune*, May 3, 1867.

44. *Chicago Tribune*, May 3 and 4, 1867.

45. *Chicago Tribune*, May 4, 1867; *Chicago Times*, May 4, 1867; *Chicago Republican*, May 4, 1867.

46. *Chicago Tribune*, May 3–9, 1867; *Chicago Republican*, May 3–9, 1867.

47. PCCCC, May 3, 1867, doc. 1220A.

48. Flinn, *History of the Chicago Police*, 114–115.

49. Montgomery, *Beyond Equality*, 311.

50. Schneirov, *Labor and Urban Politics*, 35–40.

Chapter 4. The Native-Born Protestant Elite's Bid for Control in the 1870s

1. For Chicago, see especially John Jentz and Richard Schneirov, *Chicago in the Age of Capital: Class, Politics, and Democracy during the Civil War and Reconstruction* (Urbana: University of Illinois Press, 2012), chapter 4.

2. Sven Beckert, *The Monied Metropolis: New York City and the Consolidation of the American Bourgeoisie, 1850–1896* (Cambridge: Cambridge University Press, 2001).

3. Karen Sawislak, *Smoldering City: Chicagoans and the Great Fire, 1871–1874* (Chicago: University of Chicago Press, 1995), 29.

4. Ibid.

5. *Chicago Times*, October 23, 1871, quoted in ibid., 46.

6. Sawislak, *Smoldering City*; Carl Smith, *Urban Disorder and the Shape of Belief: The Great Chicago Fire, the Haymarket Bomb, and the Model Town of Pullman* (Chicago: University of Chicago Press, 1995).

7. John Flinn, *History of the Chicago Police* (1887; repr. New York: AMS Press, 1972), 127.

8. Chicago Relief and Aid Society, *Report of the Chicago Relief and Aid Society of Disbursement of Contributions for the Sufferers by the Chicago Fire* (Chicago: Riverside Press, 1874), 15.

9. Flinn, *History of the Chicago Police*, 127.

10. Chicago Relief and Aid Society, *Report*, 16–18.

11. Throughout April 1871, the *Chicago Tribune* and *Chicago Times* covered the Paris Commune in detail. These papers also carried extensive coverage of the New York draft riots in July 1863.

12. Iver Bernstein, *The New York City Draft Riots: Their Significance for American Society and Politics in the Age of the Civil War* (Oxford: Oxford University Press: 1990); Barnet Schecter, *The Devil's Own Work: The Civil War Draft Riots and the Fight to Reconstruct America* (New York: Walker and Company, 2007).

13. Flinn, *History of the Chicago Police*, 128–129.

14. Chicago Relief and Aid Society, *Report*, 20.

15. Ibid., 20–21.

16. Ibid., 22.

17. Flinn, *History of the Chicago Police*, 130.

18. Ibid., 130; Elias Colbert and Everett Chamberlain, *Chicago and the Great Conflagration* (Cincinnati, Ohio: C. F. Vent, 1872), 242.

19. *Chicago Tribune*, December 27, 1871.

20. Chicago Relief and Aid Society, *Report*, 21.

21. PCCCC, May 31, 1872, doc. 13.

22. *Chicago Tribune*, December 27, 1871.

23. John Jentz, "Class and Politics in an Emerging Industrial City, Chicago in the 1860s and 1870s," *Journal of Urban History* 17 (May 1991): 238–239.

24. *Chicago Tribune*, January 16, 1872.

25. Ibid.

26. In *The Limits of Power: Great Fires and the Process of City Growth in America* (New York: Cambridge University Press, 1986), 100–103, Christine Meisner Rosen argues that this clash was open class conflict, while in *Smoldering City*, Karen Sawislak sees it as a conflict between a native-born commercial class and a largely immigrant mix of skilled workers, small business owners and more substantial merchants (146). John B. Jentz called the clash a "political battle with profound class and ethnic dimensions" ("Class and Politics in an Emerging Industrial City, Chicago in the 1860s and 1870s," 239).

27. Jentz and Schneirov, *Chicago in the Age of Capital*, 139.

28. The *Chicago Tribune* even declared that the mob had been "communistic" in nature (January 16, 1872.)

29. *Chicago Tribune*, January 18, 1871.

30. PCCCC, February 21, 1872, doc. 194, enclosed letter dated January 17.

31. PCCCC, June 15, 1872, doc. 492.

32. PCCCC, April 17, 1872, doc. 293.

33. PCCCC, March 31, 1873, doc. 13.

34. PCCCC, July 3, 1872, doc. 603.

35. *Chicago Tribune*, June 4, 1872.

36. *Chicago Tribune*, July 8, 1872.

37. *Chicago Tribune*, July 29, 1872.

38. *Chicago Tribune*, July 23, 1872.

39. Chicago Police Department Homicide Record Index, available at http://homicide .northwestern.edu (accessed September 2007).

40. Jeffrey Adler, *First in Violence, Deepest in Dirt: Homicide in Chicago, 1875–1920* (Cambridge, Mass.: Harvard University Press, 2006).

41. The *Tribune* paid particular attention to the New York Committee of Seventy. It covered the New York committee almost every day in September 1871, and frequently thereafter. For an account of the Committee of Seventy's role in New York, see Sven Beckert, *The Monied Metropolis: New York City and the Consolidation of the American Bourgeoisie, 1850–1896* (Cambridge: Cambridge University Press, 2001).

42. See Judge S. B. Gookins obituary, *Chicago Tribune*, June 16, 1880; J. V. Farwell was the director of the dry-goods business where Marshall Field got his start. He also invested in textiles.

43. See especially the *Chicago Tribune*, September 5, 1873, for a list of members of the Committee of Seventy.

44. *Chicago Tribune*, July 30, 1872.

45. Flinn, *History of the Chicago Police*, 138.

46. *Chicago Tribune*, August 4, 1871.

47. *Chicago Tribune*, August 4 and 13, 1871.

48. *Chicago Tribune*, September 17, 1872; M. L. Ahern, *The Great Revolution: A History of the Rise and Progress of the People's Party in the City of Chicago and County of Cook* (Chicago: Lakeside Publishing and Printing Company, 1874), 30–31.

49. *Chicago Tribune*, September 17, 1872; Ahern, *Great Revolution*, 30–31.

50. Francis O'Neil, *Chief O'Neill's Sketchy Recollections of an Eventful Life in Chicago* (Evanston, Ill.: Northwestern University Press, 2008), 48–49.

51. Ibid., 42–43.

52. Jack Blocker Jr., *"Give to the Winds Thy Fears": The Women's Temperance Crusade, 1873–1974* (Westport, Conn.: Greenwood Press, 1985).

53. Jeffrey D. Mason, "Poison It with Rum; Or, Validation and Delusion: Antebellum Temperance Drama as Cultural Method," *Pacific Coast Philology* 1, no. 1 (1990): 96–105.

54. Roy Rozenweig, *Eight Hours for What We Will: Workers and Leisure in an Industrial City, 1870–1920* (Cambridge: Cambridge University Press, 1983), 101.

55. *Chicago Tribune*, September 17, 1872.

56. See, for instance, *Chicago Tribune*, October 3, 1872. See also the description of the communications between the Committee of Seventy and Mayor Medill in Ahern, *Great Revolution*, 32.

57. Quoted in Flinn, *History of the Chicago Police*, 140.

58. *Chicago Tribune*, November 16, 1872; *Chicago Tribune*, January 28, 1873.

59. PCCCC, February 10, 1873, doc. 334.

60. *Chicago Tribune*, November 16, 1872.

61. Ahern, *Great Revolution*, 33–35.

62. *Chicago Tribune*, October 12, 1872.

63. *Chicago Tribune*, October 14, 1872.

64. *Chicago Tribune*, October 21, 1872.

65. PCCCC, May 26, 1873, doc. 886.

66. *Chicago Tribune*, October 18, 1872.

67. *Chicago Tribune*, October 28, 1872.

68. *Chicago Tribune*, October 29 and 30, 1872.

69. *Chicago Tribune*, December 5 and 6, 1872.

70. PCCCC: January 13, 1873, doc. 211; January 6, 1873, doc. 228.

71. PCCCC, February 26, 1873, doc. 366.

72. *Chicago Tribune*, January 5, 1873.

73. *Chicago Tribune*, January 21, 1873.

74. PCCCC, January 27, 1873, doc. 332.

75. PCCCC, April 8, 1873, doc. 472.

76. Ibid.

77. Ibid.

78. *Chicago Tribune*, February 1, 1873.

79. *Chicago Tribune*, February 2, 1873.

80. *Chicago Tribune*, February 5, 1873.

81. Flinn, *History of the Chicago Police*, 141.

82. *Chicago Tribune*, February 27, 1873; Flinn, *History of the Chicago Police*, 142.

83. Flinn, *History of the Chicago Police*, 142.

84. PCCCC, April 8, 1873, doc. 472.

85. *Chicago Tribune*, April 29, 1873; Flinn, *History of the Chicago Police*, 142.

86. *Chicago Tribune*, May 4, 1873.

87. PCCCC, April 29, 1873, doc. 679.

88. *Chicago Tribune*, May 8, 1873.

89. *Chicago Tribune*, May 18, 1873.

90. *Chicago Tribune*, May 24, 1873.

91. PCCCC, May 26, 1873, box 6 (no document number).

92. PCCCC: July 14, 1873, doc. 1053; July 17, 1873, doc. 1082; July 17, 1873, doc. 1066.

93. *Chicago Tribune*, August 5, 1873.

94. PCCCC, July 14, 1873, doc. 1059.

95. Ibid.

96. PCCCC, April 7, 1873, doc. 494.

97. PCCCC, September 8, 1873, box 6, folder 7 (no document number).

98. *Chicago Tribune*, August 5, 1873.

99. *Chicago Tribune*, June 1, 1873.

100. Ahern, *Great Revolution*, 24.

101. Ibid., 24.

102. *Chicago Tribune*, August 5, 1873.

103. PCCCC, August 25, 1873, doc. 54; *Chicago Tribune*, August 8 and 10, 1873.

104. *Chicago Tribune*, August 20, 1873.

105. Flinn, *History of the Chicago Police*, 146.

106. Jentz, "Class and Politics in an Emerging Industrial City, Chicago in the 1860s and 1870s"; Sawislak, *Smoldering City*; Richard Schneirov, *Labor and Urban Politics:*

Class Conflict and the Origins of Modern Liberalism in Chicago, 1864–97 (Urbana: University of Illinois Press, 1998).

107. Rehm actually had enough of a political base of his own that from his position of power as superintendent he eventually challenged Hesing for political control of the North Side. See *Chicago Tribune*, March 14, 1875.

108. Flinn, *History of the Chicago Police*, 147.

109. Ibid., 150–151.

110. Ibid., 151.

111. Ibid., 151.

112. In their campaign against the People's Party, the committee's Law and Order Party vehemently denied charges of Know-Nothingism. See *Chicago Tribune*, September 5, 1873.

Chapter 5. 1877 and the Formation of a Law-and-Order Consensus

1. This is essentially Robert Bruce's interpretation in *1877: Year of Violence* (Indianapolis: Bobbs-Merril, 1959).

2. Allan Pinkerton, *Strikers, Communists, Tramps and Detectives* (New York: G. W. Carleton & Co., 1878; repr. Arno Press and the New York Times, 1969), 387–388.

3. Sheldon Stromquist, "'Our Rights as Workingmen': Class Traditions and Collective Action in a Nineteenth-Century Railroad Town, Hornesville, NY, 1869–82," in *The Great Strikes of 1877*, ed. David Stowell (Urbana: University of Illinois Press, 2008).

4. Richard Schneirov, "Chicago's Great Upheaval of 1877: Class Polarization and Democratic Politics," in Stowell, *Great Strikes of 1877*, 76.

5. Howard Myers, "The Policing of Labor Disputes in Chicago: A Case Study," PhD diss., University of Chicago, 1929, 112.

6. John Flinn, *History of the Chicago Police* (1887; repr. New York: AMS Press, 1972), 147–148.

7. PCCCC, Dec. 26, 1873, doc. 123, doc. 124.

8. John Jentz, "Class and Politics in an Emerging Industrial City, Chicago in the 1860s and 1870s," *Journal of Urban History* 17 (May 1991): 248.

9. *Chicago Times*, December 14, 1874.

10. *Chicago Times*, February 19, 1874.

11. *Chicago Tribune*, April 25, 1874, quoted in Jentz, "Class and Politics in an Emerging Industrial City, Chicago in the 1860s and 1870s," 250.

12. For the composition of the CAC, see also Richard Schneirov, *Labor and Urban Politics: Class Conflict and the Origins of Modern Liberalism in Chicago, 1864–97* (Urbana: University of Illinois Press, 1998), 58.

13. *Daily Inter Ocean*, May 14, 1888.

14. RCAC, box 2, folder Committee on Public Safety; John Jentz and Richard Schneirov, *Chicago in the Age of Capital: Class, Politics, and Democracy during the Civil War and Reconstruction* (Urbana: University of Illinois Press, 2012), 179–193.

15. The above analysis is assembled primarily from three sources: Schneirov, *Labor and Urban Politics*; Jentz, "Class and Politics in an Emerging Industrial City"; and

Flinn, *History of the Chicago Police*. The most comprehensive treatment can be found in Jentz and Schneirov, *Chicago in the Age of Capital*.

16. *Chicago Tribune*, June 27 and July 18, 1875.

17. *Chicago Tribune*, June 27, 1875.

18. Richard Schneirov describes the social composition of this militia in *Labor and Urban Politics*, 59.

19. Proclamation issued by *Vorbote*, published in the *Chicago Times*, February 24, 1875.

20. *Chicago Times*, February 24, 1875.

21. See, for instance, *Chicago Times*, March 19, 1875.

22. *Chicago Arbeiter Zeitung*, August 3, 1880, WPA-FLPS, category I E, German.

23. John Jentz and Richard Schneirov, *Chicago in the Age of Capital: Class, Politics, and Democracy during the Civil War and Reconstruction* (Urbana: University of Illinois Press, 2012), 169.

24. Schneirov, *Labor and Urban Politics*, 59.

25. *Illinois Staats Zeitung*, April 11, 1879, WPA-FLPS I E, German.

26. *Chicago Arbeiter Zeitung*, July 2, 1879, WPA-FLPS I F 2, German; *Illinois Staats Zeitung*, June 26, 1879, WPA-FLPS I E, German; *Chicago Tribune*, June 25 and July 2, 1879.

27. Albert R. Parsons, *Autobiography*, 1886, HADC-CHM, http://www.chicagohistory.org/hadc/manuscripts/M07/M07.htm, accessed January 12, 2009.

28. PCCCC, March 14, 1877, doc. 1338.

29. *Chicago Tribune*, April 17, 1876, quoted in Schneirov, *Labor and Urban Politics*, 61.

30. See *Illinois Staats Zeitung*, October 10, 1874, WPA-FLPS I F 6.

31. Quoted in Flinn, *History of the Chicago Police*, 157.

32. PCCCC, August 13, 1877, doc. 458.

33. PCCCC, April 30, 1878, doc. 34.

34. PCCCC, June 4, 1877, doc 153.

35. PCCCC, June 4, 1877, box 33, folder 5.

36. Ibid.; PCCCC, July 2, 1877, doc. 175; PCCCC, July 12, 1877, doc. 177; *Chicago Tribune*, June 2 and 19, and July 10, 1877.

37. Myers, "Policing of Labor Disputes in Chicago," 112.

38. Flinn, *History of the Chicago Police*, 162.

39. Richard Schneirov, "Chicago's Great Upheaval of 1877: Class Polarization and Democratic Politics," in Stowell, *Great Strikes of 1877*, 86.

40. The following narrative of the events in 1877 is drawn especially from Superintendent Michael Hickey, *Annual Report for 1877*, PCCCC, February 4, 1878, doc. 1288; Flinn, *History of the Chicago Police*, 153–177; Myers, "Policing of Labor Disputes in Chicago"; and the *Chicago Tribune*, July 24–27, 1877. It is also informed especially by Schneirov, *Labor and Urban Politics*; and Robert Bruce, *1877: Year of Violence* (Indianapolis: Bobbs-Merril, 1959).

41. See *Daily Inter Ocean*, August 6, 1875, for an account of Colyer's lyceum meetings.

42. Quoted in Flinn, *History of the Chicago Police*, 181.

43. Allan Pinkerton's figure comes from *Strikers, Communists, Tramps, and Detectives*, 393; Hickey's figure is reported in the *Annual Report for 1877*.

44. PCCCC, July 25, 1877, doc. 390.

45. Superintendent Hickey quoted in *Annual Report for 1877*.

46. Dixon quoted in Flinn, *History of the Chicago Police*, 192.

47. Quote from Superintendent Hickey, *Annual Report for 1877*.

48. *Illinois Staats Zeitung*, April 25, 1879; WPA-FLPS I D 2 a (4); *Chicago Tribune*, May 6, 1879.

49. Allan Pinkerton, *Strikers, Communists, Tramps and Detectives* (1878; repr. New York: Arno Press, 1969), 392–393.

50. Myers, "Policing of Labor Disputes in Chicago," 126–131.

51. Ibid., 126.

52. Figures from Superintendent Hickey, *Annual Report for 1877*.

53. *Chicago Tribune*, July 28.

54. PCCCC, August 6, 1877, doc. 394.

55. The signature on this document is nearly illegible but appears to read "Goppeh-wading."

56. PCCCC, August 13, 1877, doc. 452. For another example of a similar petition, see doc. 451.

57. PCCCC, August 20, 1877, doc. 468.

58. This figure includes $469.14 paid out later to special policemen not remunerated by the initial disbursement, PCCCC, October 29, 1877, doc. 871. The council continued to receive petitions from individuals requesting payment for services in suppressing the riot well into January.

59. *Report of the General Superintendent of Police for the Fiscal Year Ending December 31st, 1878*, Municipal Reference Collection, HWL.

60. *Chicago Tribune*, July 27, 1877.

61. PCCCC, July 30, 1877, doc. 392.

62. PCCCC, August 13, 1877, doc. 454. In fact, a state law had initially created such a fund in all Illinois cities, but the corporation counsel ruled that Chicago's city council was not required to act on the state law, so the proposed ordinance was acted upon, but not actually passed into law.

63. Flinn, *History of the Chicago Police*, 202.

64. *Report of the General Superintendent of Police*, 1878.

65. The petition is from the PCCCC, January 1, 1878, box 38, folder 2. The resolution is from the PCCCC, March 14, 1878, doc. 1337.

66. PCCCC, December 27, 1877, doc. 1055.

67. RCAC, box 1, folder 1.

68. Ibid.

69. RCAC, box 5, folder 1.

70. RCAC, box 1, folder 1, and box 5, folder 1.

71. *Report of the General Superintendent of Police*, 1878.

72. RCAC, box 1, folder 1.

73. RCAC, box 5, folder 1.

74. Constitution of the Chicago Commercial Club, box 1, folder 1, Records of the Chicago Commercial Club, CHM.

75. Records of the Chicago Commercial Club, General Club meetings minutes, box 1, folder 4, CHM.

76. Records of the Chicago Commercial Club, Executive Committee of the Commercial Club, March 29, 1879, 11, box 7, folder 1, CHM.

77. Records of the Chicago Commercial Club, Executive Committee of the Commercial Club, 11–85, box 7, folder 1, CHM.

78. "History of the Chicago Commercial Club," Records of the Chicago Commercial Club, box 1, folder 1, CHM.

Chapter 6. Carter Harrison Remakes the Chicago Police Department

1. *Report of the General Superintendent of Police of the City of Chicago to the City Council for the Fiscal Year ending December 31st, 1878*, Municipal Reference Collection, HWL.

2. *Report of the General Superintendent of Police*, 1880.

3. See, for instance, *Illinois Staats Zeitung*, August 8, 1879, WPA-FLPS, I F 3.

4. *Chicago Tribune*, July 23, 1878.

5. *Chicago Tribune*, April 6, 1878.

6. *Illinois Staats Zeitung*, April 25, 1879, WPA-FLPS I D 2 a (4); *Chicago Tribune*, May 6, 1879.

7. *Chicago Arbeiter Zeitung*, July 2, 1879, WPA-FLPS, I F 2, German; *Illinois Staats Zeitung*, June 26, 1879, WPA-FLPS I E, German; *Chicago Tribune*, June 25 and July 2, 1879.

8. *Chicago Arbeiter Zeitung*, August 3, 1880, WPA-FLPS I E, German; *Alarm*, June 13 and July 27, 1885; Bruce Nelson, *Beyond the Martyrs: A Social History of Chicago's Anarchists, 1870–1900* (New Brunswick, N.J.: Rutgers University Press, 1988), 127–153; Richard Schneirov, *Labor and Urban Politics: Class Conflict and the Origins of Modern Liberalism in Chicago, 1864–97* (Urbana: University of Illinois Press, 1998), 76, 87.

9. *Report of the General Superintendent of Police*, 1878.

10. Ibid.

11. *Chicago Tribune*, May 19, 1878.

12. *Chicago Tribune*, March 2, 1879.

13. Schneirov makes this point in *Labor and Urban Politics*, 114 and 163. For an example, see the *Daily Inter Ocean*, October 21, 1881.

14. Claudius Johnson, *Carter Henry Harrison I: Political Leader* (Chicago: University of Chicago Press, 1928).

15. *Chicago Tribune*, March 29, 1879; Harrison's first inaugural address, reprinted in the *Chicago Tribune*, April 29, 1879.

16. *Report of the General Superintendent of Police*, 1878.

17. John Flinn, *History of the Chicago Police* (1887; repr. New York: AMS Press, 1972), 88.

18. PCCCC, November 17, 1862, doc. 203A.

19. Flinn, *History of the Chicago Police*, 98.

20. *Report of the General Superintendent of Police*, 1880.

21. Ibid.

22. Open letter from Superintendent McGarigle to the public, reprinted in the *Chicago Tribune*, December 19, 1880.

23. *Report of the General Superintendent of Police*, 1880.

24. Open letter from Superintendent McGarigle.

25. Ibid.

26. *Report of the General Superintendent of Police*, 1883.

27. Ibid.

28. *Report of the General Superintendent of Police*, 1882.

29. *Report of the General Superintendent of Police*, 1883.

30. "The Chicago Police Alarm System," *Manufacturer and the Builder* 13, no. 2 (1881): 29; *Harper's Weekly*, August 12, 1882.

31. *Chicago Tribune*, February 5, 1884.

32. *Report of the General Superintendent of Police*, 1883–1885.

33. *Daily Inter Ocean*, October 21, 1881.

34. Richard Schneirov suggests this in *Labor and Urban Politics*, 168.

35. *Report of the General Superintendent of Police*, 1883.

36. *Report of the General Superintendent of Police*, 1884.

37. Ibid.

38. *Chicago Daily News*, December 8 and 10, 1884.

39. PCCCC, July 11, 1885, doc. 190, box 101.

40. Flinn, *History of the Chicago Police*, 329–336.

41. Ibid., 210–212.

42. See, for instance, James Green, *Death in the Haymarket: A Story of Chicago, the First Labor Movement, and the Bombing that Divided Gilded Age America* (New York: Pantheon Books, 2006); and Paul Avrich, *The Haymarket Tragedy* (Princeton, N.J.: Princeton University Press, 1986).

43. Flinn, *History of the Chicago Police*, 344.

44. This is essentially the portrayal of Bonfield in Avrich, *Haymarket Tragedy*; Green, *Death in the Haymarket*; and Schneirov, *Labor and Urban Politics*.

45. Flinn, *History of the Chicago Police*, 344–346.

46. Claudius Johnson, *Carter Henry Harrison I, Political Leader* (Chicago: University of Chicago Press: 1928), 252–255.

47. These figures come from Mark Haller's computations in Mark Haller, "Historical Roots of Police Behavior, Chicago, 1890–1925," *Law and Society Review* 10, no. 2 (1976): 303–324. Haller derived his figures from an analysis of Flinn's History and his computations fit with my observations.

48. *Report of the General Superintendent of Police*, 1883.

49. Ibid.

50. *Chicago Tribune*, April 15, 1881.

51. PCCCC, July 11, 1885, doc. 190, box 101.

52. *Chicago Arbeiter Zeitung*, May 31, 1883, WPA-FLPS I D 2 a (4), German.

53. *Chicago Times*, March 1, 1882; *Chicago Tribune*, March 7, 1882; Schneirov, *Labor and Urban Politics*, 111.

54. *Chicago Tribune*, December 6, 1882, and February 2, 1883.

55. Cyrus McCormick Jr. to Mrs. C. H. McCormick, undated letter, Cyrus H. Mc-Cormick Papers, MCCMSS2A, box 57, Wisconsin Historical Society. Robert Ozanne, *A Century of Labor Management Relations at McCormick and International Harvester* (Madison: University of Wisconsin Press, 1967), 25, 28, and 29. *Alarm*, April 18, 1885, clipping, Cyrus H. McCormick Papers.

56. Special Report of J. C. Harris, April 14, 1885, Cyrus H. McCormick Papers.

57. Ibid.

58. Ibid.

59. This was a frequent accusation in the *Chicago Tribune*. See, for instance, January 7 and 8, August 29, and October 9, 1880.

60. PCCCC, April 18, 1885, box 100.

61. *Illinois Staats Zeitung*, July 15, 1881, WPA-FLPS I F 6, German.

62. Robert M. Fogelson, *Big City Police* (Cambridge, Mass.: Harvard University Press, 1977), 17.

63. In 1884, the categories of "drunk," "drunk and disorderly," and "disorderly" were collapsed into the single category, "disorderly conduct." To facilitate comparison, I have collapsed the categories for the years before 1884, as well.

64. *Report of the General Superintendent of Police*, 1883.

65. *Report of the General Superintendent of Police*, 1878–1886.

66. See, for instance, PCCCC, June 22, 1885, doc. 83, box 101. This is one in a series of weekly orders issued by the mayor listing individuals to be released from the bridewell and why.

67. PCCCC, September 14, 1885, box 107.

68. This case is similar to the celebrated case of Hester Vaughn, arrested for infanticide in New York in 1869 and eventually pardoned after Susan B. Anthony and the Workingwomen's Association investigated the case.

69. *Chicago Tribune*, August 3, 1857.

70. *Chicago Inter Ocean*, July 8, 1875.

71. *Chicago Inter Ocean*, January 9, 1878.

72. James Mohr, *Abortion in America: The Origins of National Policy, 1800–1900* (New York: Oxford University Press, 1978), 20–25.

73. Leslie Reagan, *When Abortion Was a Crime: Women, Medicine, and Law in the United States, 1867–1973* (Berkeley: University of California Press, 1997), 13.

74. Ibid., 15, 46–70.

75. *Report of the General Superintendent of Police*, 1886 and 1888.

76. See *Chicago Tribune*: November 6, 1880; September 13, 1881; December 26, 1882; June 7, 1883; May 17, 1884.

77. *Chicago Tribune*, December 25, 1882.

78. *Chicago Tribune*, April 15, 1883.

79. *Chicago Tribune*, October 18, 1885.

80. Ibid.

81. Ibid.

82. *Chicago Tribune*, November 22, 1883.

83. *Chicago Tribune*, March 1, 1885.

84. *Chicago Tribune*, April 19, 1885.

85. *Chicago Tribune*, March 8, 1885.

86. *Chicago Tribune*, March 21, 1885.

87. *Chicago Tribune*, April 19, 1885.

88. PCCCC, December 31, 1885, doc. 2279.

89. *Chicago Tribune*: September 18, 1881; February 9, 1882; April 22, 1882; and September 19, 1882.

90. *Chicago Tribune*, February 26, 1882.

91. *Chicago Tribune*, April 3, 1883.

92. *Chicago Tribune*, May 20, 1882.

93. *Chicago Tribune*, October 16, 1883.

94. *Chicago Tribune*, July 17, 1884.

95. *Chicago Tribune*, November 7, 1884.

96. Ruth Allen, *The Great Southwest Strike* (Austin: University of Texas, 1942); Frank Morn, *The Eye That Never Sleeps: A History of the Pinkerton National Detective Agency* (Bloomington: University of Indiana Press, 1982).

97. Schneirov, *Labor and Urban Politics*, 169.

98. Ibid., 168. Schneirov points out that the 1885 annual report of the Citizens' Association blamed politicians pandering for the potential votes of strikers for their reluctance to break strikes, and urged significant police reform to solve this problem.

99. *Chicago Times*, July 1–3, 1885. This led to a meeting between the sheriff and the mayor at which they agreed that the Chicago Police Department had jurisdiction over events in Chicago, especially since the mayor had a "drilled force of men at his command, while the Sheriff had not."

100. Quoted in *Chicago Times*, July 2, 1885.

101. *Chicago Times*, July 1–3, 1885; *Chicago Tribune*, July 1–3, 1885; PCCCC, November 23, 1885, doc. 2162, box 105.

102. *Chicago Times*, July 3, 1885; *Chicago Tribune*, July 3, 1885.

103. *Chicago Times*, July 3 and 4, 1885; *Chicago Tribune*, July 3 and 4, 1885.

104. *Chicago Tribune*, July 4, 1885.

105. *Chicago Tribune*, October 16, 1885.

106. Flinn, *History of the Chicago Police*, 340–343.

107. PCCCC, November 23, 1885, doc. 2162, box 105.

108. *Chicago Tribune*, July 4, 1885.

109. PCCCC, November 23, 1885, doc. 2162, box 105.

110. Ibid.

111. Ibid.

112. *Chicago Tribune*, January 31, 1886.

113. *Chicago Tribune*, February 21, 1886; Schneirov, *Labor and Urban Politics*, 172.

114. *Chicago Tribune*, February 18, 1886; *Chicago Times*, March 1, 1886.

115. Schneirov, *Labor and Urban Politics*, 192.

116. *Chicago Tribune*, March 2, 1886.

117. *Chicago Tribune*, March 6, 1886.

118. Ibid.

119. Flinn, *History of the Chicago Police*, 263.

Chapter 7. Chicago's Anarchists Shape the Police Department

1. The meaning of the word *anarchist* has changed considerably since this period. In the 1870s and 1880s, the anarchist movement included a diverse group of Chicagoans organized around the International Working People's Association (IWPA). While they were later usually referred to as anarchists, at the time they themselves, the police, and the newspapers alternately called them socialists, communists, or anarchists with little distinction. In *Beyond the Martyrs: A Social History of Chicago's Anarchists, 1870–1900* (New Brunswick, N.J.: Rutgers University Press, 1988), Bruce Nelson argues that there were no anarchists of the Bakunin type in Chicago in the nineteenth century. The unifying ideological strand among these political activists was their belief that class struggle was the only way working people could solve their problems.

2. Carl Smith, *Urban Disorder and the Shape of Belief: The Great Chicago Fire, the Haymarket Bomb, and the Model Town of Pullman* (Chicago: University of Chicago Press, 1995), 137.

3. Karl Marx, *The Civil War in France* (1871; repr. New York: International Publishers, 1940), 96.

4. Francis O'Neil, *Chief O'Neill's Sketchy Recollections of an Eventful Life in Chicago* (Evanston, Ill.: Northwestern University Press, 2008), 42–43, 48–49.

5. Eric Hirsch, *Urban Revolt: Ethnic Politics in the Nineteenth Century Chicago Labor Movement* (Berkeley: University of California Press, 1990), 117–139; Richard Schneirov, *Labor and Urban Politics: Class Conflict and the Origins of Modern Liberalism in Chicago, 1864–97* (Urbana: University of Illinois Press, 1998), 99–138.

6. John Flinn, *History of the Chicago Police* (1887; repr. New York: AMS Press, 1972).

7. See PCCCC, March 31, 1866, doc. 262A, and *Report of the General Superintendent of Police of the City of Chicago, December 31st, 1886*, Municipal Reference Collection, HWL.

8. Hirsch, *Urban Revolt*, 113–116; Schneirov, *Labor and Urban Politics*, 46–68, 139–161, and 236–259.

9. Hirsch, *Urban Revolt*, 145.

10. *Chicago Tribune*, July 25, 1877; Albert R. Parsons, *Autobiography* (1886; HADC-CHM, http://www.chicagohistory.org/hadc/manuscripts/M07/M07.htm, accessed January 12, 2009).

11. Allan Pinkerton, *Strikers, Communists, Tramps and Detectives* (1878; repr. Arno Press & New York Times, 1969), 387, 388, 389–390, 388.

12. Michael Schaack, *Anarchy and Anarchists: A History of Red Terror in America and Europe* (1889; repr. New York: Arno Press, 1977), 112.

13. Ibid., 104–112.

14. Smith, *Urban Disorder and the Shape of Belief*, 148–155.

15. Nelson, *Beyond the Martyrs*, 81.

16. Parsons, *Autobiography*; Nelson, *Beyond the Martyrs*; James Green, *Death in the Haymarket: A Story of Chicago, the First Labor Movement, and the Bombing that Divided Gilded Age America* (New York: Pantheon Books, 2006).

17. *Alarm*, November 15, 1884.

18. Ibid.

19. See, for example, Timothy Messer-Kruse, *The Trial of the Haymarket Anarchists: Terrorism and Justice in the Gilded Age* (New York: Palgrave-Macmillan, 2011).

20. Messer-Kruse, *Trial of the Haymarket Anarchists*.

21. Ibid., 15, 181.

22. Richard Schneirov, "Still Not Guilty," *Labor: Studies in Working-Class History of the Americas* 9, no. 3 (2012): 29–33.

23. Timothy Messer-Kruse, *The Haymarket Conspiracy: Transatlantic Terrorist Networks* (Urbana: University of Illinois Press, 2012).

24. John Jentz and Richard Schneirov, *Chicago in the Age of Capital: Class, Politics and Democracy during the Civil War and Reconstruction* (Urbana: University of Illinois Press, 2012), 239–241. In addition, Messer-Kruse relies heavily on Michael Schaack's book, *Anarchy and the Anarchists*. Over the years, Schaack's reliability has been called into question repeatedly; Superintendent Ebersold called his whole book a fabrication. See chapter 8, plus Harold Myers, "The Policing of Labor Disputes in Chicago: A Case Study," PhD diss., University of Chicago, 1929, 158; *Chicago Tribune*, May 11, 1889; C. A. Siringo, *Two Evil-Isms, Pinkertonism and Anarchism* (Chicago: C. A. Siringo, 1915), 3; Frank Donner, *Protectors of Privilege Red Squads and Police Repression in Urban America* (Berkeley: University of California Press, 1990), 14.

25. Nelson, *Beyond the Martyrs*, 127–153; *Alarm*, June 13 and July 27, 1885.

26. *Chicago Tribune*, July 27, 1885.

27. *Alarm*, July 27, 1885.

28. *Alarm*, December 13, 1884; *Chicago Tribune*, December 7, 1884.

29. *Alarm*, December 13, 1884; *Chicago Tribune*, December 8, 1884.

30. *Chicago Daily News*, February 3 and 4, 1885.

31. *Chicago Tribune*: December 20 and 21, 1884; February 4–6, 8, and 10, 1885; and May 11, 1885. *Chicago Daily News*: December 8, 10, and 20, 1884; and February 3–5, 1885.

32. Nelson, *Beyond the Martyrs*, 93–94.

33. Schaack, *Anarchy and Anarchists*, 207.

34. Ibid., 207.

35. *Alarm*, November 28, 1885.

36. *Alarm*, November 8, 1884.

37. *Alarm*, February 21, 1885.

38. *Alarm*, May 7, 1885.

39. Timothy Gilfoyle, *A Pickpocket's Tale: The Underworld of Nineteenth-Century New York* (New York: W. W. Norton, 2006), 47.

40. *Alarm*, November 8, 1884.

41. "The Pinkerton Army," *Alarm*, October 17, 1885.

42. *Alarm*, February 6, 1886.

43. *Alarm*, January 23, 1886.

44. *Chicago Tribune*, April 29, 1885.

45. Harrison quoted in *Chicago Tribune*, May 9, 1886.

46. Inaugural address of Mayor Carter Harrison Sr., April 28, 1879, HWLMRC.

47. *Chicago Arbeiter Zeitung*, September 23, 1882, WPA-FLPS I F 2, German.

48. Nelson, *Beyond the Martyrs*, 52–77, 153–174.

49. *Alarm*, November 8, 1884.

50. *Alarm*, July 11, 1885.

51. *Alarm*, December 12, 1885.

52. *Alarm*, March 6, 1886.

53. See, for instance, the Pinkerton report submitted to Cyrus McCormick Jr. following the 1885 strike at the McCormick Reaper Works discussed in the previous chapter.

Chapter 8. The Eight-Hour Strikes, the Haymarket Bombing, and the Consolidation of the Chicago Police Department

1. This atmosphere of fear is discussed in all the major secondary works on Haymarket, and is given particular attention by Carl Smith in *Urban Disorder and the Shape of Belief: The Great Chicago Fire, the Haymarket Bomb, and the Model Town of Pullman* (Chicago: University of Chicago Press, 1995).

2. The anarchists' frequent discussions of dynamite and street fighting have already been discussed in some detail. The *Alarm* also published directions for making dynamite and attacking Gatling guns, and advertised the practice drills of the revolutionary militias.

3. *Chicago Tribune*, January 14 and 15, 1886.

4. Bruce Nelson, *Beyond the Martyrs: A Social History of Chicago's Anarchists, 1870–1900* (New Brunswick, N.J.: Rutgers University Press, 1988), 186.

5. In ibid., Nelson gives a nuanced picture of the complicated relationship between the various labor organizations and the anarchists (27–51).

6. Records of the Commercial Club of the City of Chicago, General Club Meetings, Minutes, 71, box 1, folder 4, CHM.

7. Records of the Commercial Club, box 22, folder 2.

8. Records of the Commercial Club, General Club Meetings, Minutes, 85, box 1, folder 4.

9. Ibid., 87.

10. *Chicago Tribune*, May 1, 1886.

11. Howard Myers, "The Policing of Labor Disputes in Chicago: A Case Study," PhD diss., University of Chicago, 1929, 142; Richard Schneirov, *Labor and Urban Politics:*

Class Conflict and the Origins of Modern Liberalism in Chicago, 1864–97 (Urbana: University of Illinois Press, 1998), 200; *Chicago Tribune*, May 2, 1886.

12. *Chicago Tribune*, May 3, 1886.

13. Myers, "Policing of Labor Disputes in Chicago," 142.

14. John Flinn, *History of the Chicago Police* (1887; repr. New York: AMS Press, 1972), 271–278; Michael Schaack, *Anarchy and Anarchists: A History of Red Terror in America and Europe* (1889; repr. New York: Arno Press, 1977), 125–128; James Green, *Death in the Haymarket: A Story of Chicago, the First Labor Movement, and the Bombing that Divided Gilded Age America* (New York: Pantheon Books, 2006), 169–171; Myers, "Policing of Labor Disputes in Chicago," 142–144.

15. Green, *Death in the Haymarket*, 171.

16. Bonfield quoted in Flinn, *History of the Chicago Police*, 278.

17. Schaack, *Anarchy and Anarchists*, 124–125.

18. People's Exhibit Six, HADC-CHM.

19. Flinn, *History of the Chicago Police*, 278.

20. Schaack, *Anarchy and Anarchists*, 127–128.

21. Schneirov, *Labor and Urban Politics*, 200.

22. *Chicago Tribune*, May 5, 1886.

23. Green, *Death in the Haymarket*, 176–177.

24. Illinois vs. August Spies et al. trial transcript no. 1, Testimony of William Seliger (first appearance), July 21, 1886, HADC-CHM.

25. This meeting is widely discussed in all of the secondary works on Haymarket, in the trial records in the HADC-CHM, in Flinn's *History of the Chicago Police*, and in Schaack's *Anarchy and Anarchists*.

26. Green, *Death in the Haymarket*, 178.

27. Every work on this period includes a description of these events, and this account was re-created from them.

28. Timothy Messer-Kruse, *The Trial of the Haymarket Anarchists: Terrorism and Justice in the Gilded Age* (New York: Palgrave Macmillan, 2011).

29. Paul Avrich, "The Bomb-Thrower: A New Candidate," in *Haymarket Scrapbook*, ed. David Roediger and Franklin Rosemont (Chicago: Charles H. Kerr Publishing, 1986), 71–74; Messer-Kruse, *Trial of the Haymarket Anarchists*.

30. Schaack, *Anarchy and Anarchists*, 50.

31. Daily Police Report of Michael Marks to Superintendent Ebersold, May 30, 1886, Haymarket Collection, CHM.

32. Schaack, *Anarchy and Anarchists*, 156–157.

33. Daily Police Report of Patrick Costelle to Superintendent Ebersold, May 28, 1886, Haymarket Collection, CHM.

34. Daily Police Report of Horace Elliot to Superintendent Ebersold, May 30, 1886, Haymarket Collection, CHM.

35. Schneirov, *Labor and Urban Politics*, 199–205; Myers, "Policing of Labor Disputes in Chicago," 147–158.

36. PCCCC, May 31, 1886, doc. 351.

37. Schaack, *Anarchy and Anarchists*, 49.

38. Melville E. Stone, *Fifty Years a Journalist* (Garden City, N.Y.: Doubleday, Page, 1921), 172–173.

39. Frank Donner, *Protectors of Privilege: Red Squads and Police Repression in Urban America* (Berkeley: University of California Press, 1990), 14–15.

40. *Chicago Tribune*, May 7, 1886.

41. *Chicago Tribune*, May 30, 1886.

42. *Report of the General Superintendent of Police, December 31, 1886*, Municipal Reference Collection, HWL.

43. Ibid.

44. *Chicago Tribune*, July 14, 1886; *Report of the General Superintendent of Police*, 1886.

45. William Adelman, "The Haymarket Monument at Waldheim," in Roediger and Rosemont, *Haymarket Scrapbook*, 167; Lara Kelland, "Putting Haymarket to Rest?," *Labor: Studies in Working Class History of the Americas* 2 (2005).

46. Records of the Commercial Club, General Club Meeting Minutes, 88–89, box 1, folder 4.

47. Records of the Commercial Club, box 22, folder 1.

48. Records of the Commercial Club, box 22, folder 7.

49. Records of the Commercial Club, General Club Meeting Minutes, 103, box 1, folder 4.

50. *Chicago Tribune*, January 21, 1887.

51. *Chicago Tribune*, January 23, 1887.

52. *Chicago Tribune*, January 30, 1887.

53. *Chicago Tribune*, March 27, 1887.

54. *Chicago Tribune*, January 21, 1887.

55. *Harper's Weekly*, May 15, 1886, 306.

56. *Century* 36, no. 2 (1888): 253–254.

57. C. A. Siringo, *Two Evil-Isms, Pinkertonism and Anarchism* (Chicago: C. A. Siringo, 1915), 3, quoted in Donner, *Protectors of Privilege*, 14.

58. Myers, "Policing of Labor Disputes in Chicago," 158.

59. The considerable evidence that the police manufactured evidence and exaggerated the scale of the anarchist plot casts doubt on Timothy Messer-Kruse's assertion that the subsequent trial was fair by the evidentiary standards of the day. Most of this evidence, like that cited, comes from police sources.

60. The *Alarm* published a "notice to our readers" explaining the interruption of publication on October 8, 1886, and resumed regular publication on November 5, 1887.

61. *Alarm*, November 19, 1887.

62. *Abenpost*, January 12, 1891, WPA-FLPS 1 E German.

63. *Illinois Staats-Zeitung*, November 12, 1891, WPA-FLPS 1 E German.

64. *Chicago Tribune*, June 21, 1888.

65. PCCCC, June 7, 1886, doc. 352.

66. PCCCC, June 7, 1886, no document number.

67. PCCCC, June 7, 1886, doc. 337.

68. PCCCC, May 17, 1886, doc. 217.

69. "The Late Significant Elections," *Harper's Weekly*, April 16, 1887.

70. John A. Roche Inaugural Address, filed in the PCCCC, April 18, 1887, doc. 7.

71. Ibid.

72. See *Harpers Weekly*, April 16, 1887; *Chicago Tribune*, April 2–8, 1887.

73. John A. Roche letterbook, 5, CHM.

74. Ibid., 25–26, 28, 43, 58, CHM.

75. *Arbeiter Zeitung*, October 9, 1888, WPA-FLPS I D 2 (a)4, German.

76. John A. Roche letterbook, October 15, 1888, 168, CHM.

77. *Harpers Weekly*, October 20, 1888, 802; *Chicago Tribune*, October 6–15, 1888.

78. *Chicago Tribune*, October 15, 1888.

79. *Chicago Tribune*, October 10, 1888.

80. *Chicago Tribune*, October 8 and 9, 1888.

81. *Arbeiter Zeitung*, December 28, 1888, WPA-FLPS I D 2 (2) German; *Chicago Tribune*, January 16, 1889.

82. *Report of the General Superintendent of Police*, 1888.

83. *Report of the General Superintendent of Police*, 1885–1887.

84. *Chicago Tribune*, February 15, 1888.

85. *Chicago Times*, January 4, 1889; *Chicago Tribune*, January 9, 1889.

86. *Chicago Tribune*, January 5, 1889.

87. *Chicago Tribune*, April 14, 1889.

88. *Chicago Tribune*, May 11, 1889.

89. Donner, *Protectors of Privilege*, 15.

90. *Chicago Tribune*, May 27, 1891.

91. *Chicago Tribune*, July 19, 1891.

92. William Stead, *If Christ Came to Chicago! A Plea for the Union of All who Love in the Service of All Who Suffer* (Chicago: Laird and Lee Publishers, 1894), 312.

Epilogue

1. William Novak, "The Myth of the 'Weak' American State," *American Historical Review* 113, no. 3 (June 2008): 765.

2. Howard Myers, "The Policing of Labor Disputes in Chicago: A Case Study," PhD diss., University of Chicago, 1929, 244–245.

3. Carl Smith, *Urban Disorder and the Shape of Belief: The Great Chicago Fire, the Haymarket Bomb, and the Model Town of Pullman* (Chicago: University of Chicago Press, 1995), 221–222.

4. Richard Schneirov, *Labor and Urban Politics: Class Conflict and the Origins of Modern Liberalism in Chicago, 1864–97* (Urbana: University of Illinois Press, 1998), chapter 11.

5. Stanley Buder, *Pullman: An Experiment in Industrial Order and Community Planning, 1880–1930* (New York: Oxford University Press, 1967), xi.

6. Ibid., 30–31.

7. *New York World*, December 25, 1892, quoted in Buder, *Pullman*, 39.

8. Buder, *Pullman*, 69.

9. Richard T. Ely, "Pullman: A Social Study," *Harpers New Monthly Magazine*, February 1885.

10. Almont Lindsay, *The Pullman Strike: The Story of a Unique Experiment and a Great Labor Upheaval* (Chicago: University of Chicago Press, 1967), 92.

11. Ibid., 67.

12. Ely, "Pullman."

13. Smith, *Urban Disorder and the Shape of Belief*, 203–208.

14. Lindsay, *Pullman Strike*, 94.

15. Ibid., 130–144.

16. Ibid., 130; Schneirov, *Labor and Urban Politics*, 338.

17. Myers, "Policing of Labor Disputes in Chicago," 248.

18. Ibid., 244.

19. Francis O'Neil, *Chief O'Neill's Sketchy Recollections of an Eventful Life in Chicago* (Evanston, Ill.: Northwestern University Press, 2008), 65.

20. Ibid., 66.

21. Schneirov, *Labor and Urban Politics*, 339.

22. Lindsay, *Pullman Strike*, 143.

23. John Egan quoted in Ibid., 144.

24. Richard Schneirov, Shelton Stromquist, and Nick Salvatore, "Introduction," in *The Pullman Strike and the Crisis of the 1890s*, ed. Richard Schneirov, Shelton Stromquist, and Nick Salvatore (Urbana: University of Illinois Press, 1999), 1.

25. John Jentz and Richard Schneirov, *Chicago in the Age of Capital: Class, Politics, and Democracy during the Civil War and Reconstruction* (Urbana: University of Illinois Press, 2012), 243.

26. Victoria Brown, "Advocate for Democracy: Jane Addams and the Pullman Strike," in Schneirov, Stromquist, Salvatore, *Pullman Strike and the Crisis of the 1890s*, 132.

27. This echoes William Novak's insight about the power of the multilayered U.S. state.

28. Shelton Stromquist, *A Generation of Boomers: The Pattern of Railroad Labor Conflict in Nineteenth-Century America* (Urbana: University of Illinois Press, 1987), 267–275.

29. Robert M. Fogelson, *America's Armories: Architecture, Society, and Public Order* (Cambridge, Mass.: Harvard University Press, 1989).

30. William Forbath, *Law and the Shaping of the American Labor Movement* (Cambridge, Mass.: Harvard University Press, 1989), 59–98.

31. Andrew Cohen, *The Racketeer's Progress: Chicago and the Struggle for the Modern American Economy, 1900–1940* (New York: Cambridge University Press, 2004), 111–118; David Montgomery, *The Fall of the House of Labor: The Workplace, the State, and American Labor Activism, 1865–1925* (New York: Cambridge University Press, 1989), 312–314; Myers, "Policing of Labor Disputes in Chicago," 581–637.

32. Douglass C. North makes this point in *Structure and Change in Economic History* (New York: W. W. Norton, 1981).

INDEX

abortion: criminalization of, 154; police arrest practitioners of, 152
Addams, Jane, 209, 213–214
Alarm, 175; founded, 172; reappears, 198
alcohol regulation, 14. *See also* Sunday Closing laws; temperance
Altgeld, John, 211–212, 214–215
American Federation of Labor, 186
American Fur Company, 7
American Medical Association, 152–153
American Party, 14. *See also* Know Nothing Party; Law and Order Party
American Railway Union (ARU), 211, 214
American Tract Society, 85
Amozonian Hosiery Corporation, 178
anarchist banners: photo of, 108
anarchist militias: clashes with police, 80; criticize prisons and jails, 177; growing influence of, 181; impact on Chicago police, 166–184; nature of movement, 169–170; pardoned by Altgeld, 211; photo of, 108; reaction to repression, 198–199; repression of, 193–194; support use of dynamite, 173; suppression of, 198–199
Anarchy and Anarchists, 171; on women anarchists, 176; reaction to, 205–206
Ancient Order of Hibernians, 147
anti-skating movement, 156–157
Arbeiter Bund, 203–204
Arbeiter Zeitung, 169, 172, 175
Armour, Philip, 7, 132, 160, 162; contributes to anti-strike fund, 186; contributes to Commercial Club, 187; as member of CA, 116; one who controlled CA, 117; supports upper class, 70
Astor, John Jacob, 7
Astor Place Riot, 2

Averill, Superintendant: and McCormick reaper strike, 164

Barrett, John, 140, 194
Baus, Lieutenant, 124, 125
Bell, Lieutenant, 125
Bernstein, Abraham, 96
Billings, C. K., 161
Bishoff, Sergeant, 92
Bissell, William, 25
Black, S. I., 196
Board of Public Works, 48
Bohemian Sharpshooters, 119
bombings: by anarchists, 172–173
Bond, Lester, 98
Bonfield, James, 170
Bonfield, John, 142, 151, 161, 163; accused of corruption, 205; attacked by alarm, 198; career of, 143; defends actions, 162; donates to police, 195; effective against anarchists, 198; keeps people from rally, 203; leads raid on newspaper, 192; and McCormick reaper strike, 164–165; in national spotlight, 194; photo of, 109; promoted, 160; on prostitution, 155; put in charge of new alarm system, 138–139; retained as inspector, 201; thinks militia not necessary, 188; wishes to persecute anarchists, 184
Bonney, Edward, 17
Boone, Levi, 7, 24, 34, 144; appoints leaders of police, 29; blames alcohol for disorder, 26–27; on ethnic rivalries, 26; led Law and Order ticket, 14; most important legacy of, 33; policies disliked, 36; proposes enlargement of police force, 14; on strikes of 1877, 126; supports anti-drinking program, 15

Boston Massacre, 1
bourgeois morality, 177
Boyle, Billy, 205
Bradley, Cyrus, 84, 138; appointed police
captain, 29; attempts to prevent draft
dodger, 55; career of, 29–30; and efficiency of police, 53; fired as police superintendent, 36; as first superintendent of
police, 35; insures effectiveness of police,
52–54; as leader of Chicago police, 30–31;
supported idea of a professional police
force, 35–36
Brennan, Sergeant, 127
brothels, map of, 107
Buckley, William, 130, 135; accused Hickey
of corruption, 122–123
Burlington Railroad, 25
business class in Chicago: growth of, 6–8
Bustar, Gustav, 95–96

Caffrey, John, 38
Caffrey, Mrs. John, 38, 39
Callahan, Lieutenant, 124, 125
Cameron, Andrew, 60, 189; editor of *Work-
ingman's Advocate,* 59; not hostile to po-
lice, 61; supports eight-hour movement,
63; supports free labor ideology, 67
Cameron, Charles S., 45
Cameron, James: holds mass rally, 69
Camp Douglas, 55, 60
Catholic Benevolent Legion, 142
Central Labor Union, 186–187
Chandler, Zachariah, 9
Chase, Salmon, 62
Chicago, Burlington and Quincy Railroad,
125
Chicago, Milwaukee and St. Paul Railroad,
143
Chicago and Alton Railroad, 84
Chicagoan trinity, the, 8
Chicago Board of Trade, 7; and Albert Par-
sons, 170; and Committee of Seventy, 83;
donates to police, 131, 194; protest at new
building, 180
Chicago City Council: attacked on brick
building proposal, 79; denies police bias,
61; march against, 79
Chicago Historical Society, 8
Chicago Light Artillery, 15, 24, 30
Chicago Light Guards, 15, 24
Chicago Light Infantry, 55

Chicago Passenger Railway Company, 161
Chicago Police Board: attempts to establish
police bureaucracy, 48–49; established
to remove police from mayor, 48; impact
of, 50–51; and sexual behavior, 157
Chicago Police Department: authority
of, 19–20; boundaries established, 204;
charged with social problems, 121; class
bias denied by city council, 61; class bias
of, 61–62; consolidation of, 185–207;
could not break Pullman strike, 208;
divided along ethnic lines, 10–11; effective in strikes of 1877, 128; evaluated,
215–218; force as primary tool, 151; force
cut, 130–131; founded, 19; gets uniforms,
28; growth of, 141–142; has monopoly on
publicity after Haymaket, 193; immediate
impact of Haymarket, 185–186; impact
of anarchists on, 166–184; interests tied
to mayor, 34–35; lacks legitimacy among
many Chicagoans, 137; main activity
regarded disorderly conduct, 150–151;
monument to, 195; national reputation
of, 197; nature of, 73–74; pension fund
established for, 195–196; poor reputation
of, 135–136; receive money from private
citizens, 194; reorganization of, 27–28;
stress on, 122; unable to break Pullman
strike, 212; unable to handle problems
for 1857 panic, 46; undermanned and
disliked, 113; under Roche's leadership,
200–201; used to obtain labor movement, 60; violence of, 22, 128; weakness
of, 79–80
Chicago Relief and Aid Society, 8, 77, 115,
121, 166; demonstrated against, 118, 119;
riot outside of, 114–115
Chicago Republican, 63
Chicago Roller Skating Association, 156
Chicago Streetcar Company, 202
Chicago West Division Railway Company,
160
Chicago Workingmen's Party: holds mass
meeting, 123
Chisolm, William: early member of Commercial Club, 132
Citizens' Association (CA), 118, 136, 137,
182, 214; fears resistance to authority,
182; formed, 114, 116; policies of, 117–118;
raises funds for police, 131; reforms hurt
machine politics, 123

Citizens' Association Committee on Police, 141

Citizens' League: founded to fight underage drinking, 136

civil service reform, 145

Cleland, James, 61

Cleveland, Grover, 213

Colvin, Harvey Doolittle, 120, 142; becomes mayor, 98–99; elected mayor, 98

Colyer, Robert, 125

Commercial Club of the City of Chicago, 137, 187, 209, 214; anticipates conflict, 186; formed, 114; founded, 132; on Haymarket affair, 195

Committee of Nine, Special, 89

Committee of Seventy, 83–85, 90, 93–94, 95, 112, 115, 116, 120, and Sunday closing laws, 88–89; attempts to control police, 83; calls mass meeting to support mayor, 92; created, 73; divided over temperance, 86–87; fails to accomplish goals, 100; power over police limited, 84

Committee on Police: organized to keep order among workers, 27

communists: influence on radical movement, 170. *See also* anarchists

Congress of Industrial Organizations (CIO), 214

Connerton, Peter, 22

Corliss, Carlton, 26

Costelle, Patrick, 192

Coyne, Luke, 202

craft unions in Chicago, 59

Crane, Richard Teller, 8

Crescent Steel Works, 162

Cribben and Sexton Company, 158

crime wave fears grips Chicago, 82

Crowe, Officer, 192

Cullerton, Alderman, 94

Daggy, Alderman, 80

Darrow, Archibald, 163

Debs, Eugene, 213, 214

Deering, William, as member of CA, 116

Degan, Mathias, 191

depression of the 1870s, impact, 114–115

Deshow, Albert, 23–24

disorderly conduct, 6, 31–32, 36, 61, 136, 150, 238n63; abuse of category, 96

Dixon, Superintendent, 126

Douglas, Stephen, 25

Douglass, Sergeant, 92

Doyle, Austin, 138, 140, 142, 160, 161, 162; background of, 43; donates to police, 195; on number of arrests, 150; proposes pay grade system, 144–145; reports lost children found, 141; resists anarchists, 180

Drake, John: early member of Commercial Club, 132

Dyer, Thomas, 7, 35, 36; elected mayor of Chicago, 36; and election of 1857, 40; policies toward police, 36–37; policy on pardons continues, 42; policy toward release of prisoners, 36–37; removes Bradley from position, 30; replaced as mayor by Republican, 39; support of, 34

Ebersold, Frederick, 143, 163–164; asked to resign, 205; becomes superintendent, 160; believes anarchist threat exaggerated, 198; blames anarchists, 184; expects no trouble at Haymarket, 187; on Haymarket, 191; immigrates from Bavaria, 142; on prostitution, 154–155; and repression of anarchists, 193; resisted Schaack, 193–194; retained as supt, 201; and strikes of 1877, 125; supports pension bill, 196; as target of ridicule, 205

economic crisis of 1873, 112

economic panic of 1857, 46

Edward III, King of England, 2

Egan, John, 213

eight-hour day movement of 1867, 57–71; supported laws for, 62–63

eight-hour law: in Chicago, 63

eight-hours leagues: formed, 58

Eight-hour strikes of 1886, 185–207

Einhorn, Robin, 18

electoral violence, 40

Elliot, Horace, 192

Ellis, Robert, 161

Ely, Richard, 210

Ender, John, 144

Engel, George, 198

English, Ann, 95–96

ethnic divisions in Chicago, 113–114

ethnicity in labor movement, 168

ethnicity in police, 10–11

Excelsior Iron Works, 162

Fargo, Charles: early member of Commercial Club, 132

Farwell, John V., 8, 83, 84
Field, Marshall, 8, 123, 132, 160; contributes to Commercial Club, 187; criticized by *Alarm*, 178; early member of Commercial Club, 132; as member of CA, 116; one who controlled CA, 117; reimbursed for contributions, 129
Fielden, Samuel, 182, 191
First Regiment: drill, 183; founding, 118
Fischer, Adolph, 192, 198
Flinn, John, 20, 123, 143, 161; on Great Fire, 77; on strikes of 1877, 130
force: as primary tool of police, 151
Fort Sheridan, 195
free-speech rights restored, 203–204
French, Captain, 92
Furniture Makers' Association, 189

Gage, Lyman, 116; contributes to Commercial Club, 187
Garrigan, Catherine, 96
gender in police, 11–12
General Managers' Association, 211, 213, 214
Gerbing, Lieutenant, 124, 125
Germans in anarchist movement, 169
Germans in Chicago, 9–10, 33; divided along class lines, 113–114
Gonzalez, Lucy, 172
Gookins, S. B., 83
Goppehwading, Francis, 129
Gore, Mr., 94
Gould, Jay, 158; defeats strike, 188
Gray, Charles, 21
Great Chicago Fire, 45; looting and rioting disputed, 75–76; most disorderly night in Chicago history, 74–77; reaction to, 75–77
Great Southwest Strike, 158
Grinell, States Attorney, 189
Grosvener, Thomas, 77
Gund, Captain: dismissed by Medill, 92; reinstated, 93

Haines, John C., 42, 43; elected mayor, 46; policies toward police, 46
Hanchett, Seth, 160
Harknett, Daniel, 130
Harmonia Union, 127, 136
Harris, J. C., 147–148

Harrison, Carter, 131; anarchists willing to antagonize, 175; assassinated, 211; attempts to continue cross-alliance, 189; attends Haymarket, 191; begins civil service reform, 145; changes position on strike neutrality, 160–161; clarified position after Haymarket, 181; downplays threat of anarchists, 181–182; ends police of excluding immigrants from police, 144; evaluated on Haymarket, 200; gives police new incentives, 144–145; impact on police department, 134–164; as machine politician, 149–150; maintains police neutrality in strikes, 159; never public approved repression, 193; police reforms, 166–167; Republicans criticize, 180; on streetcar strike, 183; on strikes of 1877, 125–126; supported, 186; wins mayor's race, 137
Harrison Street Police Station: photo of, 103
Haymarket affair, 5, 185–207; meeting begins, 190–191; national impact, 197; repression of anarchists after, 193–194
Heath, Monroe, 136, 182; cuts police force, 130–131; elected mayor, 120; orders unmuzzled dogs killed, 121; reduces police force, 135; refuses to stop mass meeting, 123
Henry, Alexander, 42
Hesing, Anton, 79, 80, 98, 100, 115; caught up in whiskey ring trial, 120; protests Medill's policies, 86
Hibman, D. L., 42
Hickey, Michael C., 135, 170; accused by Medill of wrongdoing, 89; becomes minor hero, 130; dismissed by Medill, 92; helps subdue bread riot, 114; on homeless men, 120–121; indicted for corruption, 122–123; rank restored and replaces Rehm, 99; reinstated, 93; required to lay off policemen, 100; and strikes of 1877, 125–127; sued, 127
History of Chicago Police, 20
Hopkins, John, 211, 212–213, 214–215
Householder, Policeman, 127
Hubbard, George, 204
hungry people in Chicago, 114–115
Hutcheson, Francis, 2
Hutchinson, Thomas, 1, 3

ice skating rink: photo of, 102
Illinois Central Railroad, 25, 64, 83; needed protection, 25
Illinois Staats Zeitung, 79, 115
Illinois Stone Company, 69
Industrial Workers of the World (IWW), 215
Ingraham, Mattie Ross, 152
International (labor movement), 172, 173, 174
International Working Men's Association, 148
International Working People's Association, 172, 175, 182; leads parade, 187; women in, 12
Irish in Chicago, 10
Irish Labor Guard, 119

Jacoby, Andrew, 96
Jaeger Werein, 119
Jehm, Jacob, 142
Jones, J. Russell: early member of Commercial Club, 132
Joy, Hiram: rejects requests for pardons, 41–42
Judas, Stanislaus, 151, 156
Judd, Norman, 46
justice of the peace: development of in England, 2

Kane, Edward, 42–43
Kansas-Nebraska Act, 39
Keleher, Lieutenant, 212
Kellogg, George, 153–154
Kennedy, Superintendent, 83
Kinzie, James, 7
Kinzie, John H., 7
Kinzie family, 7
Kipley, Chief, 54
Klokke, Ernst, 89, 92; appointed by Mayor Medill, 81; charges against shelved, 93; joins against Washburn, 91; reinstated, 99
Knights of Labor, 9, 164; defeated by Gould, 188; defeat Jay Gould, 158; end of, 193; and Haymarket bombing, 186; membership of, 186–187; takes less radical position, 168; women in, 11–12
Know Nothing Party, 14, 16. *See also* American Party, Law and Order Party

Lager Beer Riot, 5, 24, 28, 29, 30, 33, 70, 97; as example of disorder, 16; impact of on police, 15–16
Larson, Regnat, 152
Lasalle, Ferdinand, 172
Law and Order Party, 15, 24, 33, 83; formed to opposed People's Party, 98. *See also* American Party, Know Nothing Party
Law and Order ticket: reemerges, 200–201
Lawles, Alderman, 156
Lehr und Wehr Verein, 119, 136
Leigh, C. W., 151
Leiter, Levi, 8, 132, 160; contributes to Commercial Club, 187; reimbursed for contributions, 129; wants paper suspended, 123
Lincoln, Abraham, 25, 47
Lingg, Louis, 190, 205
Lowenthal, A., 42
Ludington, Mayor, 98
Lum, Dyer D., 198
Lumberman's Exchange, 194

Macauley, Sergeant, 92
MacKellroy, James, 42
MacVeagh, Franklin: CA's first president, 116; contibutes to Commercial Club, 187; early member of Commercial Club, 132; map of brothels, 107; one who controlled CA, 117
Marks, Michael, 192
Mason, Roswell B.: blames alcohol for disorder, 26–27; calls in troops, 76; reacts to Great Fire, 75
Maxwell Box Factory strike, 163
May Day March, 1867, 57–71, 64–65, 65–67; fails, 70
Mayor's Police: created by Wentworth, 43
McAllister, Judge, 127
McCormick, Cyrus, 7, 8, 16, 58; contributes to Commercial Club, 187; donates to police, 194; as member of CA, 116; one who controlled CA, 117; reimbursed for contributions, 129; on strike at his plant, 164; supports upper class, 70; withdraws support of Harrison, 137
McCormick Reaper Works: strike at, 66, 124, 146–147, 163–164; violence at, 188
McDonald, Mike, 98, 149
McGarigle, Superintendent, 138–139, 143

McVickers, J. H., 195
meatpacking: Chicago becomes center of, 58
Medill, Joseph, 79, 83, 116, 117, 120; committed to liquor policy, 94; defeated for reelection, 98; elected mayor, 77; on police control, 81; proposes all buildings be of brick, 78- 79; as representative of elite as mayor, 77–78; and Sunday closing laws, 86–87; supports temperance, 122; supports Washburn, 91; vetoes liquor ordinance, 95
Meng, George, 192
Metal Manufacturers' Association, 190
Meyer, Michael, 131
Milliken, Isaac, 20
Molly Maguires, 12, 147, 148
monument to police, 195
Mooney and Boland private security, 203
Moore, Lizzie, 122
Mueller, George, 194

National Guards, 15, 24
National Labor Union, 58, 61
nativism: rise of, 14
Nelson, Robert S., 200
New Orleans Police Department, 19
New York Police Department, 2, 19, 73; and draft riots, 76; and police board, 49
North Side brick yards strike, 146

O'Donnell, Michael, 151
O'Donnell, Simon, 147, 164; replaces Hickey, 92
O'Farrell, Dr., 152
Ogden, M. D.: opposes brick building proposal, 79
Ogden, William, 7, 44, 57
Oglesby, Governor, 190
Oikonomikos, 2
O'Leary, Mrs., 75
O'Neill, Francis, 84–85, 168, 212
Owens, Peter, 38–39; request for pardon of wife denied, 41–42

Palmer, Potter, 8; contributes to Commercial Club, 187; donates to police, 195
Paris Commune, 76, 119, 167
Parsons, Albert, 116, 148, 163, 174; arrested, 124; attends Haymarket, 191; background of, 172; executed, 198; first member of Knights of Labor, 187; gaining strength among anarchists, 159; gains support,

165; given control of militias, 119; joins radical movement, 169; leads demonstration, 180; most representative of anarchist threat, 172; prominence among anarchists, 171
Parsons, Lucy, 116, 176, 198; continues as anarchist, 21, 99
Patton, William, 175
Pennsylvania Hall, 28
pension fund: established for police, 195–196
Peoples Gas Light and Coke Company, 161; donates to police, 195
People's Party, 97, 166; administration of collapses, 119; promotes new charter, 118; takes office, 115; win election in a landslide, 98
Personal Liberty League, 88–89, 95
Phelps, E. M.: early member of Commercial Club, 132
Philadelphia police, 13; founding, 28–29; whole department fired, 81
Pinkerton, Allan: blames communists, 170; blames outside agitators, 113; faces competition, 158; hired to protect railroads, 25; moves to Chicago, 18; on strike police, 128; on strikes of 1877, 126
Pinkerton, William, 194
Pinkerton Detective Agency, 12; criticized by Alarm, 178–179; distributes Schaack's book, 206; gets reputation as strikebreakers, 158–159; used in strikes, 146–147
Police Alarm Telegraph System, 143; allows police more social involvement, 139–140; introduced, 138; made police effective, 193; used against anarchists, 180; used at McCormick strike, 188
Police and Firemen's Relief Fund, 130
police as heroes: photo of, 111
police as victims of violence: photo of, 110
police fighting rioters: photo of, 110
Policemen's Benevolent Association, 195
police prehistory: did not exist in colonial period, 1; duties of, 11; history of growth, 2–13
Police Rules in Chicago, 20
police technology: increasing use of, 137–140
Police Telegraph Call Box, photos of, 105
police violence, 22, 92, 127, 160–161, 164; photos of, 104

police wagon: photo of, 106
Pork Packer's Association, 58
Porter, Horace, 197
Prairie Avenue houses: photo of, 102
prison escapes, 47–48
private security firms, 12, 18. *See also*
    Pinkerton Detective Agency
progressivism: influence on police, 157
property: protection of, 3
prostitution: anarchists critique of, 177; ar-
    rests of, 11–12, 32, 44, 54; and police cor-
    ruption, 122, 205; police move against,
    154–155
Pullman, George, 8; creates model town,
    208–209; early member of Commercial
    Club, 132; as member of CA, 116; refuses
    demand of workers, 189
Pullman Palace Car Company, 197
Pullman Strike, 5, 195, 208–215; like no
    other, 211
Pullman town: description of, 209–210;
    fails, 210
pure and simple: unionism, 186

Race, Officer, 137–138
Raster, Hermann, 202
rebuilding Chicago, 80–81
red squad, first, 194
Rehm, Jacob, 92; allows appointment of
    citizens deputies, 68; becomes police su-
    perintendent, 99; caught up in whiskey
    ring trial, 120; controls police, 118; forced
    to resign, 89; insures effectiveness of
    police, 52–54; reduce pay of police com-
    missioners, 78; retires, 81
Reno, C. A., 88, 92; charges against
    shelved, 93; orders suspension by Medill,
    91
Republican Party: coming into existence in
    Chicago, 35; elects first mayor, 39; fears
    resistance to authority, 182
revolution, threat of, 167
Reynolds, Floyd, 152
Richard I, King of England, 2
Roche, John A.: asks Ebersold to resign,
    205; policies as mayor, 201–202; supports
    pension bill, 196; urges compromise in
    streetcar strike, 202; wins mayor's race,
    200
Rock Island Railroad, 25
roller-skating fad, 155–156
Russel, Alderman, 68

Saloonkeepers' Association of Chicago, 149
Sands district: as vice district of Chicago, 44
Sanger, Harriet, 209
Schaack, Michael, 176, 190; accused of
    corruption, 205; becomes force within
    police, 194; blames anarchists, 191; claims
    credit after Haymarket, 193–194; effective
    against anarchists, 198; helps suppress
    anarchists, 169; influence of, 206; leads
    attack at Haymarket, 192; in national
    spotlight, 194; on nature of labor move-
    ment, 171; replaces Ebersold, 206; thinks
    anarchists planned attack, 189; wishes to
    persecute anarchists, 184
Schilling, George, 202
Schmidt, Ernst, 137, 182
Schnaubelt, 191, 192
Schwaab, Michael, 192, 196
Seavey, V. A., 125, 135
Seidle, Martha, 175
Seliger, William, 190
Shays, Daniel, 1
Shea, Lieutenant, 206
Sheridan, Commissioner, 92, 94, 96, 118
Sheridan, Philip: does not see need for
    troops, 76; on threats to country, 172–173
Short Introduction to Moral Philosophy, 2
Socialist Labor Party, 136, 182
Socialist Party, 215
Someweicks, Mr., 42
Special Committee of Nine, 89
Spies, August, 159, 174, 175, 182, 189, 191; ar-
    rested, 192; executed, 198; and strike, 188
Spies, Chris, 192
Stager, Anson: early member of Commer-
    cial Club, 132
Stamp Act, 1
Stead, William, 207
Stone, Melville E., 194
Story, Albert, 26
streetcar strike of 1885, 182–183
streetcar strike of 1888, 202–203; continu-
    ing perception of anarchist influence,
    202; reduces influence of private secu-
    rity, 203
*Strikers, Communists, Tramps and Detec-
    tives*, 170
strikes: Chicago police face first, 20–21
strikes of 1877, 123–125; cost of, 129; impact
    of, 133; impact of police on, 112–113;
    impact on elite, 131; resistance against,
    124–125

Sullivan, Thomas, 196
Sunday closing laws, 86–89
Swank, Lizzie, 176, 198
Swift, Gustavus: contibutes to Commercial Club, 187
Swift and Company, 212
Sylvis, William, 58

Talcott, Mancel, 88, 89; supports saloon closing law, 94
Tammany Hall, 49, 50, 73, 149
Teamsters' strike of 1905, 215
temperance, 24, 85–86; continues as political issue, 136; failure of, 32; Mayor Dyer opposed, 36; as political issue, 134. *See also* alcohol regulation, Sunday closing laws
Temperance Party, 83
Tessman, Karl, 127
Torrence, Joseph, 124
Trades and Labor Assembly, 161, 162, 165, 169, 180, 186
Treat, Mr., 77
Tree, Lambert, 145
Tuley, Judge, 204
Tweed, William, 73
Typographical Union, 59

union development in Chicago, 59–60
Union Fire-Proof ticket: elects Joseph Medill as mayor, 77
Union Iron and Steel Company strike, 146
Union Pacific Railroad, 116
Union Stockyards and Transit Company, 58
United States Express Company, 143

Vannornum, Madam, 153–154
Van Patten, Philip, 170; arrested, 124
Verein der Wirthe von Chicago, 149
Verona Tool Works, 162
Vesey, Lieutenant, 124
Vigilance Committee of San Francisco, 49–50

Ward, Secretary, 91
Ward, Superintendent, 92
Ward, William, 191
Washburn, Elmer, 90, 95; appointed police superintendent, 83; City Council unhappy with, 90; dictated to by Committee of Seventy, 84; and Sunday closing

laws, 86–87, 89; supports saloon closing law, 94; suspended, 91
Washington Boulevard Skating Company, 195
Weimer, Peter, 55
Welter, Col, 180
Welter, Dominick, 142
Wentworth, John, 7, 36, 78, 81, 83, 93; attacks on gambling, 45; campaign against vice, 43–44; creates Mayor's Police, 43; elected mayor, 39; imperious methods of, 45; made prisoner release more difficult, 41; opposes system of pardons, 40–41; organization of police, 43; on pardons, 42; paternalistic view of crime, 43–44; reelected mayor, 46–47; resists Chicago police board, 51–52; second term overshadowed by sectional crisis, 47; supported Medill, 92; supported older idea of police, 35; unable to handle financial panic, 46; West, J. J., 205
Western Union Telegraph Company: donates to police, 195
Wheeler, Mr., 98
Whiskey Rebellion, 1
White, C. J., 196
White, Horace, 116
Williams, Miss, 152
women in labor movement, 11–12
women in revolutionary movement, 176–177
Women's Christian Temperance Union, 85
Women's Temperance Crusade, 85
Wood, John, 47
working class emergence in U.S., 57–58
Workingman's Advocate, 59, 60, 61; supports eight-hour movement, 63
Workingmen's Parties, 29
Workingmen's Party, 169–170; calls another mass meeting, 124; fails in strikes of 1877, 128; founded, 115; gets reinforcements, 125
Wright, Albert, 137
W. W. Chambers Saloon: photo of, 101

Xenephon, 2

Yates, Governor, 49
Yates, Richard, 47
Yerkes, Charles, 202
Young Men's Christian Association (YMCA), 8

SAM MITRANI is an assistant professor of history at the College of DuPage.

THE WORKING CLASS IN AMERICAN HISTORY

Worker City, Company Town: Iron and Cotton-Worker Protest
   in Troy and Cohoes, New York, 1855–84   *Daniel J. Walkowitz*
Life, Work, and Rebellion in the Coal Fields:
   The Southern West Virginia Miners, 1880–1922   *David Alan Corbin*
Women and American Socialism, 1870–1920   *Mari Jo Buhle*
Lives of Their Own: Blacks, Italians, and Poles
   in Pittsburgh, 1900–1960   *John Bodnar, Roger Simon, and Michael P. Weber*
Working-Class America: Essays on Labor, Community,
   and American Society   *Edited by Michael H. Frisch and Daniel J. Walkowitz*
Eugene V. Debs: Citizen and Socialist   *Nick Salvatore*
American Labor and Immigration History, 1877–1920s:
   Recent European Research   *Edited by Dirk Hoerder*
Workingmen's Democracy: The Knights of Labor
   and American Politics   *Leon Fink*
The Electrical Workers: A History of Labor at General Electric
   and Westinghouse, 1923–60   *Ronald W. Schatz*
The Mechanics of Baltimore: Workers and Politics
   in the Age of Revolution, 1763–1812   *Charles G. Steffen*
The Practice of Solidarity: American Hat Finishers
   in the Nineteenth Century   *David Bensman*
The Labor History Reader   *Edited by Daniel J. Leab*
Solidarity and Fragmentation: Working People
   and Class Consciousness in Detroit, 1875–1900   *Richard Oestreicher*
Counter Cultures: Saleswomen, Managers, and Customers
   in American Department Stores, 1890–1940   *Susan Porter Benson*
The New England Working Class and the New Labor History
   Edited by Herbert G. Gutman and Donald H. Bell
Labor Leaders in America   *Edited by Melvyn Dubofsky
   and Warren Van Tine*
Barons of Labor: The San Francisco Building Trades
   and Union Power in the Progressive Era   *Michael Kazin*
Gender at Work: The Dynamics of Job Segregation by Sex
   during World War II   *Ruth Milkman*
Once a Cigar Maker: Men, Women, and Work Culture
   in American Cigar Factories, 1900–1919   *Patricia A. Cooper*
A Generation of Boomers: The Pattern of Railroad Labor Conflict
   in Nineteenth-Century America   *Shelton Stromquist*
Work and Community in the Jungle:
   Chicago's Packinghouse Workers, 1894–1922   *James R. Barrett*
Workers, Managers, and Welfare Capitalism: The Shoeworkers and Tanners
   of Endicott Johnson, 1890–1950   *Gerald Zahavi*

Men, Women, and Work: Class, Gender, and Protest
in the New England Shoe Industry, 1780–1910 *Mary Blewett*
Workers on the Waterfront: Seamen, Longshoremen,
and Unionism in the 1930s *Bruce Nelson*
German Workers in Chicago: A Documentary History
of Working-Class Culture from 1850 to World War I
Edited by Hartmut Keil and John B. Jentz
On the Line: Essays in the History of Auto Work
Edited by Nelson Lichtenstein and Stephen Meyer III
Labor's Flaming Youth: Telephone Operators and Worker Militancy,
1878–1923 *Stephen H. Norwood*
Another Civil War: Labor, Capital, and the State
in the Anthracite Regions of Pennsylvania, 1840–68 *Grace Palladino*
Coal, Class, and Color: Blacks in Southern West Virginia,
1915–32 *Joe William Trotter Jr.*
For Democracy, Workers, and God: Labor Song-Poems
and Labor Protest, 1865–95 *Clark D. Halker*
Dishing It Out: Waitresses and Their Unions
in the Twentieth Century *Dorothy Sue Cobble*
The Spirit of 1848: German Immigrants, Labor Conflict,
and the Coming of the Civil War *Bruce Levine*
Working Women of Collar City: Gender, Class, and Community
in Troy, New York, 1864–86 *Carole Turbin*
Southern Labor and Black Civil Rights:
Organizing Memphis Workers *Michael K. Honey*
Radicals of the Worst Sort: Laboring Women
in Lawrence, Massachusetts, 1860–1912 *Ardis Cameron*
Producers, Proletarians, and Politicians: Workers and Party Politics
in Evansville and New Albany, Indiana, 1850–87 *Lawrence M. Lipin*
The New Left and Labor in the 1960s *Peter B. Levy*
The Making of Western Labor Radicalism:
Denver's Organized Workers, 1878–1905 *David Brundage*
In Search of the Working Class: Essays in American Labor History
and Political Culture *Leon Fink*
Lawyers against Labor: From Individual Rights
to Corporate Liberalism *Daniel R. Ernst*
"We Are All Leaders": The Alternative Unionism
of the Early 1930s *Edited by Staughton Lynd*
The Female Economy: The Millinery
and Dressmaking Trades, 1860–1930 *Wendy Gamber*
"Negro and White, Unite and Fight!": A Social History
of Industrial Unionism in Meatpacking, 1930–90 *Roger Horowitz*
Power at Odds: The 1922 National Railroad Shopmen's Strike *Colin J. Davis*

The Common Ground of Womanhood: Class, Gender,
and Working Girls' Clubs, 1884–1928   *Priscilla Murolo*
Marching Together: Women of the Brotherhood
of Sleeping Car Porters   *Melinda Chateauvert*
Down on the Killing Floor: Black and White Workers
in Chicago's Packinghouses, 1904–54   *Rick Halpern*
Labor and Urban Politics: Class Conflict and the Origins
of Modern Liberalism in Chicago, 1864–97   *Richard Schneirov*
All That Glitters: Class, Conflict, and Community
in Cripple Creek   *Elizabeth Jameson*
Waterfront Workers: New Perspectives
on Race and Class   *Edited by Calvin Winslow*
Labor Histories: Class, Politics, and the Working-Class Experience
Edited by Eric Arnesen, Julie Greene, and Bruce Laurie
The Pullman Strike and the Crisis of the 1890s:
Essays on Labor and Politics   *Edited by Richard Schneirov,
Shelton Stromquist, and Nick Salvatore*
AlabamaNorth: African-American Migrants, Community,
and Working-Class Activism in Cleveland, 1914–45   *Kimberley L. Phillips*
Imagining Internationalism in American
and British Labor, 1939–49   *Victor Silverman*
William Z. Foster and the Tragedy of American Radicalism   *James R. Barrett*
Colliers across the Sea: A Comparative Study of Class Formation
in Scotland and the American Midwest, 1830–1924   *John H. M. Laslett*
"Rights, Not Roses": Unions and the Rise
of Working-Class Feminism, 1945–80   *Dennis A. Deslippe*
Testing the New Deal: The General Textile Strike of 1934
in the American South   *Janet Irons*
Hard Work: The Making of Labor History   *Melvyn Dubofsky*
Southern Workers and the Search for Community:
Spartanburg County, South Carolina   *G. C. Waldrep III*
We Shall Be All: A History of the Industrial Workers
of the World (abridged edition)   *Melvyn Dubofsky, ed. Joseph A. McCartin*
Race, Class, and Power in the Alabama Coalfields, 1908–21   *Brian Kelly*
Duquesne and the Rise of Steel Unionism   *James D. Rose*
Anaconda: Labor, Community, and Culture
in Montana's Smelter City   *Laurie Mercier*
Bridgeport's Socialist New Deal, 1915–36   *Cecelia Bucki*
Indispensable Outcasts: Hobo Workers and Community
in the American Midwest, 1880–1930   *Frank Tobias Higbie*
After the Strike: A Century of Labor Struggle at Pullman   *Susan Eleanor Hirsch*
Corruption and Reform in the Teamsters Union   *David Witwer*
Waterfront Revolts: New York and London Dockworkers, 1946–61   *Colin J. Davis*

Black Workers' Struggle for Equality in Birmingham
Horace Huntley and David Montgomery
The Tribe of Black Ulysses: African American Men
in the Industrial South *William P. Jones*
City of Clerks: Office and Sales Workers
in Philadelphia, 1870–1920 *Jerome P. Bjelopera*
Reinventing "The People": The Progressive Movement,
the Class Problem, and the Origins of Modern Liberalism *Shelton Stromquist*
Radical Unionism in the Midwest, 1900–1950 *Rosemary Feurer*
Gendering Labor History *Alice Kessler-Harris*
James P. Cannon and the Origins of the American Revolutionary Left,
1890–1928 *Bryan D. Palmer*
Glass Towns: Industry, Labor, and Political Economy in Appalachia,
1890–1930s *Ken Fones-Wolf*
Workers and the Wild: Conservation, Consumerism,
and Labor in Oregon, 1910–30 *Lawrence M. Lipin*
Wobblies on the Waterfront: Interracial Unionism
in Progressive-Era Philadelphia *Peter Cole*
Red Chicago: American Communism at Its Grassroots, 1928–35 *Randi Storch*
Labor's Cold War: Local Politics
in a Global Context *Edited by Shelton Stromquist*
Bessie Abramowitz Hillman and the Making
of the Amalgamated Clothing Workers of America *Karen Pastorello*
The Great Strikes of 1877 *Edited by David O. Stowell*
Union-Free America: Workers and Antiunion Culture *Lawrence Richards*
Race against Liberalism: Black Workers
and the UAW in Detroit *David M. Lewis-Colman*
Teachers and Reform: Chicago Public Education, 1929–70 *John F. Lyons*
Upheaval in the Quiet Zone: 1199/SEIU and the Politics
of Healthcare Unionism *Leon Fink and Brian Greenberg*
Shadow of the Racketeer: Scandal in Organized Labor *David Witwer*
Sweet Tyranny: Migrant Labor, Industrial Agriculture,
and Imperial Politics *Kathleen Mapes*
Staley: The Fight for a New American Labor Movement
Steven K. Ashby and C. J. Hawking
On the Ground: Labor Struggles in the American Airline Industry
Liesl Miller Orenic
NAFTA and Labor in North America *Norman Caulfield*
Making Capitalism Safe: Work Safety and Health Regulation
in America, 1880–1940 *Donald W. Rogers*
Good, Reliable, White Men: Railroad Brotherhoods,
1877–1917 *Paul Michel Taillon*
Spirit of Rebellion: Labor and Religion
in the New Cotton South *Jarod Heath Roll*

The Labor Question in America: Economic Democracy
   in the Gilded Age   *Rosanne Currarino*
Banded Together: Economic Democratization in the Brass Valley   *Jeremy Brecher*
The Gospel of the Working Class: Labor's Southern Prophets
   in New Deal America   *Erik Gellman and Jarod Heath Roll*
Guest Workers and Resistance to U.S. Corporate Despotism   *Immanuel Ness*
Gleanings of Freedom: Free and Slave Labor
   along the Mason-Dixon Line, 1790–1860   *Max Grivno*
Chicago in the Age of Capital: Class, Politics, and Democracy
   during the Civil War and Reconstruction   *John B. Jentz and Richard Schneirov*
Child Care in Black and White: Working Parents
   and the History of Orphanages   *Jessie B. Ramey*
The Haymarket Conspiracy:
   Transatlantic Anarchist Networks   *Timothy Messer-Kruse*
Detroit's Cold War: The Origins of Postwar Conservatism   *Colleen Doody*
A Renegade Union: Interracial Organizing and Labor Radicalism   *Lisa Phillips*
Palomino: Clinton Jencks and Mexican-American Unionism
   in the American Southwest   *James J. Lorence*
Latin American Migrations to the U.S. Heartland:
   Changing Cultural Landscapes in Middle America
   Edited by Linda Allegro and Andrew Grant Wood
Man of Fire: Selected Writings   *Ernesto Galarza,*
   ed. Armando Ibarra and Rodolfo D. Torres
A Contest of Ideas: Capital, Politics, and Labor   *Nelson Lichtenstein*
Making the World Safe for Workers:
   Labor, the Left, and Wilsonian Internationalism   *Elizabeth McKillen*
The Rise of the Chicago Police Department:
   Class and Conflict, 1850–1894   *Sam Mitrani*

The University of Illinois Press
is a founding member of the
Association of American University Presses.

———————————————————————

Composed in 10.5/13 Minion Pro
by Lisa Connery
at the University of Illinois Press
Manufactured by Sheridan Books, Inc.

University of Illinois Press
1325 South Oak Street
Champaign, IL 61820–6903
www.press.uillinois.edu